100 Hikes in the

Central Oregon
CASCADES

SECOND EDITION

William L. Sullivan

Navillus Press
Eugene

Fog on the trail to Mt. June.

Published by the Navillus Press
1958 Onyx Street
Eugene, Oregon 97403

Printed in USA

Cover: Gentian, South Sister from the Green Lakes
Spine: Jefferson Park
Frontispiece: Three Fingered Jack from Black Butte

SAFETY CONSIDERATIONS: Many of the trails in this book pass throughWilderness and remote country where hikers are exposed to unavoidable risks. On any hike, the weather may change suddenly. The fact that a hike is included in this book, or that it may be rated as easy, does not necessarily mean it will be safe or easy for you. Prepare yourself with proper equipment and outdoor skills, and you will be able to enjoy these hikes with confidence.

Every effort has been made to assure the accuracy of the information in this book. The author has hiked all 100 of the featured trails, and the trails' administrative agencies have reviewed the maps and text. Nonetheless, construction, logging, and storm damage may cause changes. Corrections to this guide are welcomed and often rewarded; please write in care of the publisher. Updated versions of this book are printed almost every year.

Contents

⅍ - Horses OK ∞ - Bicycles OK
C - Crowded or restricted backpacking area

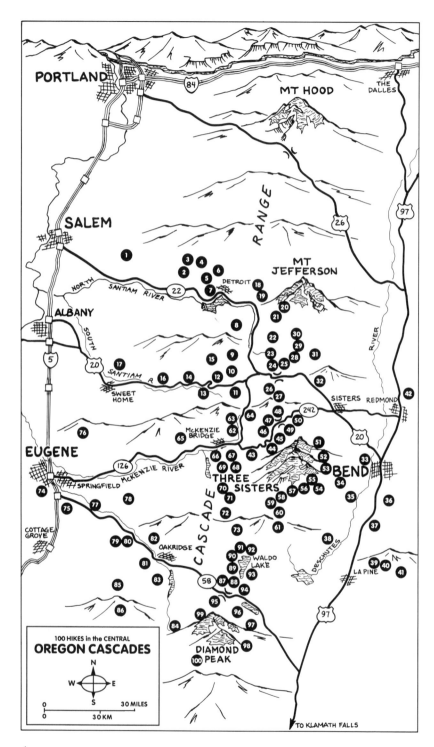

100 HIKES in the CENTRAL
OREGON CASCADES

🐴 - Horses OK   🚴 - Bicycles OK
C - Crowded or restricted backpacking area

🐎 - Horses OK   🚲 - Bicycles OK
C - Crowded or restricted backpacking area

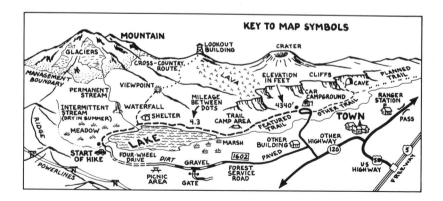

KEY TO MAP SYMBOLS

Introduction

Welcome to Oregon's favorite hiking area, the mountains between the Willamette Valley and Bend. Few regions pack such a variety of trails into an area crossable by a two-hour drive. This guide covers more than just the well-known Wilderness Areas from Mt. Jefferson to Diamond Peak. You'll discover paths to a natural rock arch near Detroit, a cluster of lava caves near Bend, and a gold-mining ghost town near Cottage Grove. Twenty-three of the trips are open even in winter.

The guidebook features several difficulty levels. Hikers with children will find 50 hikes carefully chosen for them. As a parent, I understand how enthused children become about chipmunks or splashing creeks, and how curiously uninspired they seem by steep trails. On the other hand, a quarter of the hikes included are unabashedly difficult, with outstanding beauty and challenge. Fifty-six of the trails are rated as suitable for backpackers as well as day hikers. At the back of the book you'll find a list of 20 all-accessible trails suitable for strollers and wheelchairs. And if you really want to get away from it all, there's an appendix describing 100 *more* hikes in the Central Oregon Cascades—little known but interesting paths for adventurous spirits.

HOW TO USE THIS BOOK

It's Easy to Choose a Trip

The featured hikes are divided into 7 regions, from the Santiam Foothills to Willamette Pass. To choose a trip, simply turn to the area that interests you and look for the following symbols in the upper right-hand corner of each hike's heading. Whether you're hiking with children, backpacking, or looking for a snow-free winter trail, you'll quickly find an outing to match your tastes.

 Children's favorites—walks popular with the 4- to 12-year-old crowd, but fun for hikers of all ages.

 All-year trails, hikable most or all of winter.

 Hikes suitable for backpackers as well as day hikers. Crowds unlikely.

 Crowded or restricted backpacking areas. Expect competition for campsites, especially on summer weekends.

The Information Blocks

Each hike is rated by difficulty. **Easy** hikes are between 2 and 7 miles round-trip and gain less than 1000 feet in elevation. Never very steep nor particularly remote, they make good warm-up trips for experienced hikers or first-time trips for novices.

Trips rated as **Moderate** range from 4 to 10 miles round-trip. The longer hikes in this category are not steep, but shorter trails may gain up to 2000 feet of elevation—or they may require some pathfinding skills. Hikers must be in good condition and will need to take several rest stops.

Difficult trails demand top physical condition, with a strong heart and strong knees. These challenging hikes are 8 to 15 miles round-trip and may gain 3000 feet or more.

Distances are given in round-trip mileage, except for those trails where a car or bicycle shuttle is so convenient that the suggested hike is one-way only, and is listed as such.

Elevation gains tell much about the difficulty of a hike. Those who puff climbing a few flights of stairs may consider even 500 feet of elevation a strenuous climb, and should watch this listing carefully. Note that the figures are for each hike's *cumulative* elevation gain, adding all the uphill portions, even those on the return trip.

The **hiking season** of any trail varies with the weather. In a cold year, a trail described as "Open May through October" may not yet be clear of snow by May 1, and may be socked in by a blizzard before October 31. Similarly, a trail that is "Open all year" may close due to storms.

All hikers should carry a **topographic map,** with contour lines to show elevation. Maps listed as "USFS" are available from U.S. Forest Service offices. Those tagged "USGS" are published by the U.S. Geological Survey and can be found at many outdoor stores. Or you can write to the USGS, PO Box 25286, Denver, CO 80225 to have maps sent postpaid. Order Geo-Graphics maps by calling (503) 591-7635; for Imus maps call (541) 344-1431. It also pays to pick up a Willamette National Forest map (for the west side of the mountains) or a Deschutes National Forest map (for the east) at a ranger station for a few dollars.

TRAIL PARK PASSES

A Trail Park Pass is required to park within 1/4 mile of the trailheads for 85 of the featured hikes in this book, including nearly all those in the Willamette National Forest and Deschutes National Forest. The permit costs $3 per car per day, or $25 per year, and can be purchased at ranger stations or outdoor stores. Some state parks and the Newberry National Volcanic Monument have their own permit fee systems, described in the entries for the affected hikes.

WILDERNESS RESTRICTIONS

From the last weekend in May to the end of October, permits are required to enter Wilderness Areas, including Mt. Jefferson, Mt. Washington, the Three Sisters, and Waldo Lake. In most cases you can fill these out at the trailhead, but two trails require advance reservations: the Pamelia Lake Trail (Hike #21) and the Obsidian Trail (Hike #44). Many other restrictions apply to Wilderness Areas, and affect 46 of the hikes featured in this guide:

- Groups must be no larger than 12.
- Campfires are banned within 100 feet of any water source or maintained trail.
- No one may enter areas posted as closed for rehabilitation.
- Bicycles and other wheeled vehicles (except wheelchairs) are banned.
- Horses and pack stock cannot be tethered for more than a short break

McKenzie River Trail near Tamolitch Dry Falls (Hike #62).

within 200 feet of any water source or trail.
- Motorized equipment and fireworks are banned.
- Live trees and shrubs must not be cut or damaged.

In addition, some rules apply to all federal lands:

- Collecting arrowheads or other cultural artifacts is a federal crime.
- Permits are required to dig up plants.

SAFETY ON THE TRAIL

Wild Animals

Part of the fun of hiking is watching for wildlife. Lovers of wildness rue the demise of our most impressive species. Wolves and grizzly bears are extinct in Oregon. The little black bears that remain are so profoundly shy you probably won't see one in 1000 miles of hiking. In this portion of the Cascades, the main reason for backpackers to hang their food from a tree at night is to protect it from ground squirrels. Likewise, our rattlesnakes are genuinely rare and shy—and they never were as venomous as the Southwest's famous rattlers.

Mosquitoes can be a nuisance on hikes in the Mt. Jefferson, Three Sisters, and Willamette Pass sections. To avoid them, remember that these insects hatch about 10 days after the snow melts from the trails and that they remain in force 3 or 4 weeks. Thus, if a given trail in the High Cascades is listed as "Open mid-June," expect mosquitoes there most of July.

Drinking Water

Day hikers should bring all the water they will need—roughly a quart per person. A microscopic paramecium, *Giardia,* has forever changed the old custom of dipping a drink from every brook. The symptoms of "beaver fever," debilitating nausea and diarrhea, commence a week or two after ingesting Giardia.

If you're backpacking, bring an approved water filter or purification tablet, or boil your water 5 minutes.

Car Clouting

Parked cars at trailheads are sometimes the targets of *car clouters,* thieves who smash windows or jimmy doors. The simplest solution is to leave no valuables in the car and to leave doors unlocked, especially if you are backpacking and must park a car overnight.

Proper Equipment

Even on the tamest hike a surprise storm or a wrong turn can suddenly make the gear you carry very important. Always bring a pack with the 10 essentials:

1. Warm, water-repellent coat (or parka and extra shirt)
2. Drinking water
3. Extra food
4. Knife
5. Matches in waterproof container
6. Fire starter (butane lighter or candle)
7. First aid kit
8. Flashlight
9. Map (topographic, if possible)
10. Compass

Before leaving on a hike, tell someone where you are going so they can alert the county sheriff to begin a search if you do not return on time. If you're lost, stay put and keep warm. The number one killer in the woods is *hypothermia*— being cold and wet too long.

COURTESY ON THE TRAIL

As our trails become more heavily used, rules of trail etiquette become stricter. Please:

- Pick no flowers.
- Leave no litter. Eggshells and orange peels can last for decades.
- Do not bring pets into Wilderness areas. Dogs can frighten wildlife and disturb other hikers.
- Step off the trail on the downhill side to let horses pass. Speak to them quietly to help keep them from spooking.
- Do not shortcut switchbacks.

For backpackers, low-impact camping was once merely a courtesy, but is on the verge of becoming a requirement, both to protect the landscape and to preserve a sense of solitude for others. The most important rules:

- Camp out of sight of lakes and trails.
- Build no campfire. Cook on a backpacking stove.
- Wash 100 feet from any lake or stream.
- Camp on duff, rock, or sand—never on meadow vegetation.
- Pack out garbage—don't burn or bury it.

GROUPS TO HIKE WITH

If you enjoy the camaraderie of hiking with a group, contact one of the organizations that leads trips to the trails in this book. None of the groups requires that you be a member to join scheduled hikes, and when trip fees are charged they're rarely more than a dollar or two. Hikers generally carpool from a preset meeting place. If you have no car, expect to chip in for mileage.

Chemeketans. Three to 8 hikes a week. Cabin near Mt. Jefferson, meetings at 360-1/2 State Street, Salem. Founded 1927. Write to P.O. Box 864, Salem OR 97308.

City of Eugene. One to 3 hikes or other outings a week, usually from River House, 301 N. Adams St., Eugene OR, 97402. Call (541) 687-5329.

Mazamas. Three to 10 hikes a week. Cabin at Mt. Hood, office and meetings at 909 NW 19th Ave., Portland, OR 97209. Founded 1894. Call (503) 227-2345.

Obsidians. Two to 5 hikes a week. Monthly potluck meetings at Eugene lodge. Check bulletin board at Eugene Family Y, 2055 Patterson St., Eugene, or write P.O. Box 322, Eugene OR 97440.

U of O Outdoor Program. Two to 4 hikes or other outings a week. Non-students welcome. Office, library, and programs in the basement of the Erb Memorial Union, University of Oregon, Eugene OR, 97403. Call (541) 346-4365.

FOR MORE INFORMATION

To check on permit requirements, trail maintenance, snow levels, or other questions, call directly to the trail's administrative agency. These offices are listed below, along with the hikes in this book for which they manage trails.

Hike	Managing Agency
33	Bend Metro Park and Rec. District — (541) 389-7275
34-41, 54-61	Bend & Fort Rock Ranger District — (541) 388-5664
65, 69-72	Blue River Ranger District — (541) 822-3317
76	Bureau of Land Mgmt., Eugene — (541) 683-6481
79, 85, 86	Cottage Grove Ranger District — (541) 942-5591
94, 96-98	Crescent Ranger District — (541) 433-2234
2-8, 18-25	Detroit Ranger District — (503) 854-3366
74	Eugene Parks — (541) 682-4800
75, 86	Lane County Parks — (541) 341-6940
17	Linn County Parks — (541) 967-3917
78, 80-82	Lowell Ranger District — (541) 937-2129
26, 27, 43-48, 62-64	McKenzie Ranger District — (541) 822-3381
66-68	McKenzie Ranger District — (541) 822-3381
75	Mount Pisgah Arboretum — (541) 747-3817
73, 87-93, 95, 99	Oakridge Ranger District — (541) 782-2291
1, 16, 42, 77	Oregon State Parks — (503) 378-6305
83, 84, 100	Rigdon Ranger District — (541) 782-2283
28-32, 49-53	Sisters Ranger District — (541) 549-2111
9-15	Sweet Home Ranger District — (541) 367-5168

Santiam
Foothills

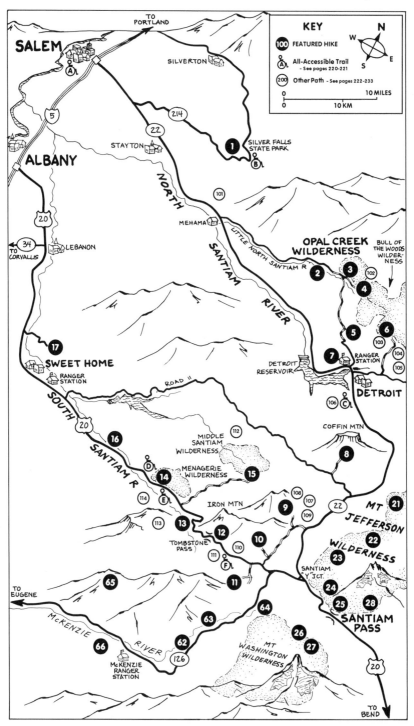

Opposite: Lower South Falls of Silver Creek (Hike #1).

1   Silver Creek Falls

Easy
7-mile loop
600 feet elevation gain
Open all year
Map: Drake Crossing (USGS)

This popular hike through Silver Falls State Park's forested canyons visits 10 spectacular waterfalls, 5 more than 100 feet high. The path even leads through mossy caverns *behind* the falls' shimmering silver curtains.

This loop is a good spring conditioner for experienced hikers. Yet it's also suitable for families with beginners, because side trails provide shortcuts back to the car, trimming the total distance to 5.1, 2.4, or just 0.7 miles. The park is usually snow-free even in mid-winter. From May through September, a $3 parking fee is charged throughout the park.

Drive 10 miles east of Salem on North Santiam Highway 22, turn north at a sign for Silver Falls Park, and follow Highway 214 for 16 miles to the large park entrance sign at South Falls. (Coming from the north, exit Interstate 5 at Woodburn and follow Highway 214 southeast through Silverton for 30 miles.)

When entering the South Falls parking complex, keep to the right for 0.6 mile and park at the last, least crowded lot. At the end of the turnaround, take the trail into the woods and walk left to an overlook of South Falls. From here take the paved trail to the right, switchbacking down into the canyon and behind 177-foot South Falls.

All waterfalls in the park spill over 15-million-year-old Columbia River basalt. As the lava slowly cooled, it sometimes fractured to form the honeycomb of columns visible on cliff edges. Circular indentations in the ceilings of the misty caverns behind the falls are *tree wells,* formed when the lava flows hardened around burning trees. The churning of Silver Creek gouged the soft soil from beneath the harder lava, leaving these caverns and casts.

A few hundred yards beyond South Falls is a junction at a scenic footbridge. Don't cross the bridge; that route merely returns to the car. Instead take the unpaved path along the creek. This route eventually switchbacks down and behind Lower South Falls' broad, 93-foot cascade.

Beyond Lower South Falls the trail forks again. Tired hikers can turn right and climb the steepish ridge trail to the canyon rim and parking lot, for a total of 2.4 miles. If you're ready for a longer hike continue straight, heading up the north fork of Silver Creek to 30-foot Lower North Falls. At a footbridge just above the falls, take a 250-yard side trail to admire tall, thin Double Falls. Then continue on the main trail past Drake and Middle North Falls to the Winter Falls trail junction.

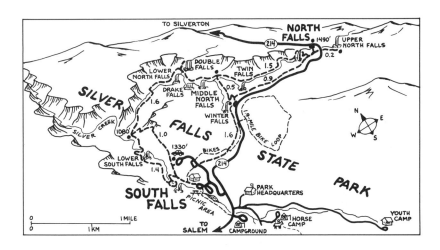

Wearing down? Then opt for the 5.1-mile loop by turning right, climbing to Winter Falls, and taking the return trail to the South Falls parking area. Still not tired? Then continue straight on the 7-mile loop, passing Twin Falls and finally hiking behind North Falls' inspiring 136-foot plume. At a junction above North Falls, turn right onto the return trail, which parallels the highway along the canyon rim for 0.9 mile to the Winter Falls parking pullout. At the far end of the pullout the trail continues along the highway, at times meandering into the woods and crossing a paved bike path. When the trail meets the parking lot entrance road, turn right for 0.2 mile to the car.

Other Hiking Options

Crowds are thinner if you start at the North Falls parking area instead. And while there, don't overlook the 0.2-mile side trail which leads under the highway bridge to less-visited Upper North Falls' quiet pool.

Trail beneath North Falls.   Opposite: Maidenhair fern.

2   Little North Santiam

Moderate
9 miles round-trip
900 feet elevation gain
Open all year
Map: Elkhorn (USGS)

The Little North Santiam has long been known for its swimmable green pools, so tempting on hot summer days. This trail, recently built by Salem volunteers along a less well-known portion of the scenic river's bank, reveals that the river has other charms as well: hidden waterfalls, spring trilliums, and mossy, old-growth forests lit with autumn-reddened vine maple. To shorten this trip to 4.5 miles, bring a second car as a shuttle and hike the trail one-way.

To find the lower trailhead, drive east from Salem on North Santiam Highway 22 for 23 miles to Mehama's second flashing yellow light. Opposite the Swiss Village Restaurant, turn left on Little North Fork Road for 14.5 paved miles. Then turn right onto a gravel road signed "Elkhorn Drive SE," drive across the river bridge, continue 0.4 mile farther, and park on the left at a brown post marking the trailhead.

The trail begins by skirting a tree plantation for 0.2 mile, then plunges into an ancient Douglas fir forest carpeted with sword ferns, vanilla leaf, and shamrock-shaped sourgrass. At the 0.7-mile mark, notice a small waterfall in the river to the left. For a fun detour take a faint side trail to the falls—a chute with a deep, clear pool and a shoreline of river-rounded bedrock ideal for sunbathing.

Return to the main trail, which now begins climbing steeply to bypass a precipitous narrows in the river canyon. Look across the canyon for glimpses of Henline Creek's triple falls and Henline Mountain's cliffs (see Hike #3). The

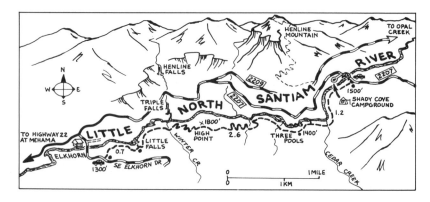

trail switchbacks down to the river again at the 2.3-mile mark and remains relatively level thereafter.

At the 3.3-mile mark, a short side trail to the left leads to a remarkable view of 3 emerald pools separated by small waterfalls. Though the pools are inaccessible here, the trail soon descends within a short scramble of a pebble beach.

The trail reaches gravel Road 2207 at the south end of a historic wooden bridge rebuilt in 1991. To bring a shuttle car to this trailhead, drive up the Little North Santiam Road 1.8 miles past the Elkhorn Drive turnoff (continue 1.3 miles past the end of pavement), and then turn right on Road 2207 for 2 miles.

Little North Santiam River. *Opposite: Sourgrass* (Oxalis).

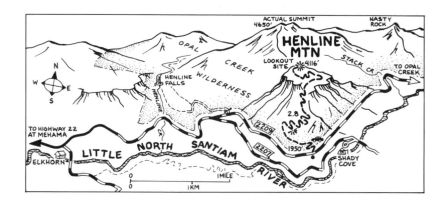

3   Henline Mountain

Difficult
5.6 miles round-trip
2200 feet elevation gain
Open April to mid-November
Map: Elkhorn (USGS)

This delightful climb, handy for a quick bit of exercise, leads to the site of a lookout tower on the rocky shoulder of Henline Mountain. The tower is gone, but the view is still here, extending beyond the Little North Santiam's forest-rimmed valley to Mt. Jefferson. To find the trailhead, drive east from Salem on North Santiam Highway 22 for 23 miles to Mehama's second flashing yellow light. Opposite the Swiss Village Restaurant, turn left on Little North Fork Road for 15 paved miles and continue straight on gravel for another 1.3 miles to a fork. Veer left on Road 2209 past the sign "Road Closed 6 Miles Ahead." Precisely one mile past this fork—watch the odometer!—look sharply for a hiker-symbol sign on a steep, unlikely-looking roadcut to the left. Park on the shoulder here.

The trail climbs up the roadcut, switchbacks several times in the forest (enlivened by rhododendron blooms in June), and traverses a large rockslide. At 0.7 mile, after another switchback, take a short side trail to the right to a rock outcropping. The view here overlooks both the rockslide and the Little North Santiam Valley.

The trail climbs steadily to the 2-mile mark, where it briefly levels to traverse a ridge to the right toward another viewpoint, this one with a first glimpse of Mt. Jefferson's snowy summit. Shortly thereafter, the trails grows rockier and switchbacks up more steeply. Just 0.3 mile from the top, take a breather at a

View from Henline Mountain trail.   *Opposite: Rhododendron.*

viewpoint by an interesting rock pinnacle on the left. Then continue on to the trail's end atop a rocky ridge inhabited by a few struggling manzanita bushes. Though the actual summit of Henline Mountain is a mile north and 530 feet higher, the lookout tower was built on this more visible knoll. Small bolts and bits of broken glass mark the site.

The snowless, square-topped mountain on the eastern horizon is Battle Ax (see Hike #6). To the west, try to spot the golf course at Elkhorn and, on a clear day, Marys Peak in the Coast Range 65 miles away.

4   Opal Creek

Easy (to Opal Pool)
7 miles round-trip
200 feet elevation gain
Open all year
Maps: Battle Ax, Elkhorn (USGS)

Moderate (to Beachie Creek)
10.2 miles round-trip
500 feet elevation gain

Opal Creek's ancient forest, on the edge of the Bull of the Woods Wilderness, was thrust to fame in the 1980s by controversy over Forest Service logging proposals. National television crews and thousands of visitors hiked to Jawbone Flats' rustic mining camp and scrambled over a rugged "bear trail" to view the endangered old-growth groves towering above this creek's green pools. By the time Opal Creek finally won Wilderness protection in 1996 an improved path had been built to make the area more hiker-friendly. The new trail shortcuts from the Little North Santiam River to Opal Creek, bypassing Jawbone Flats.

Start by driving east from Salem on North Santiam Highway 22 for 23 miles to Mehama's second flashing yellow light. Opposite the Swiss Village Restaurant, turn left on Little North Fork Road for 15 paved miles and an additional 1.3 miles of gravel. At a fork, veer left on Road 2209 past the sign "Road Closed 6 Miles Ahead." Then drive 6 miles to the locked gate. Residents of Jawbone Flats are allowed to drive the dirt road ahead; others must park and walk.

The pleasantly primitive road crosses Gold Creek on a 60-foot-high bridge, skirts dramatic cliffs above the Little North Santiam River, and winds through an old-growth grove as impressive as any found farther upstream.

At the 2-mile mark, stop to inspect the rusting machinery of Merten Mill on the right. The mill operated briefly during the Depression, using winches from the battleship *USS Oregon,* but folded after two of the mill's lumber trucks fell

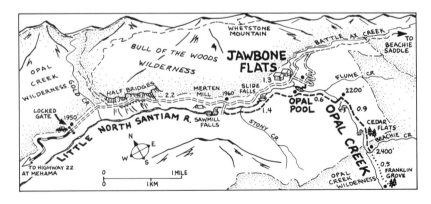

Sawmill Falls.   Opposite: Jawbone Flats.

off the narrow canyon road. Now a camping area for backpackers, the mill site has one small empty building that can serve as emergency shelter. A short side trail behind the building leads to Sawmill Falls, a 30-foot cascade pouring into a deep green pool ideal for swimming.

The road forks 0.2 mile beyond Merten Mill, offering two options. Day hikers interested in the area's mining history may wish to continue straight on the main road 1.3 miles to Jawbone Flats, a well-preserved collection of 27 buildings dating from 1929-1932. Jawbone Flats has been donated to the Friends of Opal Creek as an old-growth study center. Respect the residents' privacy by staying on the road. Cross a bridge, turn right at a building with a humming water-power generator, and walk 0.2 mile further to a sign indicating a short side trail to Opal Pool's scenic gorge—a rewarding goal for an easy hike.

If you're headed for the trail up Opal Creek, however, don't go to Jawbone Flats. Instead, turn right at the road fork beyond Merten Mill, cross the river on an old log bridge, and turn left onto the Opal Creek Trail. The path follows the Little North Santiam River a mile, crosses a forested bench to an overlook of Opal Pool, and then continues up Opal Creek 1.5 miles before petering out. Along the way you'll pass several small waterfalls and Cedar Flat's trio of ancient red cedars, 500-1000 years old. The Beachie Creek crossing, on a mossy log, makes a good turnaround point.

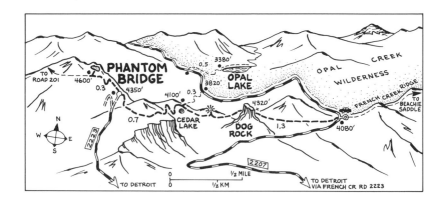

Phantom Bridge. *Opposite: Avalanche lilies.*

5   Phantom Bridge

Moderate
4.6 miles round-trip
1400 feet elevation gain
Open late June to mid-November
Use: hikers, horses, bicycles
Map: Battle Ax (USGS)

This natural rock arch, hidden on a ridgetop cliff between Detroit and the Bull of the Woods Wilderness, spans a 50-foot chasm, yet is solid enough that some daring souls creep to its middle. Admittedly, the hike along the ridge to the arch has a few rough, steep spots, but the route compensates with avalanche lilies, huckleberries, and views of the High Cascades from Mt. Hood to the Three Sisters.

Start by driving 50 miles east of Salem on North Santiam Highway 22. Just before the town of Detroit, at the west end of the Breitenbush River bridge, turn north onto French Creek Road 2223. Follow this paved, one-lane road 4.2 miles and turn right onto gravel Road 2207 for 3.7 miles. Watch for a hiker-symbol sign at the trailhead on the left, just before a saddle. Park at a turnout 100 feet farther and walk back to the trail.

The trail begins in an old clearcut, but soon heads left around a wooded hill. After traversing a rockslide at the base of Dog Rock's monolith, the path follows a ridgecrest amid masses of white avalanche lilies (in late June) and huckleberries (in late August). A small rocky knoll to the right has a particularly fine view of Opal Lake and a dozen notable peaks, including Battle Ax (Hike #6) to the north, Mt. Jefferson to the east, and square-topped Coffin Mountain (Hike #8) to the south.

The trail then descends steeply to Cedar Lake, a small pond, and switchbacks up to an open plateau. Follow cairns across this highland. Then descend through a clearcut, cross a gravel turnaround at the end of Road 2223, and climb the ridge 0.3 mile farther to a "Phantom Bridge" sign pointing to the right. A 50-foot scramble to the ridgecrest finally reveals the arch.

Other Hiking Options

A different trailhead is just 0.3 mile from Phantom Bridge, although this shortcut misses most of the flowers and views. The drive is a little trickier, too. From Detroit, take French Creek Road 4.2 miles to the end of pavement and fork left to stay on Road 2223. After another 4 miles keep right at an unmarked fork. In another 0.5 mile you'll reach an three-way fork in a saddle just before a set of powerlines. Veer left, but avoid spur Road 535. The trailhead is 2.1 miles farther, at road's end.

6   Battle Ax and Twin Lakes

Moderate (to Battle Ax)
5.6-mile loop
1600 feet elevation gain
Open mid-June through October
Use: hikers, horses
Map: Bull of the Woods Wilderness
(USFS)

Difficult (to Twin Lakes)
12.4 miles round-trip
2200 feet elevation gain

Tallest peak in the Bull of the Woods Wilderness, Battle Ax not only commands views from Mt. Hood to Diamond Peak, it also hosts an interesting rock garden of subalpine wildflowers and weather-stunted trees. The loop trail to the summit returns around the mountain's base, past a collection of tranquil ponds. For a longer hike, bypass the summit and head for forest-rimmed Twin Lakes.

Some say Battle Ax won its name because of the peak's sharp, hatchet-shaped silhouette. Others note that "Battle Ax" was a brand of chewing tobacco popular when gold prospectors scoured this area in the 1890s.

To find the trailhead, drive 50 miles east of Salem on North Santiam Highway 22 to a "Breitenbush River" pointer in the town of Detroit. Turn left on paved Breitenbush Road 46 for 4.4 miles to a small sign for Elk Lake. Then turn left onto gravel Road 4696 for 0.8 mile, turn left again mile onto Road 4697 at a sign "Elk Road Not Maintained For Trailer Travel," and after 4.7 miles of good but steep gravel, turn left at another sign for Elk Lake.

Here the road abruptly worsens. Though level, the track has big potholes and buried boulders that slow travel to a grueling crawl. After 2 miles of this agony, reach the far end of the lake. Passengers cars should probably park here, at the fork to the Elk Lake Campground. More rugged vehicles may drive up the right-hand fork 0.4 mile to a sign for the Bagby Hot Springs Trail. Parking is tight but possible on the shoulder 100 yards beyond the sign.

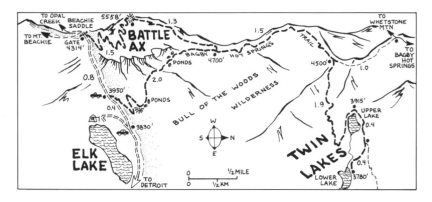

Elk Lake and Mt. Jefferson from Battle Ax.   Opposite: Cat's ear.

Start by walking up this rough road to its gated end at Beachie Saddle. Then turn right and take the trail up the ridge, switchbacking amid trees dwarfed by winter winds. Watch for huckleberries, strawberry blooms, red Indian paint-brush, and fuzzy cat's ears.

At the summit, only foundation piers remain of the old fire lookout. Take a short side trip out a shaley ridge to the east for a breathtaking view down to Elk Lake. To continue the loop, return to the lookout site and follow a faint trail along a ridge to the north. After 1.3 miles you'll meet the Bagby Hot Springs Trail. To complete the loop, turn right for 2 miles back to the road. Along the way you'll pass froggy subalpine ponds, yellow fawn lilies, and rockslides inhabited by pikas—the little, round-eared "rock rabbits" that *meep!* at hikers.

If you prefer lakes to peaks, start this hike by setting off on the Bagby Hot Springs Trail. After 3.5 miles of gradual, up-and-down climbing along a ridge you'll reach a junction in a forested saddle. Turn right on the 1.9-mile path down to Upper Twin Lake. Then keep right for another 0.8 mile to find its lower partner, an even prettier pool in deep hemlock woods.

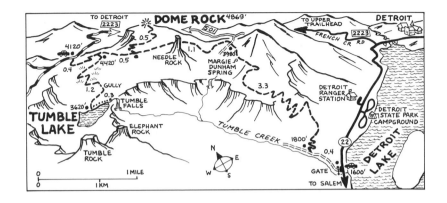

7   Dome Rock and Tumble Lake

Moderate (from upper trailhead)
5.2 miles round-trip
1550 feet elevation gain
Open June through October
Maps: Detroit, Battle Ax (USGS)

Difficult (to Dome Rk from lower trailhead)
10.6 miles round-trip
3270 feet elevation gain

High on a quiet ridge above Detroit Lake's powerboats and campgrounds, the old lookout site atop Dome Rock commands a view across jagged foothills to snowy Mt. Jefferson. Nearby, a steep trail dives into Tumble Lake's hanging valley, amid rare Alaska cedars and the area's best huckleberry fields. For a moderate hike to these enticing goals, start at an upper trailhead on a gravel backroad. For an easier drive but a much tougher hike, start at a lower trailhead on Highway 22, just a stone's throw from Detroit Lake.

To find the convenient lower trailhead, drive east of Salem on Highway 22 to Detroit Lake. Near milepost 48, just 0.8 mile before the Detroit Ranger Station, park in a pullout on the left marked "Tumble Creek Road." Walk around a locked gate, follow the old road up Tumble Creek 0.4 mile, and turn right on the Tumble Ridge Trail. This path climbs relentlessly, switchbacking up through regrowing clearcuts and patches of old growth woods. Because the first two miles of the trail are usually free of snow all year, some hikers tackle this portion for midwinter exercise. By June, when the entire trail is clear, wildflowers brighten the route: white bells of salal, yellow sprays of Oregon grape, white plumes of beargrass, and red stalks of fireweed.

At the 3.7-mile mark you'll cross a brushy road in an old Santiam State Forest clearcut known as Margie Dunham. The next 1.1 mile is less steep, traversing along a ridge and ducking behind Needle Rock's pillar to the Dome Rock Trail junction. Fork uphill to the right for half a mile to the rocky summit, where the lookout's concrete foundations remain amid windswept stonecrop blooms. Look south across Detroit Lake to spot flat-topped Coffin Mountain (Hike #8) and the humps of the Three Pyramids (Hike #9). You can also see Tumble Lake glinting enticingly in the valley to the west. But the truth is, after climbing 5.3 tough miles to Dome Rock from Highway 22, most hikers will be too bushed to continue 2.2 miles down to Tumble Lake. The trick is to start at the Tumble Ridge Trail's upper trailhead.

To find the upper trailhead, drive Highway 22 east around Detroit Lake two miles past the lower trailhead. Near milepost 50, just before crossing a bridge to the town of Detroit, turn left onto French Creek Road 2223. Follow this one-lane road for 4.2 paved miles. Then fork to the left to follow a gravel continuation of Road 2223 another 3.9 miles. Watch the odometer carefully, because the trailhead is marked by a mere post on the left, and it's easy to miss. The only parking is a wide spot on the right beside a cliff edge.

This upper end of the trail starts by scrambling 50 feet to a saddle. Then it traverses 0.4 mile along a scenic ridge to a fork. Keep left if you're headed for Dome Rock's summit viewpoint, a mile away. Keep right if you're taking the steep 1.2-mile trail down to Tumble Lake. This path dives down through brushfields of red thimbleberries, fireweed, and huge blue huckleberries (ripe in August). When the path appears to vanish in a washout, simply go straight downhill; this gully *is* the trail. The path ends at deep, 20-acre Tumble Lake. Shaggy-barked Alaska cedars, uncommon this far south, droop branches over shoreside lilypads. The massive outcrops of Elephant Rock and Tumble Rock loom across the lake. Alder brush blocks lakeshore exploration to the right, but a scramble trail follows the shore 0.3 mile left to a 100-foot waterfall in the lake's outlet creek.

Tumble Lake.   Opposite: Tumble Lake from Dome Rock.

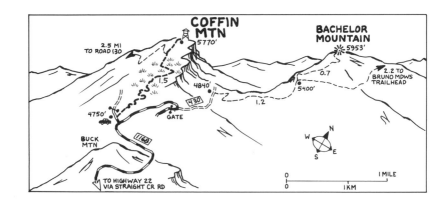

COFFIN
MTN
5770'

2.5 MI
TO ROAD 130

1.5

4840'

430

4750'

GATE

BUCK
MTN

1168

TO HIGHWAY 22
VIA STRAIGHT CR RD

BACHELOR
MOUNTAIN
5953'

2.2 TO
BRUNO MDWS
TRAILHEAD

0.7

5400'

1.2

N
W E
S

0   1 MILE
0   1 KM

Coffin Mountain's lookout with Three Fingered Jack on horizon.   Opposite: Beargrass.

8   Coffin Mountain Lookout

Moderate
3 miles round-trip
1000 feet elevation gain
Open late June through October
Use: hikers, horses, bicycles
Map: Coffin Mountain (USGS)

Coffin Mountain's square-topped silhouette seems to be on the horizon wherever one goes in the western Cascade foothills. Towering cliffs make the summit appear unreachable. Yet those who actually visit the peak discover a surprisingly well-graded trail climbing to the lookout tower through a meadow of cheerful wildflower blooms. Along the way, a string of snowy High Cascade peaks is constantly in view.

From Salem, take North Santiam Highway 22 east for 69 miles. Beyond Marion Forks 2.9 miles, near milepost 69, turn right on paved Straight Creek Road. (If you're coming from the east, take Highway 22 past the Santiam Y junction 12.7 miles and turn left.) Follow Straight Creek Road 4.2 miles to a sign for the Coffin Mountain Trailhead. Then turn right for 3.8 miles on gravel Road 1168 to a trailhead sign and parking area at a spur road on the left. Remember to pack extra water since the lookout staff cannot share their limited supply.

The hike starts on an old bulldozer track, but turns left after 200 yards onto a friendlier hiking path. Wildflowers are profuse here in early summer. Expect blue iris, red paintbrush, purple larkspur, fuzzy cat's ears, blue penstemon, and yellow violets. To the east, Mt. Jefferson rises apparently at arm's length. The view to the west is even more striking: ridge upon desolate ridge of clearcut National Forest, hidden here in the hills behind Detroit Reservoir.

After 0.9 mile begin two long switchbacks across a vast meadow of beargrass. This lily family member blooms in cycles; about every third July the hillside erupts with stalks of white flowers.

When you reach the mountain's summit ridgecrest, ignore the communications building to the left and instead head right for 0.2 mile through the trees to the fire lookout. This lonely 16-foot-square outpost becomes a miniature home in the summers it is staffed, with a tiny kitchen, a visitor's register, and all the books one never had time to read: *Alaska, Little Women, Spanish Through Pictures,* and once, *Is This Where I Was Going?*

Other Hiking Options

If Coffin Mountain's view seems unequaled, try scaling the peak's fraternal twin, nearby Bachelor Mountain. It's a trifle taller but less cliffy. Drive 0.7 mile past Coffin Mountain on Road 1168 and turn left on rugged Road 430 for 0.5 mile to its end. The trail climbs past white snags left by the 1970s' Buck Mountain Burn. It's 1.9 miles to the top and 1100 feet up.

9   The Three Pyramids

Moderate
4 miles round-trip
1800 feet elevation gain
Open late June through October
Maps: Echo Mtn., Coffin Mtn. (USGS)

Like a smaller version of the Three Sisters, this trio of ancient volcanic plugs rises in a dramatic cluster above the Old Cascades. To be sure, the Three Pyramids are only half as tall as the more famous mountain triplets, and are not draped with glaciers. But pretty, U-shaped glacial valleys remain from the Ice Age. Today, a short but strenuous section of the Old Cascades Crest Trail climbs the Middle Pyramid, switchbacking up a wildflower-spangled ridge to a former lookout tower site where the panorama stretches from Mt. Hood all the way to Diamond Peak.

To find the trailhead from Salem, drive 77 miles east on North Santiam Highway 22. Between mileposts 76 and 77, turn right on gravel Lava Lake Meadow Road 2067. (If you're coming from the other direction, take Highway 22 west from the Santiam Y junction 4.8 miles toward Salem and turn left.) Follow Lava Lake Meadow Road 1.9 miles to the Parks Creek bridge, turn sharply right at a sign for the Pyramids Trail and follow Road 560 tenaciously for 3.5 miles to a parking lot at road's end.

Start the hike by crossing a creek on a log footbridge and turning right at a T-shaped trail junction. This path climbs through a shady old-growth forest full of white woodland wildflowers: four-petaled bunchberry, delicate stalks of vanilla leaf, and tiny sprays of star-flowered smilacina. After half a mile's steady climb, cross the creek on stones and climb through a brushy meadow with

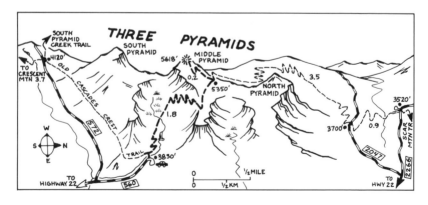

Middle Pyramid.   Opposite: Star-flowered smilacina.

bracken fern, bleeding hearts, columbine, and the giant leaves of hellebore. At the 0.7-mile mark the trail abruptly turns up the ridge, switchbacking steeply. Views now improve to cliffs across the valley and beyond to the Three Sisters.

After 1.5 miles, the trail crests the ridge and traverses a shady slope where snow and trilliums linger into July. Here the views of Mt. Jefferson begin.

The path winds around to the west face of Middle Pyramid and then switchbacks up to a rocky saddle. The trail appears to end here, between Middle Pyramid's two summits. But the path actually clambers up some rocks to the right and continues 100 yards to the lookout tower site surrounded by cliffs. Almost the entire route of the hike is visible below. To the southwest, note Iron Mountain's distinctive rock thumb. In the west, the rock monolith rising from the Middle Santiam Wilderness forests is Chimney Peak, with a stripe of Willamette Valley beyond.

Other Hiking Options
The 27-mile Old Cascades Crest Trail connects this trail with Crescent Mountain (Hike #10) to the south and the Middle Santiam Wilderness (Hike #15) to the west, opening possibilities for longer shuttle hikes and backpacking trips.

10   Crescent Mountain

Difficult
8.6 miles round-trip
2200 feet elevation gain
Open June through October
Use: hikers, horses
Map: Echo Mountain (USGS)

Sunny wildflower meadows drape the southern slopes of this huge, crescent-shaped ridge. As the trail angles up through the open fields, expect dramatic views across the High Cascade forests to Mt. Washington and the Three Sisters.

Start by driving Highway 20 east of Sweet Home 43 miles (or west of Santiam Pass 10 miles). Near milepost 71, just half a mile west of the junction with Highway 126, turn north on paved Lava Lake Road. After one mile, turn left on gravel Road 508 for 0.7 mile to a large trailhead parking lot with a horse unloading ramp.

The trail descends very gradually for its first 1.1 mile to a footbridge across lovely, 8-foot-wide Maude Creek. A small meadow on the far shore makes a nice day-hike goal for children.

After Maude Creek, the trail starts to climb. At the 2.5-mile mark it emerges from the dark woods into a steep meadow of bracken fern and blue lupine. Views open up of snowpeaks to the southeast. Soon, enter a much larger meadow. In early summer the bracken and bunchgrass grow so densely here they sometimes hide the tread.

After a total of 3.5 miles, the trail enters a weather-gnarled stand of mountain hemlock and subalpine fir. Then the path clings to a forested ridgecrest all the way to the top.

Only the wooden floor of the old fire lookout tower survives. From the

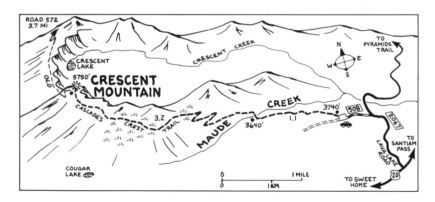

northern edge of the summit look down a cliff to Crescent Lake, curled within the curving mountain's embrace.

Other Hiking Options

Beyond Crescent Mountain's summit, the trail drops 1600 feet in 3.7 miles to a fork at Road 572. From there, equestrians can head left 5.4 miles on the South Pyramid Creek Trailhead to the Middle Santiam River (Hike #15). The right-hand fork, a continuation of the 27-mile Old Cascades Crest Trail, is for hikers only. That path leads 1.8 miles to the Pyramids Trail (see Hike #9), and continues past the tops of Middle Pyramid, Trapper Butte, and Scar Mountain.

Mt. Washington from Crescent Mountain's meadows.   Opposite: Bracken fern.

11   Browder Ridge

Moderate (to viewpoint)
3.2 miles round-trip
1150 feet elevation gain
Open June to mid-November
Use: hikers, horses
Maps: Tamolitch Falls, Echo Mtn. (USGS)

Difficult (to summit)
8.4 miles round-trip
2100 feet elevation gain

Browder Ridge, like many of its better-known neighbor peaks in the Old Cascades, sports steep wildflower meadows on its high southern slopes. But no crowds roam Browder Ridge's meadows, as they do at nearby Iron Mountain (Hike #12). And Browder Ridge's view of the High Cascades snowpeaks is second to none.

The trip provides two options: either climb the well-maintained Gate Creek Trail only as far as the viewpoint on the shoulder of Browder Ridge, or venture onward to the ridge's summit via a less well-maintained path and a cross-country meadow route.

To find the Gate Creek Trailhead, drive Highway 20 east of Sweet Home 41 miles (or west of Santiam Pass 8 miles). Near milepost 68, just 2.7 miles west of the junction with Highway 126, turn south onto Hackleman Creek Road. After 1.7 miles, turn right onto gravel Road 1598 for 2.8 miles to the well-marked trailhead.

The Gate Creek Trail abandons Gate Creek forever after a few yards and instead switchbacks steadily up toward Browder Ridge along a slope forested with ancient Douglas firs 5 feet in diameter. At the 1-mile mark, begin climbing steeply up a large meadow of bracken fern, blue mertensia, red columbine, and delicate white star-flowered smilacina. If you lose the path amid the bracken, look for it near the top of the meadow, entering the forest on the right.

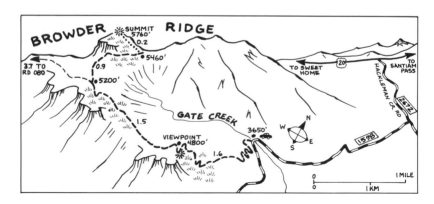

Browder Ridge meadow.   Opposite: Columbine.

After a switchback in the forest, return to the meadow at a glorious viewpoint that makes a worthy goal for a moderate hike. Here are views of Three Fingered Jack, Mt. Washington, and the Three Sisters. Rock-garden wildflowers cluster at one's feet: blue penstemon, fuzzy cat's ears, and yellow monkeyflower.

If you're going onward to the summit, follow the trail as it ambles west along the ridgecrest at a much gentler grade. The path grows faint at times in meadows on the left side of the ridge; always keep to the top of the meadows. Beyond the viewpoint 1.7 miles, at the far, upper end of a large meadow, the trail reenters the forest and immediately forks. Turn uphill to the right.

This portion of the trail is poorly maintained, with a few downed logs to step over. Follow the faint trail as it gradually ascends a broad, forested ridge for 0.4 mile to the base of a 150-foot-tall rock cliff. Then the path turns sharply right and traverses a large, steep meadow for 0.5 mile. Just before reentering the forest at a ridgecrest, climb cross-country up the steep meadow, following the ridge to the summit—a rounded knoll carpeted with heather, phlox, and cat's ears. The 360-degree view encompasses Mt. Jefferson, the South Santiam Canyon, and the entire route of the hike.

Other Hiking Options

Adventurers can follow the Browder Ridge Trail west 3.7 miles from the trail junction at elevation 5200 feet. This route can be hard to find in meadows. It finally descends to Road 080 at a trailhead just a few hundred yards from paved Road 15.

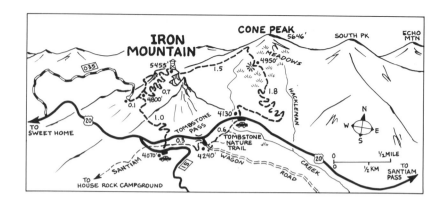

12   Iron Mountain

Easy (to Cone Peak meadows)
3.6 miles round-trip
800 feet elevation gain
Open mid-May to mid-November
Map: Harter Mountain (USGS)

Moderate (to Iron Mountain)
6.6-mile loop
1900 feet elevation gain
Open mid-June through October

Iron Mountain's lookout building is one of the Old Cascades' most popular hiking goals, but most people hike to it the wrong way—up a steep, dusty, largely viewless forest trail on the west side of Tombstone Pass. To really see the July wildflowers that make this area famous, take the longer, better graded Cone Peak Trail through the alpine meadows on the east side of Tombstone Pass. In fact, the viewpoint amid these flower-packed fields makes a worthwhile day-hike destination in itself.

Start by driving Highway 20 east of Sweet Home 36 miles (or west of Santiam Pass 13 miles). At milepost 64, just 0.4 mile east of Tombstone, park at a small pullout marked with a brown hiker-symbol sign.

The Cone Peak Trail sets out climbing steadily through an old-growth forest that includes shaggy-barked Alaska cedars, rare in Oregon but common here. The entire ridge from Iron Mountain to Echo Mountain is a biological wonderland, featuring more types of trees (17) than any other area in Oregon, and fully 60 plant species considered rare or unusual in the Western Cascades. After 1.1 mile and several switchbacks, emerge from the forests in a rock garden of early-summer wildflowers: fuzzy cat's ears, purple larkspur, yellow stonecrop, and pink penstemon. The path continues across a cinder-strewn shoulder of Cone Peak—a landscape where one wouldn't think plants could grow at all, but where red paintbrush and other flowers wash the slopes with color. The viewpoint here overlooks Iron Mountain and Tombstone Prairie.

Beyond the meadow viewpoint the trail descends slightly to a saddle and contours halfway around Iron Mountain to a junction with the Iron Mountain Trail. Turn left and climb 0.7 mile on steep switchbacks to the lookout building. To the east, all the major Cascade peaks are visible. To the west, look for Rooster Rock (Hike #14) and, on a clear day, Marys Peak in the Coast Range.

Be cautious near the summit cliffs. A lookout staffer fell to his death here in 1990. The entire building blew off the peak in a 1976 winter storm and had to be returned by helicopter.

To return from the lookout on a loop, keep left as you descend the Iron Mountain Trail. In 1.7 miles you'll reach Highway 20. Don't walk back along this busy road. Instead follow the trail across the highway, heading toward the official Iron Mountain Trailhead on Road 15, downhill another 100 yards. Just before you reach Road 15, however, turn left on the Santiam Wagon Road—a pleasant path that climbs 0.3 mile to the Tombstone Pass Sno-park. Walk to the far right end of this parking lot and angle downhill on the Tombstone Nature Trail. Then keep left for 0.6 mile to find a new connector trail that climbs to your car at the Cone Peak Trailhead on Highway 20.

Other Hiking Options

A shorter, 0.8-mile route to Iron Mountain's lookout begins from the end of a rough gravel road. To find it, drive Highway 20 a mile west of Tombstone Pass. Near milepost 62, turn north on Road 035 for 2.8 miles.

Iron Mountain from the Cone Peak Trail.   Opposite: Phlox.

13 Santiam Wagon Road

Easy (House Rock loop)
0.8-mile loop
100 feet elevation gain
Open all year

Easy (from Mountain House)
4.8 miles round-trip
300 feet elevation gain

Moderate (to knoll viewpoint)
11.2 miles round-trip
1100 feet elevation gain
Use: hikers, horses, bicycles

When the first automobile to cross North America sputtered down the old Santiam Wagon Road toward Sweet Home in 1905, dragging a tree behind it on the steepest pitches as an emergency brake, the toll gate keeper studied the begoggled New York driver of the horseless Oldsmobile runabout and charged him three cents—the going rate for hogs.

Local entrepreneurs built the for-profit wagon road up the South Santiam River canyon in 1866-67, hoping to sell Willamette Valley cattle in the gold mining boomtowns of Eastern Oregon. Riders with good horses usually made the trip from Albany to Sisters in 4 days, stopping each night at roadhouses where hay, a bed, and a meal cost less than a dollar. The route remained the main link across the Cascades until the 1920s, when the McKenzie Pass highway opened. By 1925 the Santiam Wagon Road was sold to the government, and in 1939 the state replaced it with Highway 20.

Today a 19.3-mile stretch of the old wagon road has been reopened as a trail. For a quick sample of the route's charms, try the 0.8-mile trail loop from House Rock Campground. Complete with cave and waterfall, this short path is great for families with kids. For a better taste of the historic route, start 2.1 miles away, near the Mountain House restaurant. For a longer hike (or a mountain bike ride), plan to continue up Sevenmile Hill to a canyon viewpoint atop a knoll.

If you only have time for the 0.8-mile loop, start by driving Highway 20 east of Sweet Home 25 miles. At a "House Rock Campground" pointer between mileposts 53 and 54, turn right for 0.2 mile and then turn right again at a campground entrance sign for another 0.2 mile to the hiking trail parking lot beside the river. Walk to the right 100 yards, cross a dramatic footbridge across the South Santiam River, and turn left to start the loop. Right away you'll pass House Rock, a boulder so large that entire pioneer families could camp beneath its overhang to weather storms. The forest here is a jungle of moss-draped bigleaf maples, delicate maidenhair ferns, and giant 6-foot-thick Douglas firs.

Continue upriver on the loop 0.2 mile, detour briefly on a 200-yard side trail to House Rock Falls' frothing 30-foot cascade, and then turn right on the actual roadbed of the Santiam Wagon Road. After 0.2 mile on this wide, woodsy trail, turn right to complete the loop.

If you'd prefer a longer hike—or if you've brought a mountain bike—start near the Mountain House restaurant instead. Drive Highway 20 to this old

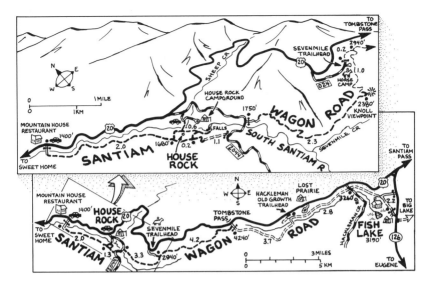

roadhouse between mileposts 52 and 53, and continue east 0.1 mile to a roadside parking area with a green metal gate. Walk around the gate, cross a wooden bridge over the South Santiam River, and follow the old wagon roadbed left. The wide dirt trail ambles through a mix of young alder woods, shaggy maples, and a few old firs. Expect some highway noise from across the river.

When you reach a post identifying the trail's 2-mile mark, a hiker-only side trail to the left leads to House Rock and the waterfall—a good goal for a moderate hike. If you opt to continue straight on the Santiam Wagon Road, you'll climb gradually 1.3 miles to a gate at gravel Road 2044. Head left along this road 0.3 mile until you cross the river, and then turn right onto a gated spur—the trail's continuation. The next mile of trail is newly built, but then you'll rejoin the original wagon track as it climbs Sevenmile Hill, a treacherous grade where Eugene's mayor rolled his car on a 1924 outing.

At a switchback beside the 5-mile marker post, take a small side trail to the right 100 yards to a rocky knoll. The view here extends across a vast forested canyonland to the cliffs of Jumpoff Joe Mountain and the rocky thumb of Iron Mountain (Hike #12). Turn back here, because much of the historic wagon route beyond has been confused or supplanted by relatively recent forest roads.

Footbridge at House Rock.   *Opposite: Wagon road sign.*

14　Rooster Rock

Difficult
6.6 miles round-trip
2300 feet elevation gain
Open April through November
Map: Menagerie Wilderness (USFS)
Left: Rabbit Ears.　Opposite: Shelter Falls

Turkey Monster, Rabbit Ears, Chicken Rock—the rock pillars and arches rising from the forests of the Menagerie Wilderness suggest a petrified zoo. In fact, the crags are remnant plugs of the volcanoes that built this portion of the Old Cascades 25 million years ago.

Today, the trail up to Rooster Rock's former lookout site offers not only a look at this ancient menagerie but also a view of the entire South Santiam Canyon from Iron Mountain to the Willamette Valley. The trail is a particularly good choice for a conditioning hike in spring, when the rhododendrons bloom.

Take Highway 20 east of Sweet Home for 21 miles. A few hundred yards east of the Trout Creek Campground entrance (near milepost 49), park at a pullout on the highway's north shoulder marked by a hiker-symbol sign. Two trails begin here. Skip the Walton Ranch Interpretive Trail, a 0.3-mile path to a decked overlook of a farm with a wintering elk herd. Instead, start at the right end of the parking pullout on the Trout Creek Trail. This path climbs at a remarkably steady grade through a Douglas fir forest with Oregon grape, salal, mossy vine maple, and crowds of May-blooming rhododendrons.

At the 2.8-mile mark, join the Rooster Rock Trail and begin climbing more steeply through a drier forest of madrone, chinkapin, and manzanita. After two quick switchbacks the trail passes Rooster Rock's spire. Uphill another 500 yards the trail forks. Ignore the route straight ahead—it's a rough climbers' trail to a

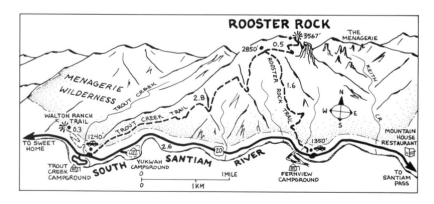

logging road near Rabbit Ears' twin 260-foot pillars. Take the right-hand fork, which promptly leads to an excellent viewpoint atop a bare rock knoll. For years this was the site of a base cabin for a tiny fire lookout shack precariously perched atop Rooster Rock's pinnacle. Only scattered boards remain of the two cabins.

Other Hiking Options

For variety, return on the Rooster Rock Trail. Though this route down to Highway 20 is 1.2 miles shorter, it's a lot steeper. The two trailheads are 2.6 miles apart on the highway—an unpleasant roadside walk, but a delightful bicycle ride if you've had the foresight to stash a pair of wheels nearby.

15 Middle Santiam River

Easy (to Shedd Camp Shelter)
1.4 miles round-trip
430 feet elevation loss
Open April through November
Use: hikers, horses
Map: Middle Santiam Wildrns (USFS)

Moderate (to Pyramid Creek)
6 miles round-trip
900 feet elevation gain

Difficult (to Donaca Lake)
13 miles round-trip
1700 feet elevation gain

One of the wildest places in Western Oregon, yet surprisingly close to the Willamette Valley, the Middle Santiam Wilderness is a hidden haven for brawling rivers and low-elevation old-growth forests. An easy 0.7-mile path leads to a rustic shelter beside a roaring waterfall's swimmable pool. Longer treks lead to rarely visited creeks and silent Donaca Lake. The price of admission to all this splendor, however, is a tedious 13-mile drive on narrow gravel logging roads through the ghastly clearcut foothills that surround the Wilderness.

From Sweet Home, drive Highway 20 east 24 miles. Just before the Mountain House restaurant (and half a mile after passing milepost 52), turn left on Soda Fork Road 2041. After 0.9 mile on this one-lane gravel road, keep left at a fork. At the 8-mile mark you'll reach a 6-way road intersection in a pass. Go straight, sticking to Road 2041. In another 4.5 miles you'll reach a 3-way fork. Take the middle route, Road 646, for 0.6 mile to its end at a large gravel parking lot for the Chimney Peak Trail.

The trail starts out amid second-growth woods, but soon descends into an ancient forest of 5-foot-thick Douglas firs and red cedars. The lush undergrowth here has attractions for all seasons: white trilliums in April, four-petaled bunchberry in May, pink rhododendrons in June, stately beargrass plumes in July, red thimbleberries in August, and orange chanterelle mushrooms in September.

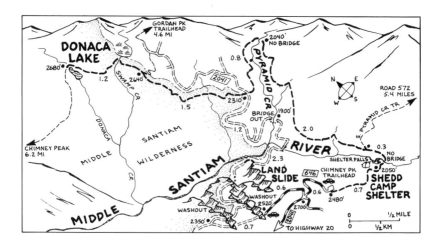

At the 0.7-mile mark you'll reach Shedd Camp Shelter, a three-sided structure with a leakless shake roof. From here the trail dives 100 feet down to the Middle Santiam River, a bridgeless torrent in a dramatic canyon of gravel bars, driftwood logs, and sculpted bedrock. Explore downstream 100 yards to a spectacular blue-green pool fed by a 20-foot waterfall. A pebbly beach here invites swimmers to a chilly dip.

For a longer hike, you'll have to cross the river above the falls. When the water's low and logs span the channel, daring hikers can cross dry-footed. Otherwise bring old tennis shoes for the wade. On the far shore, the trail climbs 0.3 mile to a fork. Keep left, traversing a hillside for another 2 miles before descending to a lovely wooded flat beside Pyramid Creek. This makes a good turnaround point, in part because the 30-foot-wide stream has no bridge. Only the most skilled of rock-hoppers can avoid wading, and only in late summer.

If you're headed onward to Donaca Lake, cross Pyramid Creek, follow the trail up to the left 0.8 mile, cross an abandoned portion of Road 2041, and amble along for 2.7 easy miles to the little green lake. House-sized boulders in the woods and a few white snags in the water reveal that Donaca Lake was dammed by a landslide long ago. Since then, giant red cedars have grown along the sandy inlet creek that meanders down to a tiny but tempting swimming beach.

Other Hiking Options

To return on a loop, consider walking back on Road 2041. This rougher, 1.6-mile longer route takes you through the astonishing moonscape of landslides and washouts triggered by Forest Service efforts to punch logging roads into the steep Middle Santiam area prior to Wilderness designation in 1984.

Instead of crossing Road 2041 on the way back from Donaca Lake, turn right for 1.2 miles to the concrete ruin of the road's washed-out Pyramid Creek bridge. Cross on a fallen log downstream if you can. Then continue on the road 0.7 mile to the toe of a half-mile-long landslide from a clearcut. In the next 2.3 miles, a dozen sections of Road 2041 have vanished into vast gullies. After scrambling across the last gap, walk 1.2 miles on drivable road to return to your car.

16   Cascadia Park

Easy
2.6 miles round-trip
450 feet elevation gain
Open all year
Maps: Cascadia (USGS)
Right: South Santiam River

Short trails to a waterfall, a mineral spring, and a South Santiam River wading beach highlight this historic state park near Sweet Home.

The area's history as a travelers' camp has been traced back 8000 years, when native Americans built campfires in nearby Cascadia Cave. Excavations in this broad hollow beneath the overhang of a cliff reveal that early visitors hunted deer, elk, and rabbits, and used hand-held stones to grind nuts and seeds.

Pioneer entrepreneurs expanded use of the South Santiam as a travel route, building a for-profit wagon road from Albany to Sisters in 1866-67. In 1895, George and Jennie Geisendorfer bought the natural soda springs here, built a bridge across the river to the wagon road, and developed a resort for weary travelers. The Geisendorfers ran their hotel, store, bath house, rental cabins, and campground for 45 years before selling to the state. Cascadia Resort's buildings are gone, but the park's picnic areas and campground are as popular as ever.

To find the park, drive Highway 20 east of Sweet Home 14 miles. At a state park sign between mileposts 41 and 42, turn left across a river bridge. Then keep right for 100 feet and park at a picnic area beneath big Douglas firs.

Two short hikes begin here. To find the trail to Lower Soda Falls, walk up the road 100 yards, veering right toward the East Picnic Area. At a "No Parking" sign where the road crosses Soda Creek, turn left on a broad footpath. This trail follows the splashing creek 0.7 mile through increasingly grand Douglas fir

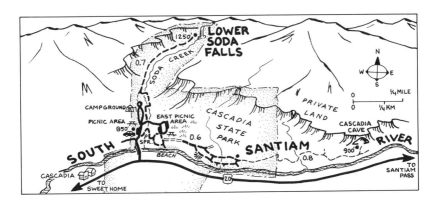

woods to the base of a 80-foot, twisting waterfall in a mossy slot.

For the second short hike, return to your car. At a "Soda Spring Trail" pointer across the road from the parking lot, take a paved path 100 yards down to a stone-paved creekside patio. A drinking fountain here squirts ordinary tap water, but if you look down an open pipe nearby you'll see Soda Spring's actual output, a churning orange brew loaded with calcium, potassium, and iron.

If you continue on the paved trail, keeping right at junctions for 200 yards, you'll reach a gravel beach beside the South Santiam River. The low water of late summer reveals bedrock benches and warm pools ideal for sunning or wading. To explore the rest of the park, walk back from the beach, head straight across the East Picnic Area lawns toward a restroom building, and turn right on an abandoned gravel road. This old road crosses the group camping lawns and becomes a wide bark dust trail in the riverside woods. The path has many forks, but keep right for 0.3 mile until the trail finally loops back away from the river, climbing 100 yards to an easy-to-miss junction. A small trail toward Cascadia Cave goes right. Keep left on the main path to complete the loop and return to your car.

Do not hike to Cascadia Cave. Although this 20-foot-deep overhanging cliff and its ancient, deeply-chiseled petroglpyhs are on the federal register of historic sites, the cave and the surrounding timberland are privately owned. A local archeological group hopes to acquire the cave for the park in the future.

17 McDowell Creek Falls

Easy
1.7-mile loop
200 feet elevation gain
Open all year
Map: Sweet Home (USGS)

This charming glen's 3 lovely waterfalls, low-elevation forest, and easy graveled paths make it ideal for family outings and Sunday strolls. Tucked in a valley near Sweet Home, this little-known miniature version of Silver Creek Falls is hikable all year long.

To drive here from the west, take Highway 20 past Lebanon 4 miles, turn left at the McDowell Creek Park exit, and follow signs for 10 paved miles. To drive here from the east, turn north off Highway 20 at the west end of Sweet Home and follow signs 8.5 miles to the park.

The county park has three parking areas accessing the falls. Stop at the first lot, marked "Royal Terrace Falls," to hike through the park on the recommended 1.7-mile loop. Cross the creek on a large footbridge and follow the main trail left

Majestic Falls on McDowell Creek.   Opposite: Bigleaf maple.

through a lush, low-elevation forest of mossy bigleaf maple, alder, and Douglas fir. Look for large white trilliums and oxalis (sourgrass) blooming in March. Sword fern, snowberry, and Oregon grape add to the greenery.

After 0.2 mile you'll reach the base of lacy Royal Terrace Falls, a 119-foot triple-decker. Turn left across a long footbridge below the falls. Then keep right at junctions for the next 0.3 mile, cross the paved road, and continue 0.2 mile along a trail to Crystal Pool's 20-foot cascade. Beyond this waterfall the trail crosses the creek and climbs two flights of stairs to a massive wooden viewpoint structure perched on the lip of 39-foot Majestic Falls. From here, climb stone steps to the upper parking lot.

To complete the hiking loop, walk down the paved road 0.2 mile to the right. Just before the highway crosses the creek, turn left onto an unmarked trail. This path switchbacks up to the canyon rim, with views across the valley through tall firs. Keep right for 0.4 mile to a fenced viewpoint at the top of Royal Terrace Falls. From here steep, dilapidated stone stairs lead down to the familiar loop trail. Turn left 0.2 mile to your car.

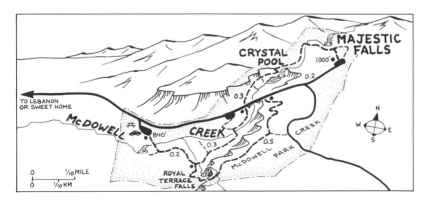

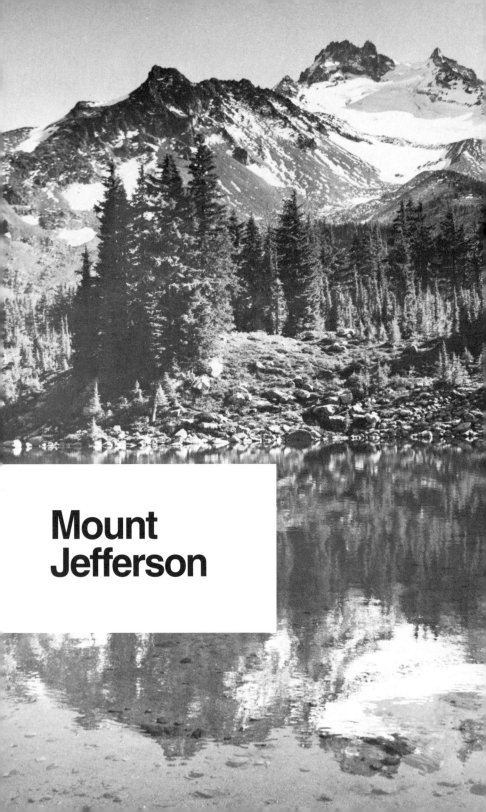

Mount
Jefferson

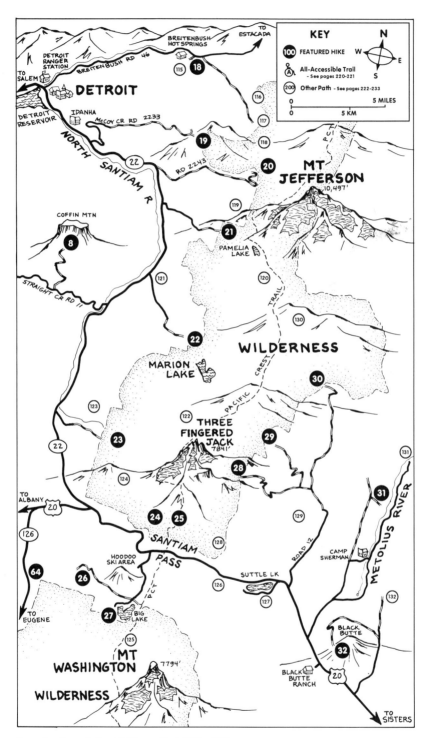

Opposite: Scout Lake at Jefferson Park (Hike #20).

18 South Breitenbush Gorge

Easy
3.6 miles one way with shuttle, or
6.2 miles round-trip to Roaring Creek
700 feet elevation gain
Open except in winter storms
Map: Breitenbush Hot Springs (USGS)

An easy walk through an old-growth forest, this hike follows the South Breitenbush River to a rocky narrows where the river churns through a 100-yard-long slot. If you shuttle a second car to the upper trailhead you can walk the path one-way. But you won't regret walking both directions along this pleasant forest trail.

Start at the old Breitenbush Guard Station. To get there, drive 50 miles east of Salem on North Santiam Highway 22 to the town of Detroit. At a sign for Breitenbush River, turn left for 11 miles on paved Road 46. Beyond Breitenbush Campground 1.6 miles, at a sign for Breitenbush Guard Station, turn sharply right onto gravel Road 050. Park at the rustic, unstaffed old guard station and walk 150 yards farther along the road to a green gate. The trailhead is to the left.

The trail promptly descends to the river, a raging, 50-foot-wide stream with broad gravel bars flanked by alders and tall red cedars. The old footbridge across the river's north fork washed out in a flood, so the trail now detours briefly downstream to a new bridge—a large fallen log with handrails. Then the trail climbs away from the river through a forest carpeted with delicate, shiny-leaved twinflowers. Rhododendrons bloom here in June. At the 2-mile mark enter an area hard hit by a 1990 winter windstorm. In places two-thirds of the large trees fell, closing the trail for over a year.

At a small sign on the right announcing the South Breitenbush Gorge, take a

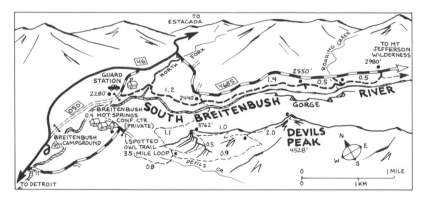

short side trail down to this water-sculpted, 40-foot-deep rock chasm. This makes a nice lunch spot, but don't turn back to the car yet. The trail's next half mile is the prettiest of all, with river views and a scenic footbridge over mossy Roaring Creek.

If you've left a shuttle car ahead, continue 0.5 mile to the upper trailhead, taking the second left-hand trail spur after Roaring Creek. To drive to this trailhead from paved Road 46, drive 0.5 mile east of the guard station's turnoff and turn right on gravel Road 4685. Ignore the first two trailheads and park at the third, a pullout on the right, half a mile past Roaring Creek.

Other Hiking Options

Like a longer hike? The trail continues 3 miles upriver, ending at Road 4685 a few hundred yards before the well-marked South Breitenbush Trailhead to Jefferson Park and Bear Point. Though scenic, this 3-mile section is unsigned and a little rough; it is the original tread used by staff of the former Bear Point lookout tower.

Footbridge at Roaring Creek.   Opposite: Vine maple leaves.

19 Triangulation Peak

Easy
4.2 miles round-trip
700 feet elevation gain
Open July through October
Use: hikers, horses
Map: Mt. Jefferson (Geo-Graphics)

The monumental view of Mt. Jefferson is reason enough to climb to Triangulation Peak's former lookout site. But there's a bonus if you're willing to scramble cross-country a few hundred yards: Boca Cave, a hidden, 60-foot-high cavern gaping from the peak's flank.

Start by driving 56 miles east of Salem on North Santiam Highway 22. A mile past the town of Idanha (and just before milepost 53), turn left onto McCoy Creek Road 2233 for 9.2 miles. This gravel road makes a right-hand turn at a winter sports building; continue 1.3 miles and park on the right at spur Road 635. The trailhead sign is 100 feet down the spur, on the right.

The hike's first 1.5 miles are a nearly level stroll through a mountain hemlock forest. Big white trilliums bloom once the snow is gone in late June. At the half-mile mark, pass a large clearcut on the left with a bumper crop of sun-loving huckleberries and a view of Mt. Hood.

The final 0.6 mile is much steeper. Turn right at a trail junction and switchback up past the base of Spire Rock's impressive monolith. Until mid-July expect to cross a few patches of snow on the trail. Finally the path reaches an open saddle and curves to the right, toward the site of the former lookout tower atop a rocky knob. Mt. Jefferson looms to the east, just 7 miles away. Snowpeaks from Diamond Peak to Mt. Rainier mark the horizon.

Boca Cave is hidden a few hundred yards from the summit, but only experi-

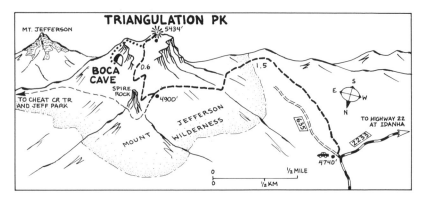

Boca Cave and Mt. Jefferson.   Opposite: Trillium.

enced hikers should attempt to find it, because there is no path and parts of the route are treacherously steep. To find it, hike back down the trail 200 yards to a saddle, turn right, and walk cross-country to Triangulation Peak's second, lower summit hump. Then continue another 200 yards toward Mt. Jefferson on a scramble trail that descends to the right around a rock outcropping, reaching a cliff edge. The cave is hidden at the bottom of this cliff. Get there by scrambling around the cliff to the right, down a steep, forested slope. The dome-shaped, 100-foot-deep cavern has a sloping floor of red cinders and a well-framed view of Mt. Jefferson. Digging or otherwise disturbing the cave is prohibited by law.

Other Hiking Options
With a car shuttle, you can descend from Triangulation Peak via the Cheat Creek Trail, upping the day's mileage to 8.2. Hike down to the trail junction by Spire Rock and turn right. This path contours to a scenic ridgecrest with fields of wildflowers and views up to Boca Cave (inaccessible from this side). After 2.6 miles, fork right onto the Cheat Creek Trail, which descends steeply through Wild Cheat Meadow, losing 1700 feet of elevation. To drive to the Cheat Creek Trailhead, follow Highway 22 east of Idanha 5.6 miles and turn left on White-water Road 2243 for 3.3 miles to the "Cheat Creek" sign.

20 Jefferson Park

Moderate
10.2 miles round-trip
1800 feet elevation gain
Open mid-July to mid-October
Use: hikers, horses
Map: Mt. Jefferson (Geo-Graphics)

Oregon's second tallest mountain rises like a wall from the lake-dotted wildflower meadows of Jefferson Park. The view of Mt. Jefferson is so impressive and the meadows are so delightful to explore that the area shows signs of overuse.

On August weekends hundreds of people roam this corner of the Wilderness. Some of the lakeshores, once green with vegetation, are closed for restoration. Wilderness rangers strictly enforce restrictions: campfires are banned throughout the area and camping within 250 feet of the lakes is only permitted at approved sites marked with an embedded post.

To visit this alpine treasure without damaging it or fighting crowds, do not come on August weekends. Wait for the clear, crisp weather of September—or come in late July, when the wildflowers (and, alas, the mosquitoes) are at their peak. Or visit only as a day trip. If you insist on backpacking, bring a stove, a permit, and the energy to seek out one of the remote, forested corners of the park for your camp.

To find the trailhead, drive 61 miles east of Salem on North Santiam Highway 22. Between mileposts 60 and 61 (beyond Detroit 10 miles or 21 miles north of the Santiam Y junction), turn left on Whitewater Road 2243. Follow this gravel route 7.4 miles to its end at a large parking area. Especially if you're leaving your car here overnight, leave no valuables inside and leave doors unlocked to

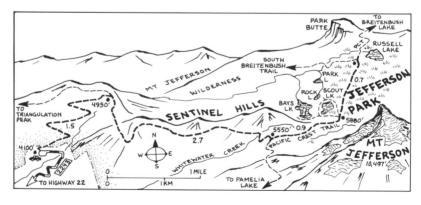

Pond in Jefferson Park.   Opposite: Shooting stars.

discourage car clouters, an occasional problem here.

The well-graded trail starts out in an old-growth Douglas fir forest with a lush mat of twinflower and prince's pine. Gradually you'll switchback up into a higher-elevation forest of true firs and beargrass. After 1.5 miles, turn right at a trail junction on a ridgecrest.

The path climbs east along the ridge for another mile, crosses a saddle, and then levels out. Breathtaking views of Mt. Jefferson begin here. At the 3.9-mile mark, a footbridge crosses Whitewater Creek in a meadow with shooting star, larkspur, and bleeding heart.

At the Pacific Crest Trail junction, turn left. For the next 0.9 mile the trailside meadows become larger and prettier until the path reaches Jefferson Park—a vast plateau of heather, red paintbrush, lupine, and clumps of wind-gnarled mountain hemlock. Here, unfortunately, a confusion of trails proliferate—left to Bays Lake, right to the head of Whitewater Creek. To follow the PCT, keep straight to the first glimpse of Scout Lake, then veer right.

One way to explore the area is to follow the PCT 0.7 mile across the park to large Russell Lake and return cross-country, either south through the heather or southwest to find the hidden lakes. Though chilly, these sandy-bottomed pools are among Oregon's most beautiful spots for a quick swim.

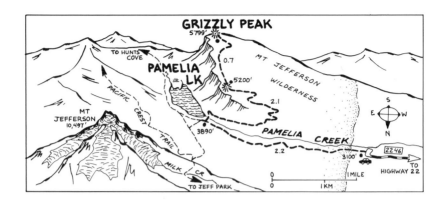

21   Pamelia Lake

Easy (to Pamelia Lake)
4.4 miles round-trip
800 feet elevation gain
Open May through November
Use: hikers, horses
Map: Mt. Jefferson (Geo-Graphics)

Difficult (to Grizzly Peak)
10 miles round-trip
2700 feet elevation gain
Open July through October

The popular trail to Pamelia Lake has something for everyone: an easy creekside forest stroll for the novice hiker, a lake with a mountain reflection for the meditative, and an optional, strenuous viewpoint climb for the go-getters. What's the catch? Only that the trail is so popular.

To limit crowds, *the Forest Service requires that trail users headed for Pamelia Lake pick up a special permit in advance at the Detroit Ranger Station.* Call them at (503) 854-3366 for information. Note that permits are issued to a limited number of groups for each day, so plan ahead if you want a weekend reservation. Camping at the lake is allowed only at approved sites marked by a post.

To find the trailhead, drive 62 miles east of Salem on North Santiam Highway 22. Between mileposts 62 and 63 (beyond Detroit 11 miles or 20 miles north of the Santiam Y junction), turn right on Pamelia Road 2246 for 3.7 miles to the trailhead parking lot at road's end.

The wide trail begins in an enchanting forest so thickly carpeted with moss that fallen trees and rocks soon become mere lumps in the green cushion. Trilliums and rhododendrons bloom profusely along the way in May and June. Vine maple and huckleberry turn scarlet in fall. In all seasons, noisy Pamelia Creek accompanies the trail with little whitewater scenes.

Your first glimpse of the lake comes at a trail junction. Signs here point right to Grizzly Peak and left to the Pacific Crest Trail. For the time being, ignore both pointers and go straight ahead to inspect the lakeshore. The lake formed after the Ice Age when a rockslide pinched off a steep valley left by a retreating glacier. Since the lake's outlet mostly seeps underground through the old rockslide, the water level varies seasonally. By summer, expect a reservoir-like beach. Walk to the right around the lakeshore for a noble view of Mt. Jefferson.

To hike to a grander viewpoint, return to the trail junction and follow the sign to Grizzly Peak. This path crosses the lake's usually dry outlet and heads steadily uphill at such an even grade that the huge elevation gain seems less difficult than might be expected. Beargrass blooms put on a spectacular display approximately every third summer along the route. After climbing 2.1 miles from the lake, the trail switchbacks at a cliff edge with the climb's first viewpoint.

Here's a secret: this first viewpoint is in many ways a better goal than the actual summit of Grizzly Peak, a difficult 0.7-mile climb beyond. The bird's-eye view of Mt. Jefferson is identical from here, and this cliff edge offers a far better look down at Pamelia Lake. What's more, the path is snow-free to this point by mid-June, when drifts still clog the route ahead. On the other hand, only the actual summit has a view south across the Wilderness to the Three Sisters.

Other Hiking Options

For a nice side trip from Pamelia Lake, hike 1.1 mile up to the Pacific Crest Trail's crossing of Milk Creek. Named for the silt-laden runoff of glaciers, Milk Creek pours down a rough-and-tumble canyon with a gaping view up Mt. Jefferson's slopes.

For a scenic backpacking trip, continue south 4 miles past Pamelia Lake to Hunts Cove. To make a 16-mile loop, return via the PCT.

Pamelia Lake and Mt. Jefferson.   Opposite: Hawk.

22   Marion Lake

Easy (to Marion Lake)
6 miles round-trip
800 feet elevation gain
Open mid-May to mid-November
Use: hikers, horses
Map: Mt. Jefferson (Geo-Graphics)

Difficult (to Marion Mountain)
11.2 miles round-trip
2000 feet elevation gain
Open mid-June through October

Generations of Oregon families have hiked to Marion Lake to escape the Willamette Valley's summer heat. Traditions die hard. For many people, this mile-long lake remains the only familiar destination in the Mt. Jefferson Wilderness—even though much of the lakeshore is roped off for restoration, the fishing is hampered by algae, and the trail is trampled to an 8-foot-wide promenade.

If you avoid the crowds by coming any time other than summer weekends, however, the easy walk to Marion Lake does have attractions. Don't miss the unmarked side trails to Marion Falls and the lake's scenic rock peninsula, with its distant view of Three Fingered Jack. A long, optional side trip up to Marion Mountain's former lookout site provides a bit more exercise and a frontal view of Mt. Jefferson, a mountain you otherwise wouldn't see.

To start, drive 66 miles east of Salem on North Santiam Highway 22 (or 16 miles north of the Santiam Y junction), to Marion Forks. Between mileposts 66 and 67, turn east onto Marion Creek Road 2255 and drive 5.4 miles to the parking lot at road's end.

The trail begins with a nearly level half-mile stretch through deep woods. Then the route climbs 1.3 miles to the outlet of forest-rimmed Lake Ann. Listen for the gurgle of water beneath the trail's rocky tread; the outlet is wholly subterranean. This portion of Lake Ann's shoreline is recovering from overuse, so camping is banned.

Beyond Lake Ann 0.4 mile bear right at a trail junction, following the Marion Lake Outlet Trail. Up this route 200 yards, watch for an unmarked side trail to the right. Follow this path 0.2 mile down to Marion Falls, an impressive but seldom visited cascade. Then return to the main trail and continue half a mile to a junction at the footbridge across the lake's outlet. Both fishing and camping are prohibited near the outlet. It's also illegal to enter any of the restoration areas cordoned off by twine and signs; seedlings have been planted to help vegetation return.

If you're just taking the easy loop trip, turn left at the outlet, following the shoreline trail 0.4 mile to a rock peninsula. This stretch of shore, and the peninsula itself, are reserved strictly for day use. On the peninsula's north side, look for smoothed, exposed bedrock—evidence this area was scoured and polished by the weight of Ice Age glaciers. At a trail junction just beyond the peninsula, turn left to return to your car.

Marion Lake.   Opposite: Sign on overused lakeshore area.

Don't try walking entirely around the lake, since swamps at the far end are impassable. Instead, if you're interested in a longer hike, why not climb to Marion Mountain's former lookout site for a look around? Return to the footbridge at the lake outlet and take the Blue Lake Trail, climbing steadily on a long traverse for 1 mile. The forest changes here to a drier mix of lodgepole pines, huckleberry bushes, and clumps of beargrass. At a junction by a pond, turn right onto the less-steep Pine Ridge Trail. After 0.8 mile, watch for a fork in the trail and turn left at a small sign for Marion Mountain. Then ascend 0.8 mile to a rocky ridgecrest with a view of Three Fingered Jack. Go left along the ridgecrest 100 yards to the lookout site and a sweeping view across Marion Lake's valley to Mt. Jefferson.

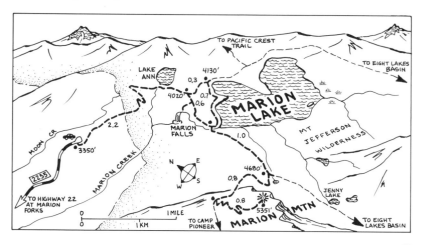

23 Duffy Lake

Moderate (to Duffy Lake)
6.6 miles round-trip
800 feet elevation gain
Open early June to early November
Use: hikers, horses
Map: Mt. Jefferson (Geo-Graphics)

Difficult (to Red Butte)
11.8 miles round-trip
1800 feet elevation gain
Open July through October

The forests west of Three Fingered Jack conceal dozens of lakes, meadows, and buttes. Of these, Duffy Lake is the easiest and most frequently visited goal, a great swimming lake with a reflection of craggy Duffy Butte. For a more challenging destination, continue past Mowich Lake to Red Butte, a cinder cone with a map-like view of the entire area.

Drive 76 miles east of Salem on North Santiam Highway 22 (or 6 miles north of the Santiam Y junction). Near milepost 76, turn east on Big Meadows Road 2267 for 3 miles to its end at a turnaround.

The wide, well-graded Duffy Trail climbs gradually for 1.5 miles through a stately forest of old Douglas fir and hemlock. Then, after the Turpentine Trail splits off to the left, the route levels along the North Santiam River for another 1.1 miles to a bridgeless river crossing.

This crossing is no problem in August or September when the river is dry. In early summer and late fall, however, the stream can flow 20 feet wide. There are stepping stones, but it's safer to bring old tennis shoes and wade.

Beyond the crossing 0.4 mile ignore a trail to the Maxwell Trailhead splitting off to the right. The main path skirts the meandering river's meadows to a 4-way trail junction. Go straight to find a footbridge across the (often dry) outlet of Duffy Lake.

If you're backpacking, note that campfires are banned within 100 feet of the

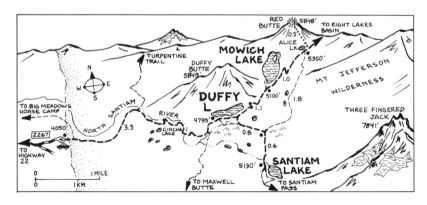

Duffy Lake and Duffy Butte.   Opposite: Townsend's chipmunk.

lake or the trail. Some overused campsites have been closed altogether for wilderness restoration.

If you're headed onward and upward to Red Butte, continue along the lake, taking the route signed to Eight Lakes. After an easy mile you'll reach the delightful sandy beach of Mowich Lake, a steep-shored lake with a large forested island. Next the trail climbs a mile to a junction. Continue straight on the Blue Lake Trail a few hundred yards to little Alice Lake, in a meadow on the left. From here Red Butte is obvious, and so is the 0.5-mile cross-country route up this steep cinder cone to a panoramic view of the Eight Lakes Basin, Mt. Jefferson, Three Fingered Jack, and the Three Sisters.

Other Hiking Options

Santiam Lake, with its wildflower meadows and its reflection of Three Fingered Jack, makes another worthwhile destination. To get there, hike 0.2 mile past Duffy Lake's outlet and turn right for 1 mile, following signs for Santiam Pass. This route connects with Hike #24, making a 9.8-mile, one-way hike possible for those with a car shuttle.

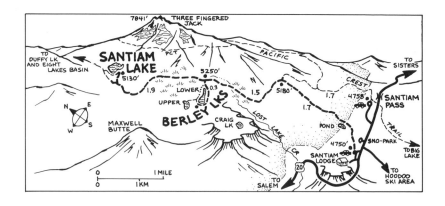

24   Berley Lakes

Easy (to Lower Berley Lake)
7 miles round-trip
500 feet elevation gain
Open July through October
Use: hikers, horses
Map: Mt. Jefferson (Geo-Graphics)

Moderate (to Santiam Lake)
10.2 miles round-trip
800 feet elevation gain

The Pacific Crest Trail is designed to bypass most of Oregon's fragile high country lakes, but an earlier route along the Cascade crest, the old Skyline Trail, intentionally dips from lake to lake. This hike follows a heavily used portion of that older crest trail from Santiam Pass to the cinder-strewn lakeshore meadows at the base of Three Fingered Jack.

Although you can start this hike at the well-marked Pacific Crest Trail parking lot, it's no farther and much less crowded to start at the Skyline Trail's original trailhead. To find it, drive Highway 20 to Santiam Pass. Opposite the turnoff for the Hoodoo Ski Area—and 100 yards west—turn north onto an unmarked road leading 50 yards to a parking lot and a sign for the Santiam Lodge Trail.

The nearly level trail traverses a subalpine forest well stocked with huckleberries, beargrass, bracken fern, and queen's cup. The wide path is dusty from long use—and from the volcanic ash that dusted this area when Maxwell Butte and Red Butte erupted several thousand years ago.

After 1.7 miles turn left at a pointer for the Eight Lakes Basin. Half a mile beyond this junction and just before a small meadow, you'll pass the almost unrecognizable, charred remains of Jack Shelter, once one of a string of historic shelters along the former Skyline Trail.

The Berley Lakes are not visible from the main trail, and no sign marks their side path, so watch closely for the turnoff. After hiking 3.2 miles from the trailhead you'll crest a rise and reach a small campsite, just before the main trail crosses a small, usually dry creekbed. Turn left here, following a side trail along the rocky creekbed 100 yards to Lower Berley Lake. Continue on the somewhat rough path to the lake's far end to a nice beach, a small meadow, and a view of Three Fingered Jack. A bit farther around the lake an even fainter route heads up to Upper Berley Lake, a few hundred yards northwest.

To find Santiam Lake, return to the main trail and continue left. This path crosses a broad sandy plain, climbs over a low forested ridge, and finally forks. The main route to the left bypasses Santiam Lake. The right fork goes along the lakeshore, featuring top-to-bottom views of Three Fingered Jack. The lake itself is picturesquely set in a broad basin with scattered meadows and subalpine firs.

Backpackers should note that campfires are banned within 100 feet of the fragile shores of Santiam Lake and the Berley Lakes. Tent in sandy openings (not on meadow vegetation!) well away from the lakes.

Other Hiking Options

This trail connects with the route to Santiam Lake described in Hike #23. With a car shuttle, the combined one-way trip is 9.8 miles.

Three Fingered Jack from Lower Berley Lake.   *Opposite: Queens cup.*

25   Three Fingered Jack

Moderate (to viewpoint)
10.4 miles round-trip
1400 feet elevation gain
Open late July to mid-October
Use: hikers, horses
Map: Mt. Jefferson (Geo-Graphics)

Difficult (return via Martin Lake)
11.7-mile loop
1600 feet elevation gain

This demanding portion of the Pacific Crest Trail climbs from Santiam Pass to a viewpoint on the timberline slopes beneath Three Fingered Jack's summit crags. Experienced hikers comfortable with a short cross-country scramble can return on a slightly longer loop trail past Martin, Booth, and Square Lakes.

Begin at the Pacific Crest Trail parking area, 0.2 mile down a paved entrance road from Highway 20 at Santiam Pass. The forest here is a high-elevation mix of lodgepole pine and subalpine fir, dotted with beargrass. Down the trail 100 yards, turn left onto the actual PCT. At the Square Lake Trail junction 0.2 mile beyond, keep left. After another 1.2 mile, reach a junction at the base of a rocky knoll. Turn right to stay on the PCT, which now heads more steeply up the side of a forested ridge.

At the 3.5-mile mark the trail finally gains the ridgetop and the first impressive views: east to Black Butte, south to the Three Sisters, west to Maxwell Butte, and ahead to the tip of Three Fingered Jack. After a few hundred yards along the ridgecrest, the path traverses a steep, rocky slope high above blue-green Martin Lake. Then come 3 switchbacks and a traverse to the left through steep alpine country. Finally the trail rounds a bend for a first view of Three Fingered Jack's west face. But don't stop yet. In another 0.2 mile the path turns a sharper corner to an even more spectacular view.

The peak's crags are actually the eroded core of a much larger, smooth-sided

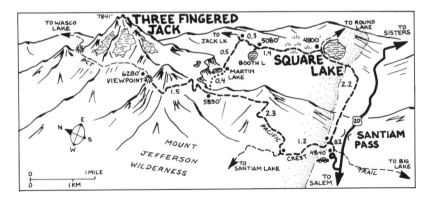

Three Fingered Jack from the Pacific Crest Trail.   Opposite: Martin Lake.

volcano. The red and black stripes are remnants of the lava layers that built up the original cone. Note the ascent trail scarring the scree high on the mountain's shoulder. You can often spot climbers on the jagged skyline above.

Of course the easiest route back is the same way you came. But experienced hikers with some extra energy can try a loop past 3 lakes instead. Hike back down the PCT 1.5 miles to the ridgecrest overlooking Martin Lake to the east. There's no trail down to Martin Lake, and the route is very steep. Start at a low spot in the ridge where the slope is the least rocky, take a good look at the lake below, and head directly downhill through the open woods. The bearing for this 0.3-mile cross-country descent is due east, but simply aiming downhill will hit the lake, since it fills the only outlet to this narrow valley.

At Martin Lake, walk around the shore to a charming meadow at the lake's far end. From here a clear trail (not shown on any topographic map) descends half a mile to the large and unmistakable Booth Lake Trail. There is no trail junction sign here, and in fact a downed tree disguises this end of the Martin Lake path, making it virtually unfindable for anyone hiking the opposite direction—so do not attempt this loop in reverse.

Turn right on the Booth Lake Trail for 1.7 miles to a junction at large, heavily used Square Lake. Then turn right on the Square Lake Trail for 2.2 less interesting miles to the PCT and the return route to the car.

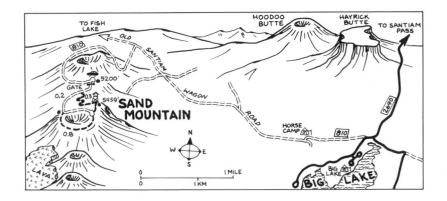

26   Sand Mountain Lookout

Easy
1.3-mile loop
400 feet elevation gain
Open July through October
Map: Clear Lake (USGS)

In the 1940s Oregon boasted more than 800 fire lookout towers, staffed each summer by isolation-tolerant souls willing to trade civilization's comforts for a glass-walled viewpoint in the wilderness. Now that most fire-spotting work is done by airplane, only about 100 towers remain, and only a fraction are staffed.

Nostalgia for the old towers runs particularly high among the children of the original staffers. Don Allen, for one, grew up spending summers on this cratered cinder cone near Santiam Pass. Years after the original tower burned in 1968, he founded the Sand Mountain Society to protect the area from off-road vehicle damage and to rebuild a tower with painstaking historical accuracy. Volunteers—many with lookout experience on other summits—joined in the effort. They salvaged a 1930s-style tower originally from Whisky Peak in the Rogue River National Forest. They rebuilt authentic furniture based on early photographs. They installed a functioning, antique fire-sighting table for locating smoke plumes.

Now these volunteers staff the finished tower each summer, welcoming visitors. And they actually do spot quite a few otherwise unreported wildfires, because this little cinder cone offers one of the most comprehensive panoramas in the entire Central Oregon Cascades.

To drive to Sand Mountain, take Highway 20 to Santiam Pass, turn south at the Hoodoo Ski Area sign, and follow the paved Big Lake Road 3.1 miles to a major fork. Keep right toward Big Lake Campground, but after another 200 yards turn right again onto dirt Road 810. This is a remnant of the Old Santiam Wagon Road, a toll route built from Albany to Central Oregon in 1866-67.

The historic track remains unimproved, and may be impassable in wet weather. Drive passenger cars with caution to avoid large rocks and ruts. Follow Road 810 as it jogs to the left at a primitive horse camp 0.9 mile from the Big Lake Road. At the 1.5-mile mark, go straight at a fork. After 2.4 miles, go straight at a 4-way junction. Finally, 2.9 miles from the paved road, turn left toward the lookout and climb 1.5 miles to a parking area at a locked gate.

Hike up the closed road 200 yards and turn left on a trail switchbacking up to the tower. Mt. Washington is particularly impressive from here, rising above Big Lake. To the west, lava flows snake from their source at Sand Mountain to Clear Lake—which formed when these flows dammed the McKenzie River 3000 years ago. In the Old Cascades beyond, look for Iron Mountain's distinctive thumb and the Three Pyramids' peaks.

After soaking up the view, hike on to the closed road's upper terminus and continue on a path around the crater rim. Watch for well-camouflaged, thumb-sized horned toads scampering among the cinders. Return to the car via the road.

Sand Mountain Lookout.   Opposite: Horned toad.

27   Patjens Lakes

Easy
6-mile loop
400 feet elevation gain
Open late June through October
Use: hikers, horses
Map: Mt. Washington Wilderness
    (USFS)

Hidden in the high lodgepole pine forests south of Santiam Pass, these small lakes reflect rugged, spire-topped Mt. Washington. The easy loop trail here also passes a remote beach of Big Lake, where you can wash off the trail dust with a refreshing swim. Mosquitoes are a problem the first half of July.

To find the trailhead, drive Highway 20 to Santiam Pass, turn south at the Hoodoo Ski Area sign, and follow paved Big Lake Road 4 miles (0.7 mile past the Big Lake Campground entrance) to a hiker-symbol sign at the trailhead on the right.

After just 0.1 mile the trail forks, with signs pointing to the Patjens Lakes in both directions—the start of the loop. Take the right-hand fork and gradually descend through a dry forest where beargrass and lupine provide occasional July blooms. After a mile the trail follows the long meadow of a (dry) snowmelt creek. Then the path gradually climbs to a low pass, offering glimpses north to Sand Mountain's double hump of red cinders (with the lookout tower described in Hike #26).

On the far side of the ridge the trail descends through several small bracken meadows brightened with stalks of scarlet gilia. Above the trees look for (left to right) Mt. Washington, Belknap Crater's black shield, the Three Sisters, the Husband, and Scott Mountain's long, low rise.

The first Patjen Lake is a pond on the right. Half a mile beyond is a more

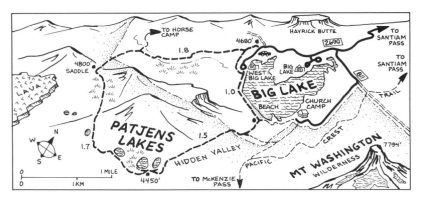

Morning at the Patjens Lakes.   Opposite: Lupine leaves.

substantial lake on the left, with a mostly brushy shore. The third lake is the largest and most attractive, surrounded by meadows. The last lake's water level varies seasonally, leaving a wide, muddy beach.

After exploring the lakes continue 1.5 miles to an unmarked trail junction. Go left and promptly come to a sandy beach with a view across Big Lake to cliff-rimmed Hayrick Butte. By late summer the water is warm enough for excellent swimming here. The trail continues 0.6 mile around the lakeshore to another unmarked fork. Either go left to return to the car via the loop trail, or go right to the West Big Lake Campground and a short walk along the road to your car.

Three Fingered Jack from the lower meadow.   Below: Marsh marigold.

28   Canyon Creek Meadows

Easy (to lower meadow)
4.5-mile loop
400 feet elevation gain
Open mid-July through October
Use: hikers, horses
Map: Mt. Jefferson (Geo-Graphics)

Moderate (to viewpoint)
7.5-mile loop
1400 feet elevation gain
Open August through October

One of the easiest routes to the High Cascades' wildflower meadows, this short loop is ideal for children and amblers. More energetic hikers can continue up a steep glacial moraine to an ice-filled cirque lake and a breathtaking viewpoint beneath Three Fingered Jack's summit pinnacles. For solitude, however, skip summer weekends when this trail attracts hundreds of visitors a day.

Turn off Highway 20 east of Santiam Pass 8 miles at the "Wilderness Trailheads" sign near milepost 88 (1 mile east of Suttle Lake or 12 miles west of

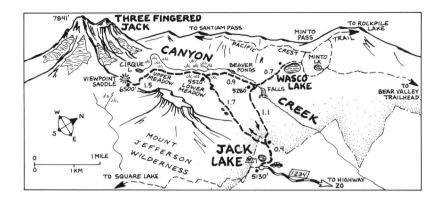

Sisters). Drive north 3.7 miles on paved Road 12, continue straight on gravel Road 1230 for 1.5 miles, and then turn left onto Road 1234, climbing 5 miles to the trailhead at the primitive Jack Lake campground.

Start hiking on the trail to the right, skirting Jack Lake's shore. This path climbs to the Wilderness boundary and a well-marked fork at the 0.3-mile point: the start of the loop.

To limit the number of people you meet, the Forest Service asks that you hike the loop clockwise. So bear left at this junction, climb gradually through the lodgepole pines, pass two ponds atop a small ridge, and descend to the lower meadow. Here the view of Three Fingered Jack's snow-clad crags emerges and the wildflower displays begin in earnest. Peak season for the masses of blue lupine and red paintbrush is the end of July—a trade-off, because mosquitoes are still a nuisance and snowdrifts usually still block the trail to the upper meadow until August. At any season, do not trample these delicate alpine gardens. Stay on the main trail and choose a picnic spot amid trees. Backpackers must camp at least 100 feet from trails or water (please, not atop fragile meadow vegetation).

If you still have plenty of energy, continue 0.7 mile up the trail to the rim of the rock-strewn upper meadow—actually a glacial outwash plain. From here the 0.8-mile route to the 6500-foot-elevation viewpoint becomes less distinct. Climb south up a steep, rocky moraine to a notch overlooking a stunning, green cirque lake at the foot of Three Fingered Jack's glacier. Next the path follows the somewhat precarious crest of the moraine, scrambling steeply up to a windy saddle, where the view stretches from Mt. Jefferson to the Three Sisters. Sharp eyes can often spot climbers on the spires of Three Fingered Jack.

To return via the loop, hike back to the bottom of the lower meadow and turn left. This path follows Canyon Creek past a fascinating beaver workshop, where dozens of large pines have been ringed and felled. Rings 6 feet above the ground prove the beavers are active even when winter snowdrifts remain.

Half a mile beyond the beaver trees join the trail from Wasco Lake—but before turning right to return to the car, follow the sound of falling water to a footbridge below the first of Canyon Creek Falls' two lovely, 12-foot cascades.

Other Hiking Options

For an easy side trip, leave the loop hike at Canyon Creek Falls and walk a nearly level 0.7 mile north to deep, clear blue Wasco Lake.

29   Rockpile Lake

Difficult (to Rockpile Lake)
10.8 miles round-trip
2100 feet elevation gain
Open August through October
Use: hikers, horses
Map: Mt. Jefferson (Geo-Graphics)

Difficult (to Minto Lake)
13.4-mile loop
2600 feet elevation gain

Even when crowds throng other parts of the Mt. Jefferson Wilderness you'll probably find solitude on a little-known trail recently built up Bear Valley. This demanding, view-packed route climbs a ridge to Rockpile Lake, a small jewel set right on the Cascade crest. For even better views on a challenging loop, follow the Cascade crest south to forest-rimmed Minto Lake and return via shallow Bear Valley Lake.

To find the Bear Valley Trailhead, turn off Highway 20 near milepost 88 at the "Wilderness Trailheads" sign 8 miles east of Santiam Pass (or 12 miles west of Sisters). Drive north 3.7 miles on paved Road 12, continue straight on gravel Road 1230 for 1.5 miles, veer left onto Road 1234 for 0.8 mile, and turn right onto Road 1235 for 3.9 miles to a turnaround at its end.

After hiking 50 yards you'll see a sign for the Two Springs Trail. Turn right on this fainter path. It soon joins a horse trail, contours through a ponderosa pine grassland, crosses a small valley, and begins climbing a sunny, open ridge. Views emerge of Three Fingered Jack, with the Three Sisters, Mt. Washington's spire, Broken Top, and Black Butte's cone arrayed to the left. Trailside bushes on this dry slope include pungent snowbrush (Ceanothus), tough-limbed manzanita, and chinkapin. The trail itself was cleared of this brush by a Redmond-based hot shot fire-fighting crew to keep in shape for building fire lines.

At the 2.6-mile mark, turn left at a T-shaped trail junction. After another 2

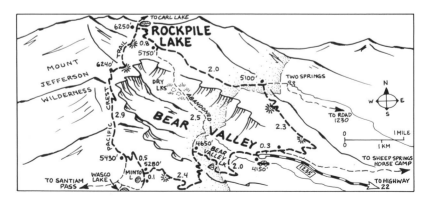

Rockpile Lake.   Opposite: Three-Fingered Jack from the trail.

miles, climbing more steeply through a forest of lichen-draped mountain hemlock, you'll pass the a signed junction with the abandoned Bear Valley Trail. Keep right for another 0.8 mile to the Pacific Crest Trail junction at Rockpile Lake. Along the way, the woods give way to alpine meadows of heather and huckleberry. Camping within 250 feet of the lake is limited to sites marked by a post, and these sites are often occupied by PCT travelers.

Hardy hikers can return from Rockpile Lake on a longer loop route past two larger, woodsier lakes. Start by heading south on the PCT for 2.9 miles. The first level mile through glorious alpine high country is packed with breathtaking mountain views. Then the trail moseys down through hemlock woods to a junction in a wooded saddle. Turn left at a Minto Lake pointer for half a mile to another junction, where a Bear Valley Trailhead sign points left toward home. But if you go left you'll miss Minto Lake. First go right for 200 yards to see the water skippers and dragonflies at circular Minto Lake, reflecting the tip of Three Fingered Jack. Then return to the junction and head down into Bear Valley. After 2.4 miles you'll join the old Bear Valley Trail and turn right. Then you'll pass shallow Bear Valley Lake on the 2-mile descent back to your car.

Other Hiking Options

For a shorter, rougher loop back from Rockpile Lake, try the abandoned Bear Valley Trail. Backtrack from the lake 0.8 mile and fork steeply downhill to the right on a trail marked "Not Maintained." Expect to step over a few fallen logs on this path as it drops through the woods and past dry lakebed meadows for 2.5 miles to the Minto Lake trail. Then turn left for 2 miles to your car.

30   Carl Lake

Moderate (to Carl Lake)
9.4 miles round-trip
1000 feet elevation gain
Open mid-July through October
Use: hikers, horses
Map: Mt. Jefferson (Geo-Graphics)

Difficult (to South Cinder Peak)
13.4 miles round-trip
2200 feet elevation gain

There's lots to do at this deep, rock-rimmed alpine lake: explore the interesting shoreline, admire wildflowers, gather huckleberries, or take a challenging side trip to a viewpoint atop South Cinder Peak.

To start, turn off Highway 20 at the "Wilderness Trailheads" sign 8 miles east of Santiam Pass (or 12 miles west of Sisters), near milepost 88. Drive north 3.7 miles on paved Road 12 and then continue straight on gravel Road 1230 for 8.3 miles to its end, following signs for the Cabot Lake Trailhead.

The trail starts out climbing very gradually through a mixed forest. Many of the Douglas firs have been killed by tiny spruce budworms burrowing within the needles. This is not as tragic as it sounds, for the extra sunshine has encouraged the huckleberry bushes to put out masses of delicious blue fruit each August.

At the 1.9-mile mark go briefly right on a short, unsigned side trail to inspect forest-rimmed Cabot Lake. Then return to the main path, which now heads uphill in earnest. After a dozen switchbacks the trail levels somewhat, passing a series of three scenic ponds. A final level stretch leads to large, blue-green Carl Lake.

The trail leads left around the south shore, past small heather meadows with purple aster and white partridge foot. Though there is no trail around the lake's north shore, the mountain views are better there, and the bared bedrock rim is quite hikable. The north shore bears the marks of the Ice Age glacier which gouged out this lake's basin, polishing the bedrock smooth and sometimes grooving the surface as smaller rocks dragged beneath the heavy ice. Only a narrow rim now holds the lake back from the steep Cabot Creek Valley beyond. Atop this natural dam, bonsaied whitebark pines struggle in cracks. Clark's nutcrackers squawk, eyeing picnickers' sandwiches. If you're backpacking, remember to camp more than 100 feet from the shore or trail.

If you're interested in the challenging side trip up South Cinder Peak, take the turnoff for Shirley Lake in the middle of Carl Lake's south shore. This trail passes above Shirley Lake and traverses steadily up the sunny side of a steep, scenic valley. Expect huckleberries here, too. At an alpine pass, turn left on the Pacific Crest Trail for 0.2 mile until the red cone of South Cinder Peak is immediately to your right. Then strike off cross-country across a cinder flat and up the steep, loose slope. Views promptly unfold of Mt. Jefferson and the Three Sisters.

Carl Lake. Opposite: South Cinder Peak.

Other Hiking Options

To return from South Cinder Peak on a slightly longer loop, follow the Pacific Crest Trail 1.7 miles north to a saddle, turn right, and descend 1.5 miles to Carl Lake on a switchbacking route.

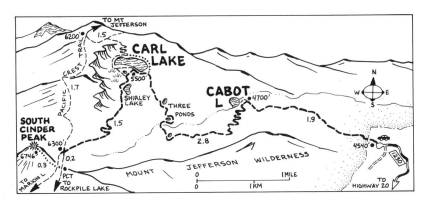

31   Metolius River

Easy (to Wizard Falls fish hatchery)
5.4 miles round-trip
100 feet elevation gain
Open except in winter storms
Map: Metolius River (Imus)

The Metolius, most magical of all Oregon rivers, emerges fully grown at 50,000 gallons a minute from the arid base of Black Butte. Sample the river's wizardry with this easy hike along a section of the oasis-like riverbank. The trail passes sudden springs, reveals colorful bird life, and leads to a wonderfully visitable fish hatchery.

Start by driving Highway 20 east of Sisters 9 miles (or west of Santiam Pass 10 miles). Just east of Black Butte, near milepost 91, turn north at a sign for the Metolius River. Drive straight on paved Road 1419, ignoring a right-hand fork after 2.5 miles labeled "Campgrounds." At a stop sign at the 5.3-mile mark, continue straight onto Road 1420. Keep going straight for another 2.6 miles. Then turn right at a sign for Canyon Creek Campground and drive 1 mile to the West Metolius Trailhead, beside the river at the far end of the campground.

Just 0.3 mile down the trail, spectacular springs enter the river from the far bank, gushing like a dozen opened fire hydrants. The river winds through a steep canyon here with old-growth ponderosa pine and lots of May-June wildflowers: purple larkspur, yellow monkeyflower, and red columbine. A mile beyond the huge springs some smaller springs seep across the trail, muddying unwary hikers' tennis shoes.

At the 2-mile point the river's whitewater splits around a series of long islands, bushy with monkeyflower, lupine, and false hellebore. Birds delight in

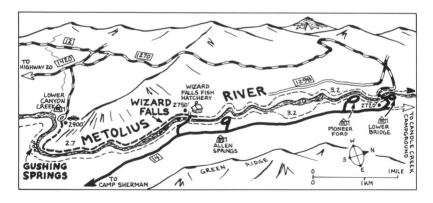

Ponderosa pine along Metolius River Trail.   Opposite: Gushing springs.

these islands. Look for broods of goslings paddling about, bright yellow tanagers hopping in streamside shrubs, and the peculiar robin-sized water ouzels that whir along the river's surface, at times diving to "fly" underwater.

Soon the trail reaches the rustic buildings and countless open-air concrete ponds of the Wizard Falls state fish hatchery. Wizard Falls itself is a humble rapids over a ledge in the river. Though the hatchery has no formal tours, friendly staff members always seem to be on hand to answer questions and show, for example, the indoor tank of two-headed fish. Fish food can be purchased from dispensing machines for 25 cents.

Other Hiking Options

Trails continue beyond the fish hatchery on both banks to the bridge at Lower Bridge Campground, making an additional 6.4-mile loop tempting. From the hatchery, continue 3.2 miles along the quiet west bank to Lower Bridge Campground, cross the river, and return on the east bank through two campgrounds.

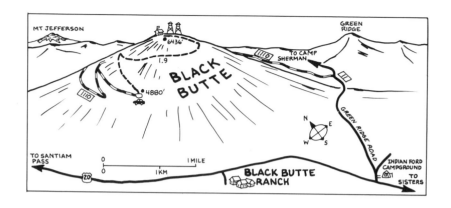

Cupola-style lookout atop Black Butte. *Opposite: Black Butte from Santiam Pass.*

32 Black Butte Lookouts

Moderate
3.8 miles round-trip
1600 feet elevation gain
Open July through October
Map: Metolius River (Imus)

Plunked in the midst of the Central Oregon plateau, Black Butte looks like a misplaced mountain. This symmetrical volcano formed before the last Ice Age along the same fault that uplifted Green Ridge's scarp to the north. The resulting 3000-foot pile of cinders is one of the tallest such cones in the state. The eruption buried the Metolius River, creating Black Butte Ranch's swampy meadows on one side of the mountain and Metolius Springs on the other, where the river now emerges.

The butte's unusual placement east of the High Cascades makes it ideal as a fire lookout site. In 1910 one of Oregon's earliest fire detection structures was built here: a simple "squirrel's nest" platform wedged between two adjacent treetops. That original lookout is gone, but later structures are intact: a cupola-style building from 1924, an 85-foot tower erected by the Civilian Conservation Corps in 1934, and a new, 65-foot tower built in 1995. In 1979 a one-room log cabin was constructed in Sisters, disassembled, and flown by helicopter to the butte's summit to provide the staff with more comfortable quarters.

A steep but view-packed trail climbs to Black Butte's summit. To find the trailhead, drive Highway 22 west of Sisters 5.5 miles (or east of Black Butte Ranch 2.5 miles) to Indian Ford Campground, near milepost 95. Turn north onto paved Green Ridge Road 11. After 3.8 miles, turn left onto gravel Road 1110 for 5.1 miles to a parking area at the road's end.

The trail climbs steadily through a forest of orange-barked old-growth ponderosa pine. After 1.1 mile, the route crosses a treeless slope that's white in June with the the blooms of serviceberry bushes. Expect other wildflowers too: big yellow balsamroot, purple larkspur, and red paintbrush. The golf courses of Black Butte Ranch appear as miniature meadows in the forest far below.

Next the path climbs sharply—a hot, dusty stretch that makes this hike tough for small children. The trail gains the butte's broad, eastern ridge amidst wind-stunted whitebark pines and follows the ridge up to the top.

Do not attempt to climb or enter the lookout structures. The 1934-vintage tower was declared unsafe and closed in 1990. The log cabin is the residence of the modern lookout tower's staff; respect their privacy. And bring your own drinking water, as the staff has none to spare. They diligently collect snow each spring and allow it to melt, filling a concrete cistern.

Bend
Area

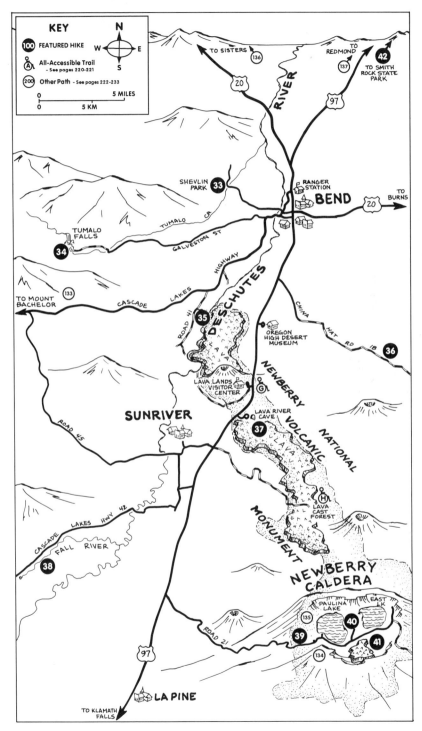

KEY

N
W · E
S

100 FEATURED HIKE

Ⓐ All-Accessible Trail
- See pages 220-221

200 Other Path - See pages 222-233

0   5 MILES
0   5 KM

TO SISTERS
136
TO REDMOND
137
42
TO SMITH ROCK STATE PARK

20
97

RIVER

SHEVLIN PARK 33

RANGER STATION
BEND
TO BURNS
20
US

TUMALO CR.

TUMALO FALLS
34
GALVESTON ST

CASCADE LAKES HIGHWAY

DESCHUTES

TO MOUNT BACHELOR
133
ROAD 41
35
LAVA
CHINA HAT RD. 18
36

OREGON HIGH DESERT MUSEUM

NEWBERRY

LAVA LANDS VISITOR CENTER
Ⓖ

LAVA RIVER CAVE
37
LAVA

SUNRIVER

ROAD 45

VOLCANIC

NATIONAL

Ⓗ
LAVA CAST FOREST

CASCADE LAKES HWY 42
FALL RIVER
MONUMENT

38

NEWBERRY CALDERA

PAULINA LAKE
135
40
EAST LK.

ROAD 21
39
41
134

97

LA PINE

TO KLAMATH FALLS

Opposite: Tumalo Falls (Hike #34).

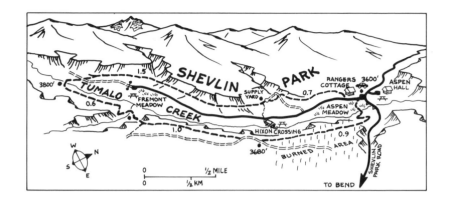

33 Shevlin Park

Easy
4.7-mile loop
300 feet elevation gain
Open all year
Use: hikers, bicycles
Map: Shevlin Park (USGS)

This canyon rim trail along Tumalo Creek begins just 4 miles from downtown Bend, yet feels surprisingly remote. Even the picnickers who gather in Shevlin Park's creekside meadows often overlook this unmarked path among the ponderosa pines. The hike is particularly welcome in winter or early spring when most other Central Oregon trails are under snow. Expect some mountain bikers, for a roadside bicycle path connects the park with Bend.

To find the park from the junction of Highways 97 and 20 in Bend, drive west through downtown on Greenwood Avenue and continue straight on what becomes Newport Avenue and then Shevlin Park Road. After 4 miles cross Tumalo Creek and promptly stop at a railed gravel parking lot on the left. Signs here note that horses, fires, and camping are banned, and that dogs must be kept on leash. Walk past the entrance gate and immediately turn left on a trail through a grove of quaking aspen and ponderosa pine. Continue 100 yards through a meadow and cross a log footbridge over rushing Tumalo Creek.

A 1990 forest fire narrowly spared the park, burning right up to this bridge. The next half mile of trail along the canyon's east rim was used as the fire line. On the left are black snags; on the right, green forest. The contrast provides an interesting look at how high desert vegetation recovers from fire. Bunchgrasses have regrown from their fireproof roots. Many old ponderosa pines also have survived. These conifers' thick bark is designed to flake off during fires, relieving the trunk of heat. Older ponderosas restrict their greenery to widely spaced needle clusters high off the ground, thus preventing most range fires from "crowning out."

After 0.9 mile the trail joins a dirt road. Follow the road 400 yards along the canyon rim before turning right into unburned forest on the continuation of the trail. The next portion of the trail is perhaps the most scenic of all, offering views across the creek to the canyon's far rim. At the 1.8-mile mark, veer right at a fork and descend steeply into an oasis-like creekside meadow among the pines. Though the popular Fremont Meadow picnic area is nearby, picnickers rarely cross Tumalo Creek to this hidden glen.

To continue on the loop, cross a footbridge over a 6-foot side creek. The trail switchbacks up to the canyon rim again and then gradually descends for 0.6 mile to a log footbridge across Tumalo Creek. Uncommon Engelmann spruce grow here amid the Douglas firs.

Beyond Tumalo Creek the trail crosses a dirt road and follows an ancient flume ditch along the canyon's dry north slope. After 1.5 miles, ignore a side trail that leads down to Hixon Crossing's covered bridge. Instead, briefly join a supply yard's road and then veer down to the right on the unmarked continuation of the main trail. In another 0.7 mile the path ends at the park's entrance road 100 yards short of the caretaker's house and the parking lot.

Tumalo Creek at the upper footbridge.   *Opposite: Ponderosa pine bark.*

Double Falls.   Opposite: Porcupine.

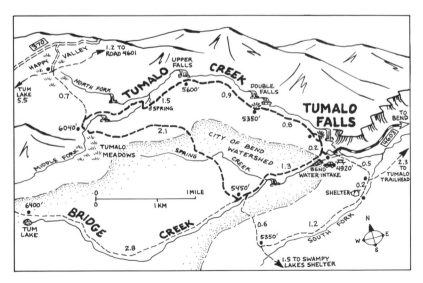

34   Tumalo Falls

Easy (to Upper Falls)
3.8 miles round-trip
680 feet elevation gain
Open late May through November
Use: hikers, bicycles
Map: Tumalo Falls (USGS)

Moderate (to Tumalo Meadows)
6.8-mile loop
1100 feet elevation gain
Open early June to mid-November

Tourists who drive out from Bend to see picturesque, 97-foot Tumalo Falls often don't realize that a dozen other waterfalls are hidden nearby on a network of woodsy trails. Even hikers with young children can usually manage the easy 1.9-mile path up Tumalo Creek to Double Falls and Upper Falls. If you continue on a 6.8-mile loop you'll pass countless smaller waterfalls. This route crosses Bend's Bridge Creek Watershed, where bikes, dogs, and tents are banned

From Highway 97 in Bend, follow "Cascade Lakes Highway" pointers west through downtown for 1.4 miles to Galveston Avenue. Keep going straight, following Galveston another 9.8 paved miles to a gate. Then turn right on gravel Road 4601, cross a one-lane bridge, and promptly veer left on Road 4603 for 3.4 miles to the Tumalo Falls Picnic Area, where the road is blocked by a gate to the City of Bend's water intake center.

The trail starts beside the gate and climbs a slope amid pungent snowbrush and young ponderosa pines. This area is still recovering from the 1979 Bridge Creek Burn, a 6-square-mile blaze sparked by a campfire. Keep right at all junctions for 0.2 mile to reach a fenced viewpoint platform beside Tumalo Falls. Purple penstemon bloom on this dramatic cliff edge in summer.

Follow the path another 0.3 mile up clear, rushing Tumalo Creek and you'll enter an older, unburned forest with Engelmann spruce, mountain hemlock, and white pine. Hang tight to kids at the 1-mile mark, because the path passes the dizzying edge of an unrailed, 200-foot cliff. Churning below is Double Falls, a pair of 20-foot drops. Then head upstream another 0.9 mile to 50-foot-tall Upper Falls, where the creek tumbles from a ledge into a rock bowl.

If you're continuing on the loop, you'll pass a spring, a footbridge, and several small falls in the next 1.5 miles before reaching a trail junction. Turn left on the Spring Creek Trail, which promptly crosses Tumalo Creek's middle fork. There is no bridge here, but you can avoid a cold, knee-deep wade by crossing on a fallen log upstream. Tumalo Meadows, incidentally, is out of sight even farther upstream. Once across the creek, follow the Spring Creek Trail an easy 2.1 miles down to Bridge Creek and turn left for 1.3 miles to your car.

Bicycles aren't allowed on this return route, and it's not encouraged to take them back downhill on the Tumalo Creek Trail, so if you're mountain biking, plan riding on up to Happy Valley. From there you can return on much longer loops, either by turning left to Swampy Lakes or by turning right to Road 4601.

35 Dillon and Benham Falls

Easy (to Big Eddy Rapids)
4.4 miles round-trip
100 feet elevation gain
Open except after winter storms
Map: Benham Falls (USGS)

Moderate (to Dillon Falls)
8.4 miles round-trip
300 feet elevation gain

Moderate (to Benham Falls, with shuttle)
8.7 miles one-way
400 feet elevation gain

The Deschutes River has many moods, at times flowing glassily between meadowed shores, and elsewhere churning angrily down lava canyons. Just minutes from Bend, this convenient trail explores both of the river's humors. Although the path is 8.7 mile from end to end, half a dozen access points along the way make it easy to sample the route in segments. The moody river serves as a reliable landmark throughout.

Mountain bikes are allowed on most of the path, but the Forest Service prefers that they use instead the designated, gated backroads shown on the map. Horse riders have their own trail a few hundred feet above the hiker path.

From Bend, drive 6 miles west on the Cascades Lakes Highway. At a "Meadow Picnic Area" pointer just before a golf course, turn left on a gravel road for 1.3 miles to a turnaround at the far end of the picnic area.

The trail starts among ponderosa pine and pungent manzanita, with views across the rugged lava that splits the river at Lava Island's rapids. At 0.5 mile reach a trail junction and turn left across a pond's dike. (The trail to the right leads up to the Inn at Seventh Mountain.) On the far end of the dike, turn left for 100 feet, then take a right-hand fork across a ditch.

In another 0.5 mile you'll reach Lava Island Rock Shelter, a 4-foot cave where archeologists found evidence of 7000 years of human habitation. A few hundred yards beyond, bypass the Lava Island Trailhead. Stick to the riverbank for

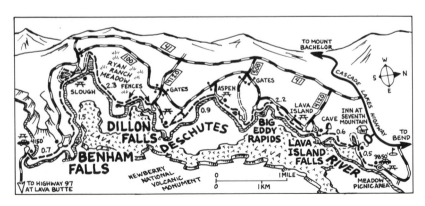

another 1.1 mile to Big Eddy Rapids, a half-mile series of riffles that commence with a churning chute—an ideal spot to watch river rafters flail and squeal.

Hikers with children may wish to turn back here, but hardier walkers will want to continue to Dillon Falls' more dramatic chasm. After Big Eddy Rapids the trail again hugs the riverbank, passing one dead-end jeep road, briefly following another, and circumventing a cattail pond to the Aspen boat launch site. From here continue 0.5 mile to a fork. Keep left for 0.4 mile to Dillon Falls, a churning rapids walled with 100-foot cliffs.

To continue, walk along Dillon Falls Picnic Area's entrance road to a boat launch junction and cross a wire fence at an unmarked gap. The trail crosses a meadow and another fence before petering out in the grass. Continue ahead between a small piney hill and a slough. Reach the riverbank again after 0.2 mile, follow a clearer tread for 0.5 mile, and then hike around the shoreline of a 10-acre lake to Slough Picnic Area. From here circumvent a 5-acre slough of pond lilies and follow the riverbank trail 1 mile to Benham Falls' turbulent cascade. A shuttle car can be left in the parking lot here (see map for driving directions), or hikers can continue another 0.7 mile along the river to a footbridge and trailhead at the Benham Falls Picnic Area. To leave a shuttle car there, drive 10 miles south of Bend on Highway 97, turn right at the Lava Lands Visitor Center exit, and immediately turn left onto gravel road 9702 for 4 miles.

Other Hiking Options

If Benham Falls is your goal, an easy and popular alternative is to park at the Benham Falls Picnic Area, cross the river on the footbridge, and walk a pleasant 0.7 mile to view the falls.

Deschutes River near Dillon Falls.   Opposite: Osprey nest at Dillon Falls.

36 Bend Lava Caves

Easy (Boyd and Skeleton Caves)
1.6 miles round-trip
200 feet elevation gain
Open all year
Map: Kelsey Butte (USGS)

Moderate (Wind Cave)
1.2 miles round-trip
600 feet elevation gain
Open May through October

This collection of short hikes explores the chilly caves riddling the ancient lava flows outside Bend. Bring one flashlight per person—and a lantern as well, if possible. And don't forget coats. Even on a hot day it's cold underground.

The lava flows here spilled thousands of years ago from the flanks of Mt. Newberry, a vast shield-shaped volcano dotted with cinder cones. When the flows were molten the basalt was so runny that even after its surface solidified, liquid rock flowed underneath. The draining lava left long, tube-like caverns. Of the 4 caves in this particular cluster, two are hikable even by children.

Drive 4 miles south of Bend on Highway 97. Opposite Ponderosa Street, turn left on paved China Hat Road 18. After 9 miles, mostly on gravel, turn left at a sign for Boyd Cave. Park at the turnaround and climb down the wooden staircase. The main cave extends to the left. Note the roof's lavacicles—stone drips caused when superheated gases long ago roared through the cave, remelting the surface rock. After 0.2 mile a rockfall obstructs the passage. By scrambling, hikers can continue another 100 feet to the cave's definitive end.

To reach the even more impressive Skeleton Cave, return to China Hat Road 18, drive east 0.5 mile, and turn left at the "Skeleton Cave" sign for 1.6 miles. Stairs lead down into the large, collapsed opening. Head left (north) along a spacious sandy-bottomed corridor often 20 feet tall and 30 feet wide. Rock climbers often practice here.

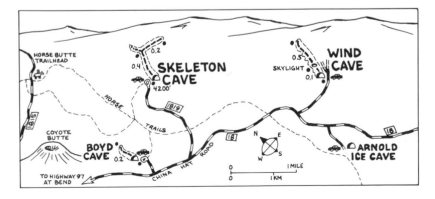

Skeleton Cave.   Opposite: Lava drips.

After 0.4 mile the cave forks. Avoid the left fork, which promptly diminishes to a low-ceilinged squeeze. Bats inhabit this cranny and deserve an undisturbed habitat. Instead take the right-hand fork, a cylindrical tube curving downhill. After 0.1 mile the floor becomes jumbled with rocks. Adequate headroom ends in another 0.1 mile, with the terminus a 100-foot scramble beyond.

Spelunkers looking for a more athletic challenge need only return to Road 18, drive another 2 miles east, and turn left at the sign for Wind Cave. This cave is floored with large, jumbled rocks, some of them wobbly. Enter only with boots, steady legs, and determination. After boulder-hopping for 0.1 mile, reach a 35-foot-tall room lit by a natural skylight. The remaining 0.5 mile of the cave consists of 5 cathedral-like halls separated by wearisome, 60-foot-tall rockpiles. Note the lines along the walls, the "high-water marks" of ebbing lava flows.

Wind Cave is closed to visitors from November to late April, when a large bat colony hibernates inside. Bats that are awakened in winter sometimes die.

The final cave is unhikable but nonetheless interesting. Return to Road 18, drive 0.6 mile east, turn right at an "Arnold Ice Cave" sign, and park after 1 mile at the end of gravel. Take a short downhill trail to the left into a large, cliff-rimmed pit to see Arnold Ice Cave's former entrance, now filled with solid ice. Earlier in this century a Bend company harvested summer ice blocks here.

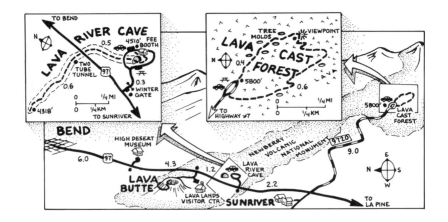

37 Lava Cast Forest and Cave

Easy (Lava River Cave)
2.2 miles round-trip
200 feet elevation loss
Open all year
Map: brochure at trailhead

Easy (Lava Cast Forest)
1-mile loop
100 feet elevation gain
Open May through November
Map: brochure at trailhead

Oregon's newest national monument, packed with the geologic curiosities of the Mt. Newberry volcano, now charges a $5-per-car Monument Pass fee to visit most attractions. But you don't need the pass to try two of the most astonishing short hikes—an underground stroll through mile-long Lava River Cave and a paved loop through the Lava Cast Forest. The two trails are short enough, and close enough together, that you can do both in a single afternoon.

Start with Oregon's longest and most hikable lava tube, Lava River Cave. Drive 11 miles south of Bend on Highway 97. A mile past the Lava Lands Visitor Center (and just before milepost 151), turn left at a sign for Lava River Cave. In summer you can drive 0.3 mile to the far side of a turnaround loop and park right beside the lantern rental booth. Although you don't need a pass to park here, there's a summertime fee to enter the cave itself: $2.50 per adult and $2 per teenager. Kids under 12 are free. Gas lanterns can be rented for $1.50.

There's no charge to visit the cave in the off-season from October to May, but because the entrance road is gated closed then, you'll have to park near Highway 97 and walk 0.3 mile to the cave mouth. In all seasons, bring warm clothes (the cave is 42 degrees Fahrenheit year-round) and plenty of flashlights.

Like many other caves near Bend (see Hike #36), this lava tube formed when molten basalt spilled from the flanks of Mt. Newberry's vast shield-shaped volcano. After a crust hardened on the surface of the runny lava flow, liquid rock continued flowing underneath, draining long, tube-shaped caverns. Lava tubes are only discovered if a roof collapse has exposed an entrance.

The cliff-rimmed pit at Lava River Cave's entrance is set in a ponderosa pine forest with scampering Townsends chipmunks and white sprays of large smilacina flowers. Several feet of slippery ice coat the entrance stairs in winter, so take extra care. Until June, three-foot-tall ice stalagmites remain in the first chamber, like frozen ghosts beside the path. Farther into the cave, dripping water doesn't freeze. Because the drips carry tiny bits of volcanic ash, they have gradually covered much of the cave floor with sand. Lines on the cave walls are "high-water marks" left by ebbing lava flows. Also look for lavacicles—inch-long stone drips left when superheated gases roared through the cave near the end of the eruption, remelting the walls' surfaces.

At the 0.4-mile mark you'll be hiking underneath Highway 97. Just beyond is Two Tube Tunnel, where the cave briefly splits into two tiers. This is a possible turnaround point, although the cave continues another 0.6 mile with an increasingly sandy floor and a lower roof. In the 1930s, two men arduously excavated sand to expose the cave's final 310 feet.

If you'd like another short hike after touring Lava River Cave, drive up to the Lava Cast Forest to see what happened when a similar basalt flow swept through a stand of trees. Go back to Highway 97 and drive south 2.2 miles to milepost 153. Opposite the Sunriver exit, turn left on Road 9720 and follow this washboard gravel road 9 miles uphill to a turnaround at road's end.

The paved path sets out across a lava flow that oozed from the side of the

Lava Cast Forest.   *Opposite: Lava River Cave entrance.*

Newberry volcano just 6000 years ago. Only a few twisted ponderosa pines, golden currant bushes, and purple penstemon flowers have colonized the five-square-mile flow's jumbled rock surface. Circular rock wells along the path remain where the runny lava washed up against trees and cooled before they could burn. At a viewpoint after 0.4 mile, notice Mt. Newberry's caldera rim looming above the lava ahead, while Mt. Bachelor and the Three Sisters line the horizon far to the west. Then continue 0.6 mile back to your car.

38   Fall River

Easy
5.6 miles round-trip
100 feet elevation gain
Open except after winter storms
Use: hikers, horses, bicycles
Map: Pistol Butte (USGS)

Like the more famous Metolius River (Hike #31), this Central Oregon stream emerges from an enormous spring and meanders in glassy curves through pungent pine woods. But unlike the Metolius, Fall River is not crowded with campers and river rafters, and its gentle riverside trail is open to all.

Drive 16 miles south of Bend on Highway 97 (or 13 miles north of La Pine). Between mileposts 155 and 156, turn west onto Vandevert Road at a sign for Fall River. After 1 mile, turn left onto South Century Drive for 0.9 mile, and then turn right on Cascade Lakes Highway (Road 42) for 9.7 paved miles. A bit beyond milepost 13, turn left into the Fall River Campground entrance for 100 yards and park at a day use area on the right, overlooking the river.

If you've brought kids, the first thing they'll want to do is run 200 yards down to a scenic river footbridge on the right. The 40-foot-wide river is so clear here you can see every fish. Lush green clumps of yellow-flowered arrowhead butterweed cluster on fallen logs in the glassy stream.

In fact, 3 riverside trails start from this alluring bridge, but none is the actual Fall River Trail, and they all deadend within a few hundred yards. Nonetheless, you might warm up for the day's hike by crossing the bridge and turning left for 0.3 mile to a bench overlooking a picturesque riverbend.

To find the real Fall River Trail, however, go back to the car and walk along the campground road to a post behind campsite #8, at the far end of a turn-around loop. The riverside trail that begins here sets off through lodgepole pine woods with bitterbrush, wild strawberries, and bunchgrass. Look for mallard ducks paddling near shore and river swallows swooping over the water from nest boxes in the trees. Also keep an eye out for elk—the source of marble-sized droppings you may see along the trail. Herds from the High Cascades rely on

Fall River.   Opposite: Footbridge near the parking area.

these riverbank meadows for winter range.

After 0.3 mile you'll briefly follow a red cinder road, and at the 1.2-mile mark a side trail leads left up to a parking lot. After 2.1 miles the trail appears to end at a roadside pullout, but the path actually continues another 0.3 mile to a pretty riffle at the end of public lands. Return as you came.

The Fall River Trail doesn't lead to the huge springs at the river's source, but it's easy enough to drive there after the hike. From the Fall River Campground, drive east 0.7 mile on the paved road and park at the old Forest Service guard station on the left. The building isn't open to the public, but if you walk 100 feet to the right around its railed yard you'll find the gushing, grassy-banked springs. Look here for tiny white orchids and water ouzels.

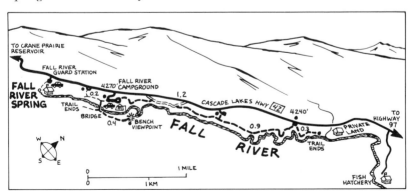

39   Paulina Creek Falls

Easy (to falls viewpoints)
1.6 miles round-trip
300 feet elevation gain
Open late June to mid-November
Map: Paulina Peak (USGS)

Easy (to McKay Crossing)
5.6 miles round-trip
500 feet elevation gain
Open all year
Use: hikers, horses, bicycles

Difficult (entire trail)
16.6-mile loop
2050 feet elevation gain

Paulina Creek spills from a caldera lake high in the Newberry National Volcanic Monument, tumbles down the volcano's slopes in a series of waterfalls, and meanders across the high desert. The 8.5-mile trail tracing the stream is a bit long for a day hike, so most hikers focus on shorter segments—either exploring the spectacular summer viewpoints up at Paulina Creek Falls, or strolling along the lower creek where trails are usually snow-free even in winter.

Start by driving Highway 97 south of Bend 22 miles (or north of La Pine 7 miles). Between mileposts 161 and 162, turn east at a sign for Newberry Caldera and Paulina Lake. For the easiest hike, drive 12.2 miles up this paved road and turn left into the Paulina Creek Falls picnic area.

The trail begins between the picnic area's upper and lower parking lots. Keep right for 100 yards to a fenced clifftop viewpoint of two massive, side-by-side 60-foot waterfalls. Most tourists turn back here, but paths lead to two other excellent viewpoints nearby. To find the first, head upstream past the picnic area. You'll discover a lovely trail that follows the creek 0.2 mile up to Paulina Lake's

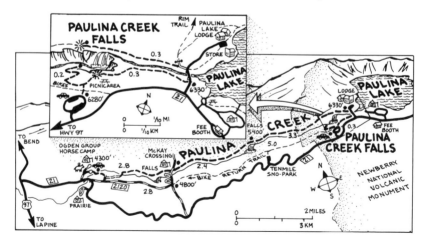

Paulina Creek Falls.   *Opposite: Golden-mantled ground squirrel.*

outlet. Horses and bicycles are banned on this path. Turn left across a road bridge and immediately turn left on a creekside trail that descends 0.3 mile to a fenced viewpoint on the far side of Paulina Creek Falls.

To find the third viewpoint, head back to your car, but turn right 50 feet before the parking lot. This trail switchbacks down through the woods 0.2 mile to its end at a decked platform wedged between creek boulders below the falls.

If you'd prefer a longer hike (or if the trail at Paulina Creek Falls is closed by winter snow) try the lower end of the creek's trail instead. To find this route, turn off Highway 97 at the Newberry Caldera exit, drive 2.8 paved miles, turn left at Ogden Group Camp, and follow "Trailhead" pointers to a large gravel parking area for the Peter Skene Ogden Trail.

This path crosses glassy, swift Paulina Creek on a bridge and heads upstream. The creek's meadowed banks form a narrow oasis here, with the dry flora of the high desert on either hand. The sagebrush-like brush is bitterbrush *(Purshia tridentata)*—a member of the rose family, as its tiny blooms reveal. The prominent trailside bunchgrass is known as "needles and thread" because of its needle-like, seed-bearing stalks and curly, thread-like basal leaves.

After 0.7 mile the trail appears to end at a road. Turn right for 50 yards to an intersection and then turn left for 0.2 mile to a footbridge where the path resumes. The next half mile of trail follows the level bed of an abandoned railroad grade, used for logging in the early 1900s. Since then, lodgepole pines have returned in force and ponderosa pines are already a proud 100 feet tall, but occasional 3-foot-thick stumps recall the earlier Central Oregon woods.

At the 2.8-mile mark you'll reach a twisting rock gorge and a 15-foot waterfall beside McKay Crossing Campground. This makes a good turnaround point for an easy hike. If you're out for a challenge, however, continue 5.7 miles upstream to Paulina Lake. Horses and mountain bikes share this route, but bicyclists aren't allowed to zoom back down the same way. Instead they have to ride back on paved Road 21 for 0.2 mile and then veer to the right on a well-marked return trail that follows a powerline 5 miles down to McKay Crossing.

40 Paulina Lake

Easy (to Warm Springs)
2.4 miles round-trip
No elevation gain
Open mid-July through October
Maps: Paulina Pk., East L. (USGS)

Moderate (around lake via Little Crater)
8.6-mile loop
500 feet elevation gain

At the heart of Oregon's newest national monument, Paulina Lake has the feel of an exotic sea. Deep, azure waters lap against rocky shores. Seagulls cry. Hidden beaches beckon. But this remarkable lake is actually well over a mile above sea level, and the forested rim that walls it from the outside world is in fact the collapsed caldera of Mt. Newberry, an enormous volcano. If all this fails to pique your curiosity, how about submarine hot springs, a gigantic flow of obsidian glass, and a miniature cinder cone crater?

To start, drive south of Bend 22 miles on Highway 97 (or drive north of La Pine 7 miles). At a "Newberry Caldera" sign between mileposts 161 and 162, turn east on a paved road for 13 uphill miles to a fee booth. Stop to buy the required Monument Pass ($5 per car for a day or $20 for a season). Then continue 1.5 miles on the main road, turn left into the Little Crater Campground entrance, and keep right for 0.9 mile to a gravel trailhead parking spur at the far end of the campground.

The trail sets off along a dramatic, rock-lined shore with the jagged face of Paulina Peak looming across the lake. The sparse forest here is an odd mix of lowland ponderosa pine and highland firs. Note that the older trees are flocked with glowing green letharia lichen, a sure sign of clean mountain air.

After 0.7 mile the trail skirts the Inter Lake Obsidian Flow, passing boulders of banded volcanic glass. Then you'll reach a long, meadowed beach at undeveloped Warm Springs Campground, accessible only by trail or boat. This makes a good turnaround point for hikers with kids. A hot springs just offshore encourages the growth of lake algae here—unpleasant for swimmers but attractive to other fauna. Watch for mallards, mule deer, gray jays, and Stellar's jays.

If you're continuing on the loop, you'll climb to a panoramic viewpoint above a red cinder rockslide. A gap in the caldera rim to the right allows a glimpse out to spire-topped Mt. Thielsen and cone-shaped Mt. McLoughlin in the distance. Then hike onward to primitive North Cove Campground, with picnic tables, an outhouse, and a fine pebble beach suitable for (chilly!) swimming.

Another 1.7 miles brings you to the Paulina Lake Lodge's rental cabins, restaurant, boat rental dock, and rustic general store. Cross a road bridge over the lake's outlet creek, immediately turn left, and stick to the lakeshore path for another 2.4 miles, following "Trail" signposts where necessary. You'll pass summer houses and campgrounds before reaching the Little Crater Campground entrance road. From there, of course, the quickest way back to your car

Paulina Peak from the trailhead.   Opposite: Viewpoint above Warm Springs beach.

is to turn left along the paved road for 0.8 mile. But if you've got the energy for
a prettier route, turn right on the road for a few yards to a sign for the Little
Crater Trail. This path climbs 0.3 mile to a tiny volcano's crater. Turn right along
the rim to a spectacular viewpoint overlooking both Paulina and East Lakes.
Then continue around the rim to a junction on the far side, turn right, and
descend 0.6 mile to your car.

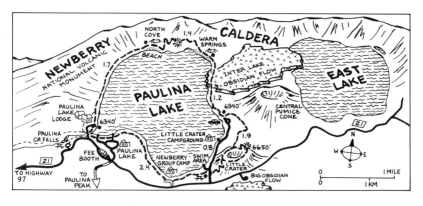

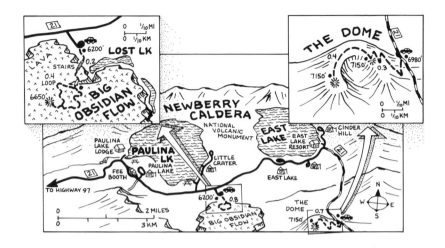

41 Obsidian Flow and The Dome

Easy (Obsidian Trail)
0.8-mile loop
450 feet elevation gain
Open mid-July through October
Map: East Lake (USGS)

Easy (to The Dome)
1.4 miles round-trip
200 feet elevation gain

High on the ruined shell of Mt. Newberry, these short hikes explore two different volcanic oddities: a gigantic flow of black glass and a U-shaped cinder cone. The two trails are easy enough that even hikers with kids can usually manage both in a day.

Mt. Newberry is probably Oregon's strangest volcano. It's the latest protrusion of a geologic "hot spot" that's been moving westward from Idaho for 10 million years, leaving a string of lava flows and volcanic buttes in its wake. Geologists theorize that North America's shearing collision with the Pacific plate has been stretching Eastern Oregon diagonally all this time, and lava has been leaking through the shifting cracks.

All that leaking lava has made Newberry the state's most massive volcano, measured by volume. Countless thin basalt lava flows have built up its 25-mile-wide shield-shaped bulk over the past half million years. Each eruption typically starts with fireworks—the explosive creation of a cinder cone where a pocket of molten rock first reaches the surface. After the fireworks subside, a lava flow oozes from the base of the cone to end the eruption.

The Dome is one of 400 such cinder cones dotting Mt. Newberry's broad flanks. The Dome's fireworks must have gone off sideways, because its cone is shaped like a giant U, with the south rim blown out.

Like many aging volcanoes, Mt. Newberry's eruptions gradually contained more silica, making the lava thicker, glassier, and more explosive. The entire mountaintop has collapsed in Crater Lake fashion at least twice, leaving a gaping, 6-mile-wide caldera. The giant lake that once filled that caldera has since been split in two by lava flows. The largest of these flows—and the most recent eruption in all of Central Oregon—is the Big Obsidian Flow, which poured more than a square mile of black glass into the caldera just 1300 years ago.

To try the easy loop trail atop the Big Obsidian Flow, start by driving south of Bend 22 miles on Highway 97 (or north of La Pine 7 miles). At a "Newberry Caldera" sign between mileposts 161 and 162, turn east on a paved road for 13 uphill miles to a fee booth. Stop to buy the required Monument Pass ($5 per car for a day or $20 for a season). Then continue 1.8 miles on paved Road 21 and turn right into the Obsidian Trail's huge parking area. Do not feed the cute, golden-mantled ground squirrels that beg for handouts here, because human food is dangerously unhealthy for them.

The trail ambles 150 yards through lodgepole pine woods, climbs metal stairs up the glinting face of the lava flow, and then bridges a jagged pressure crack in the lava. Much of the jumbled rock surface is gray pumice—the flow's frothy scum. Underneath, the silica-rich lava cooled without bubbles to leave shiny obsidian, colored black by a trace of iron oxide. Hike a final 0.4-mile loop to a viewpoint overlooking Paulina Peak (and the distant tips of snowy Mt. Bachelor and South Sister) before returning to your car.

To visit The Dome, drive east on paved Road 21 another 2.6 paved miles to a junction. Following a "China Hat Road" pointer, turn right on a continuation of Road 21 that soon becomes washboard gravel. After 2.5 miles, park at a small pullout on the right just before a large sign for The Dome Trail. This path switchbacks 0.3 mile up a gray cinder slope of struggling pines and lupines to the crater rim. Follow the level, horseshoe-shaped crest to the right for 0.4 mile to a viewpoint overlooking Fort Rock's valley to the south, several dozen nearby cinder cones, and Cascade snowpeaks from Mt. McLoughlin to Mt. Thielsen.

The Big Obsidian Flow.   Opposite: The Dome.

42 Smith Rock

Easy (along river)
5.8 miles round-trip
200 feet elevation gain
Open all year
Map: Redmond (USGS)

Moderate (across Misery Ridge)
4-mile loop
800 feet elevation gain

Smith Rock juts from the Central Oregon lava plains like an orange-sailed ship in the desert. Oregon's most popular rock-climbing area, this state park challenges mountaineers with 3 miles of rhyolite cliffs and Monkey Face, a 300-foot-tall natural sculpture overhanging on all sides.

Hikers can experience Smith Rock's scenic drama too. For an easy trip, walk along the aptly named Crooked River as it curls past the base of Monkey Face. For a steep shortcut back, climb a new loop beside Monkey Face across Misery Ridge to cliff-edge views of a string of Cascade snowpeaks.

The area is best in early spring, when high desert wildflowers bloom, or in winter when other trails are blocked by snow. Anytime you're rained out of a hike in the Cascades, Smith Rock is likely to be a dry alternative. Just avoid July and August when the park bakes in 100-degree heat.

To drive to the park, turn off Highway 97 at Terrebonne (6 miles north of Redmond or 20 miles south of Madras). Follow "Smith Rock State Park" signs east for 3.3 zigzagging miles to the parking area. An automat accepts bills or change for the $3 parking fee.

Walk past the restrooms to an overlook at the far right end of the picnic area.

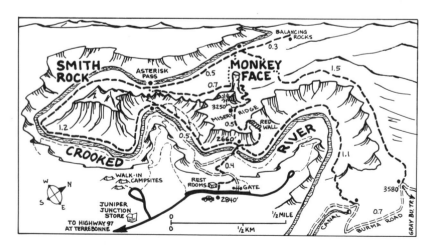

Smith Rock and the Crooked River.   Opposite: Monkey Face.

Follow a gated dirt road down through an aromatic stand of tall sagebrush, cross the river bridge to a trail junction, and turn left along the riverbank. You'll soon round a bend and come to three side trails signed for The Dihedrals and Asterisk Pass; these climb up stairs and end at cliffs where climbers dangle, jangling their gear. Explore these side trails by hiking up one and descending on the next.

Then continue downriver, watching the plentiful bird life. Black-and-white magpies swoop from gnarled junipers. Pigeons coo in rock cracks. The eagles who hunt these birds soar from aeries high on the cliffs. At the 2-mile mark the trail rounds the tip of a peninsula and soon offers the first view ahead to Monkey Face. Look for climbers resting in the mouth cave. The trail is rough for 0.2 mile, with some scree, then passes a cave and a house-sized boulder. Here the riverside trail splits into several diffuse paths. Cross a rockslide to the balancing rocks atop ash pillars—a good turnaround point.

If you'd like to try a shortcut back, hike along the river trail until you're below Monkey Face. Then leave the trail and bushwhack straight up through the sagebrush to the pillar's base. You'll find a good path there that climbs up past Monkey Face to a ridge, where views extend across Central Oregon to peaks from the Three Sisters to Mt. Hood. If you're not afraid of heights, you can take a side trail down to the right to a precipice directly opposite Monkey Face's cave-mouth. Otherwise continue straight on the loop trail, contouring 200 yards to the edge of Misery Ridge. Here several steep staircases have taken the misery out of the switchbacking descent to the Crooked River bridge.

Other Hiking Options

For a more challenging, 6.3-mile loop, hike the Crooked River trail to a house-sized boulder just beyond Monkey Face, veer right on a path up a very steep rock gully, and turn left on the ridgecrest for a mile to Burma Road. Turn right and descend this dirt track 0.7 mile. At the second switchback (where the road meets a canal) take a steep side trail down to the river. The park footbridge is a level 0.9-mile walk away.

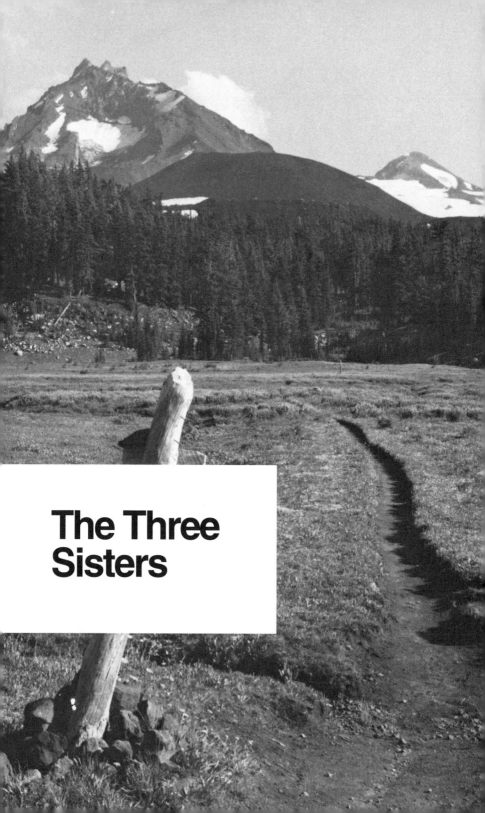

The Three Sisters

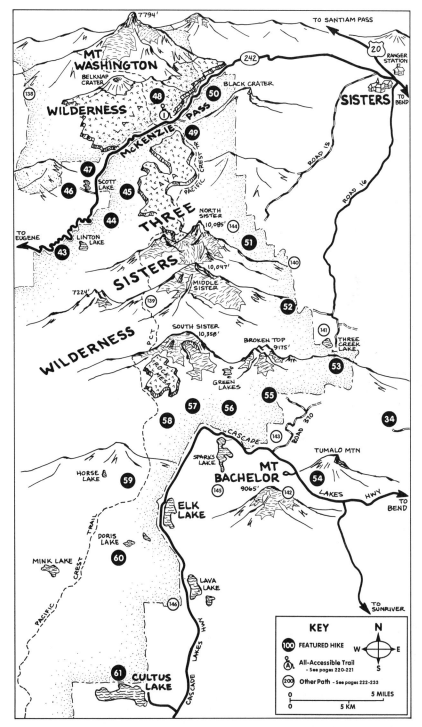

Opposite: North Sister and Middle Sister from Scott Trail junction (Hike #45).

43 Proxy Falls and Linton Lake

Easy (to Proxy Falls)
1-mile loop
200 feet elevation gain
Open May through November
Map: Three Sisters (Geo-Graphics)

Easy (to Linton Lake)
3.8 miles round-trip
300 feet elevation gain

The first of these two short walks loops across a lava flow to a pair of 100-foot waterfalls. The second trail winds through deep woods to a large lake in a steep, forest-rimmed valley.

Fire and ice have sculpted this corner of the Three Sisters Wilderness. During the Ice Age, glaciers from the Three Sisters poured down this canyon, scouring it to a deep U-shaped trough. When the ice melted some 6000 years ago, the canyon's side valleys were left hanging. Upper and Lower Proxy Falls spill over these glacier-cut cliffs. Since then, blocky basalt lava flows from cinder cones near North Sister have flooded the canyon floor, damming Linton Lake. Water seeps through the porous lava, leaving Linton Lake with no visible outlet. Likewise, the splash pool beneath Upper Proxy Falls never overflows. Apparently the water resurfaces a few miles down the canyon at the massive springs which create Lost Creek and White Branch Creek.

To find the Proxy Falls Trailhead, drive McKenzie Highway 242, the scenic old road between McKenzie Bridge and Sisters. At a hiker-symbol sign between mileposts 64 and 65 (east of the Highway 126 junction 9 miles, or west of McKenzie Pass 13.5 miles), park in a long row of roadside parking slots. Cross the road to start the loop trail up onto the lava. The flow is old enough that vine maples provide splashes of color in autumn. Near water the jumbled rock is overgrown with moss, twinflower, and yew trees. Take short side trails from the

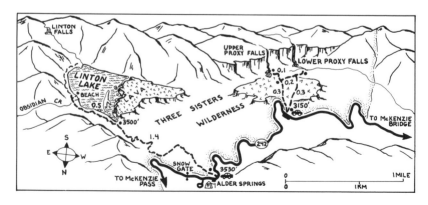

Linton Lake.   Opposite: Lower Proxy Falls.

loop to visit Lower Proxy Fall's overlook and Upper Proxy Fall's pool. Then continue on the loop 0.3 mile back to your car.

To visit Linton Lake, drive east up the winding Old McKenzie Highway another 1.5 miles to a hiker-symbol sign and a small parking area on the left at Alder Springs Campground. On weekends, parking can be tight. Walk across the highway to the trailhead. This trail sets off among old-growth hemlock and Douglas fir. Vanilla leaf and Oregon grape bloom here in June. After a mile the path climbs over a lava bluff and switchbacks back down into the forest.

The path skirts Linton Lake for half a mile, staying several hundred feet above the shore until Obsidian Creek. Here the trail ends by descending to a pleasant sandy peninsula with a view across the lake basin to distant Linton Falls.

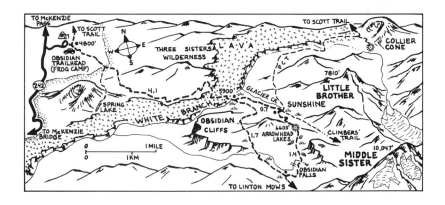

44   Obsidian Trail

Difficult
12-mile loop
1800 feet elevation gain
Open mid-July through October
Use: hikers, horses
Map: Three Sisters (Geo-Graphics)

The Obsidian Trail leads to Sunshine, one of the most beautiful and heavily used alpine areas in Oregon. Brooks meander through the wildflower meadows nestled here between Middle Sister and Little Brother. Snowmelt tarns shimmer from plateaus strewn with black obsidian glass.

To limit crowds, *the Forest Service requires that Obsidian Trail users pick up a special permit in advance at the McKenzie Ranger Station* on Highway 126 just east of McKenzie Bridge. Call them at (541) 822-3381 for information. Note that permits are issued to a limited number of groups for each day, so plan ahead if you want a weekend reservation. Also note that Wilderness rangers strictly enforce a total ban on campfires, and that tents are prohibited within 100 feet of trails or water.

To find the trailhead, drive McKenzie Highway 242, the scenic old road between Sisters and McKenzie Bridge. West of McKenzie Pass 6.2 miles (between mileposts 70 and 71), turn off at a sign for the Obsidian Trailhead and drive 0.4 mile to a maze of small parking spots.

The trail begins at a message board at the far end of the parking loop and immediately forks. Head right, following a "White Branch Creek" pointer. The first mile of the path is dusty, climbing through a hot forest of lodgepole pine and beargrass. After passing a side trail to Spring Lake, climb steadily through cooler woods of lichen-draped mountain hemlock and red huckleberry.

At the 3.4-mile mark, traverse up the face of a fresh, blocky lava flow to a viewpoint of Cascade snowpeaks from Mt. Jefferson to Middle Sister. Beyond the lava, the path crosses White Branch Creek and reaches a junction in a meadow of blue lupine wildflowers. The loop begins here.

Follow the "Linton Meadows" pointer to the right. This route climbs a mile to a plateau of flashing obsidian chips. This black volcanic glass forms when silica-rich rhyolite lava oozes to the surface without contacting water. If the lava meets water it explodes upon eruption, forming frothy pumice instead.

The trail follows a brook in a meadow decorated with western pasque flower—the early, anemone-like bloom that develops a dishmop seed head known as "old man of the mountain." At the Pacific Crest Trail junction, turn left and climb past 20-foot Obsidian Falls to a spring atop a glorious alpine plateau dotted with ponds. Pass a stunning view of North Sister and switchback down to Sunshine, a meadow nestled beside Glacier Creek. Sunshine Shelter was demolished in the 1960s but the trail junction here is still a crossroads for wilderness traffic. Turn left to continue the loop, following Glacier Creek steeply down to White Branch's meadow and the return route to the car.

Other Hiking Options

For a challenging 15-mile loop through the best of this area's volcanic landscape, follow the PCT north from Sunshine 2.2 miles to Collier Cone. At a rock cairn there, take a 0.4-mile side trail to the right to a breathtaking view of Collier Glacier. Then continue 1.8 miles north on the PCT, turn left on the Scott Trail for 4.9 miles (see Hike #45), and take a 0.6-mile connector trail left to the car at Obsidian Trailhead.

More difficult destinations are Linton Meadows (4 miles south of Obsidian Falls on the PCT) and the summit of Middle Sister (an arduous, but non-technical climb from Sunshine).

Middle Sister from above Sunshine.   Opposite: Western pasque flower seed heads.

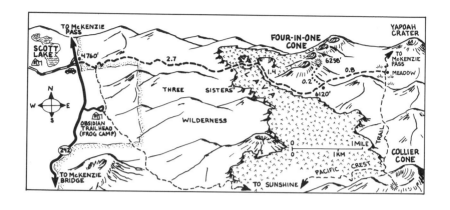

The Three Sisters from Four-In-One Cone. *Opposite: North Sister from the PCT.*

45   Four-In-One Cone

Moderate
8.6 miles round-trip
1500 feet elevation gain
Open mid-July through October
Use: hikers, horses
Map: Three Sisters (Geo-Graphics)

When Captain Felix Scott led the first wagon train through the McKenzie Pass area in 1862, he blazed a sinuous route across an alien volcanic landscape of cinder cones and lava flows beside North Sister. This hike traces his footsteps, following the Scott Trail to a viewpoint atop the crater rim of 4 connected cinder cones. If you have the energy to hike 0.8 mile further, you can picnic in a meadow with one of Oregon's best lupine displays.

To find the trailhead, drive McKenzie Highway 242, the scenic old road between Sisters and McKenzie Bridge. West of McKenzie Pass 5.6 miles (between mileposts 71 and 72), park at the turnoff for Scott Lake. The trail starts at a hiker-symbol sign on the opposite (south) side of the highway.

After 0.2 mile pass a connector trail on the right to the Obsidian Trailhead. Go straight and begin to climb, switchbacking up from a dry forest of lodgepole pine and beargrass to moister mountain hemlock woods. At the 2.7-mile mark, cross a 200-yard jumble of barren, blocky lava to a forested "island" entirely surrounded by the basalt flows. The trail then crosses another 100 yards of lava and climbs gradually for 1.4 miles along the sandy fringe between the woods and the lava flow's rugged wall.

The trail finally crests in a broad cinder barrens. North Sister dominates the horizon to the right; Four-In-One Cone is the cinder pile to the left. Boots are required for the short, steep cross-country climb up Four-In-One Cone because the cinder scree is loose and jagged. Once you're on top the crater rim, you can walk as far as you like along the summit of the 4 contiguous cones, with top-of-the-world views of half a dozen Cascade peaks.

Note how lava flows have breached each of the 4 craters. Cinder cones form when a blip of magma rises to the Earth's surface. An initial violent eruption spews cinders, with prevailing western winds usually building the cone highest on the east rim. The cinder cone dies once the magma has released its volatile gases, but a quieter basalt flow then typically pours from the cone's base.

To lunch in greener pastures, continue on the Scott Trail a relatively level 0.8 mile to a delightful meadow at the Pacific Crest Trail junction. Blue lupine blooms profusely here from mid-July through August.

Other Hiking Options

To extend this hike to a challenging, 15-mile loop, return via the PCT and the Obsidian Trail (see Hike #44).

46

Benson Lake

Easy (to Benson Lake)
2.8 miles round-trip
400 feet elevation gain
Open July through October
Use: hikers, horses
Map: Mt. Washington Wilderness (USFS)

Moderate (to Scott Mountain)
8.2 miles round-trip
1300 feet elevation gain
Open mid-July through October

Difficult (return via Hand Lake)
9.7-mile loop
1300 feet elevation gain

The hike to beautifully blue, cliff-rimmed Benson Lake is short enough for children, yet can be lengthened if you'd like more exercise. Just 1.1 miles further up the trail you can explore the somewhat less heavily visited Tenas Lakes—half a dozen swimmable pools scattered among huckleberry meadows and forests. Or you can continue another 1.6 miles to the wildflowers and mountain views at Scott Mountain's former lookout site.

Start by driving McKenzie Highway 242, the scenic old road between Sisters and McKenzie Bridge. West of McKenzie Pass 5.6 miles, between mileposts 71 and 72, turn north at a Scott Lake pointer for 1.5 gravel miles to road's end at a gravel pit and parking area. The Benson Trail climbs steadily through a mixed lodgepole pine forest graced by *Pedicularis,* a dainty stalk of beak-shaped blooms with the unbecoming common name of lousewort. After 1.4 miles, when the trail crests a ridge, take a side trail left to the lakeshore. Here dragonflies zoom, small fish jump, and northern toads lurk—particularly during the first half of July when mosquitoes, their favorite prey, are common.

There is no developed trail around Benson Lake, but routes for exploration abound. For starters, take a fishermen's path to the left, cross the lake's outlet, and scramble up a rock ridge to a viewpoint overlooking the lake, two of the

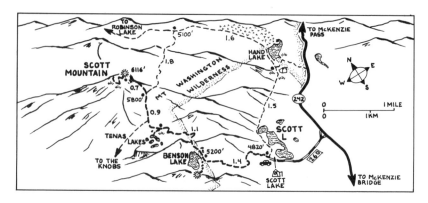

Three Sisters, and Mount Scott. Notice how the bedrock here has been rounded and smoothed by the same Ice Age glaciers that carved the lake's basin.

For a longer hike, return to the main trail, continue 1.1 mile, and take a side trail left to the Tenas Lakes. *Tenas* means "small" in Chinook jargon, the old trade language of the Northwest Indians. The first lake is actually the size of a golf fairway, with cliffs at one end. Hike around it to look for several smaller lakes on the far side. Huckleberries ripen here in August.

If Scott Mountain is your target, continue on the main trail 1.6 miles past the Tenas Lakes junction. This path aims straight for the red, barren peak, but then banks around the mountain and switchbacks up through meadows on the far side, trading cinders for cat's ears. The summit, where a lookout once stood, provides an aerial view of the entire hike's route and half a dozen Cascade peaks.

It's only 1.5 miles longer to return from Scott Mountain via Hand Lake—a delightful loop on less crowded trails. Hike down from the summit 0.7 mile to a small trail sign on the right. Turn left here on a side path that descends through woods 1.8 miles to a T-shaped junction. Then turn right for 3.1 miles back to your car, passing a lava flow, Hand Lake, and several meadows on the way.

Benson Lake with Scott Mountain on horizon.   Opposite: Scott Mountain summit.

47   Hand Lake Shelter

Easy (to shelter)
1 mile round-trip
100 feet elevation gain
Open July through October
Use: hikers, horses
Map: Mt. Washington Wilderness (USFS)

Easy (to old wagon road)
2.6-mile loop
200 feet elevation gain

If you have but one hour to spend in the Wilderness consider investing it here, because this short walk provides as much interest as a trek. In just 2.6 miles you'll pass wildflower meadows, mountain views, a rustic shelter, a lake, a lava flow, and a historic portion of the old McKenzie Wagon Road. There's even a short (but safe) trailless section to add a touch of adventure.

Start by driving McKenzie Highway 242, the scenic old road between Sisters and McKenzie Bridge. West of McKenzie Pass 4.5 miles, between mileposts 72 and 73, park at a very small roadside pullout marked with a hiker-symbol sign.

The trail sets off through subalpine woods of mountain hemlock, lodgepole pine, and red huckleberry. Flowers along the way include blue lupine, pearly everlasting, purple aster, and wild strawberry. After half a mile you'll reach the historic 3-sided, shake-roofed shelter at the edge of lovely meadow. The view here extends across Hand Lake to Mt. Washington's spire.

If you're hiking with children, you might just let them romp to the lake and explore the meadow before heading back to your car. For a longer, more interesting loop, however, continue on the path directly across the meadow. Turn right at a junction in the woods, following a "Robinson Lake" pointer. After 0.4 mile the trail begins following the sandy edge of a lava flow. Continue up alongside the lava 0.2 mile, watching closely for several small rock cairns marking the easily-overlooked wagon road that cuts across the lava to the right.

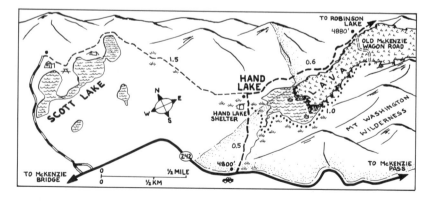

Mt. Washington from Hand Lake's meadow.   *Opposite: Hand Lake Shelter.*

The abandoned roadway is perfectly level and 15 feet wide, but so old that a few struggling plants have had time to take root. Pioneer John Craig arduously chipped this route from the lava around 1871 as a shortcut from the Willamette Valley to Central Oregon's grazing lands.

Follow the roadbed across the lava and turn right, following the sandy margin between the lava and the forest back down to Hand Lake. Though there is no trail here, the lake's water level drops in summer, leaving a wide, hikable beach. Go around the lake to the outlet, walk left along this creek until it narrows enough to be crossable, and then continue around the lake meadows to the shelter and the trail back to the car.

48   Little Belknap Crater

Moderate
5.2 miles round-trip
1100 feet elevation gain
Open mid-July through October
Use: hikers, horses
Map: Mt. Washington Wilderness (USFS)

Much of the raw-looking lava at McKenzie Pass comes from Belknap Crater and its dark twin, Little Belknap. Both mountains keep a low profile among the High Cascades' peaks, yet on average they've erupted every 1000 years since the Ice Age.

This hike along the Pacific Crest Trail follows a lava flow to its source in a

Belknap Crater from inside Little Belknap's lava caves.   *Above: Lava bomb.*

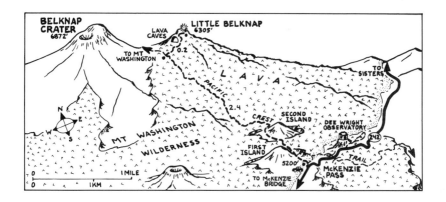

throat-shaped cave atop Little Belknap. Along the way the route passes lava bombs, pressure ridges, and forested islands left in the aftermath of the eruption. Tennis shoes aren't recommended on the path's jagged lava cinders.

Start by driving McKenzie Highway 242, the scenic old road between Sisters and McKenzie Bridge. Half a mile west of McKenzie Pass, at a hiker-symbol sign near milepost 77, turn north into a parking area.

At first the trail's tread is not clear in the sand and dust of this sparse pine forest. Walk to the message board and head left past the "Mt. Washington Wilderness" sign. Climb 0.4 mile along the edge of an "island" surrounded by lava, then cross the blocky flow for 100 yards to the second "island"—another hill that succeeded in diverting the liquid basalt. Notice how the sunny south slope of the hill has dry manzanita and ponderosa pine, while the cooler north slope is damp enough to support huckleberry and subalpine fir.

At the 0.8-mile mark the trail climbs onto the lava for good. Why is the flow so rugged? After the surface solidified, liquid basalt flowed on underneath the crust, buckling up pressure ridges and leaving caves that often collapsed. Since then, only a few intrepid whitebark pines and penstemons have managed to take root.

Views improve of North and Middle Sister as you climb. Ahead is Belknap Crater's red cone, whose eruption blanketed 100 square miles with ash. Blobs of molten rock were thrown high into the air and solidified in teardrop shapes— the lava "bombs" along the slope.

Near the trail's crest, a rock cairn with a pole marks the junction to Little Belknap. Turn right on a 0.2-mile path to the summit parapet. The last 50 feet are a steep scramble to a viewpoint of peaks from Mt. Jefferson to Broken Top.

On the way back down to the trail junction explore the lava caves—actually, 3 short remnants of a single collapsed tube. Since the caves offer the only shade on this hike, they make tempting lunch spots. The uppermost cave, 50 feet north of the path, has a 40-foot-deep throat with snow at the bottom. Don't fall in! Farther down the trail, walk through the middle cave's culvert-like tube. The lowest cave, just south of the trail, is a low-ceilinged bunker.

Other Hiking Options

For a slightly better view, scramble up Belknap Crater. Continue north on the PCT until it leaves the lava. Then head cross-country, traversing left to the cinder cone's less-steep northern slope. Total distance from the trailhead is 4 miles.

49   Matthieu Lakes

Easy
6-mile loop
800 feet elevation gain
Open mid-July through October
Use: hikers, horses
Map: Three Sisters (Geo-Graphics)

The two Matthieu Lakes seem worlds apart—one in a windswept pass with mountain views and the other in a deep forest sheltered by a craggy lava flow. Visit both on this easy loop along a heavily used portion of the Pacific Crest Trail.

Start by driving McKenzie Highway 242, the scenic old road between Sisters and McKenzie Bridge. Half a mile east of McKenzie Pass, near milepost 78, turn south at a sign for Lava Camp Lake. Follow cinder Road 900 for 0.3 mile, then turn right to the Pacific Crest Trailhead parking area. Horse hooves have churned the Matthieu Lakes loop to deep dust.

Set off on the path to the right, marked "P.C.N.S.T. 1/2" Despite the sign's estimate, the Pacific Crest Trail junction is only 0.2 mile away, at the edge of a lava flow. Turn left there for 0.7 mile to a junction marking the start of the loop.

Go left at this junction toward South Matthieu Lake. The PCT gradually climbs along a forested slope through ever-larger openings of bracken fern and red cinders. Views improve as you go. Ahead are glimpses of North and Middle Sister. Behind are spire-topped Mt. Washington and distant, snowy Mt. Jefferson. Far below in the forest is blue North Matthieu Lake.

At the 2.8-mile mark, crest a barren ridge shoulder with the best views of all. Notice the lava bombs scattered among the cinders here. These teardrop-shaped rocks—some as small as footballs, others as large as bears—were blown out of

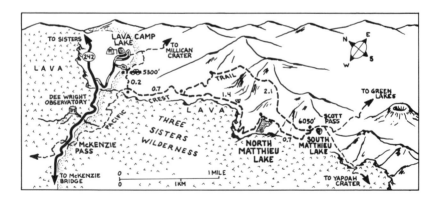

North Sister from South Matthieu Lake.   Opposite: Northern toad.

cinder cones in molten form and solidified in flight.

Continue across a black cinder field to South Matthieu Lake, set in Scott Pass like a gem in a ring. If you're backpacking, remember that campfires are banned in the lake area. Tents are only allowed within 250 feet of the lakes at approved sites marked by a post, and these few sites fill fast with PCT travelers.

To continue the loop, hike back 100 yards to a trail junction sign for North Matthieu Lake. This dusty downhill route, a portion of the old Oregon Skyline Trail, descends 0.7 mile to this larger lake in a forest enlivened by cute golden-mantled ground squirrels. Here, too, permissable campsites are designated by posts. The trail follows the lakeshore to the outlet, switchbacks down through forest, and then follows the edge of a lava flow back to the PCT.

Other Hiking Options

To extend this hike, continue 2.5 miles past South Matthieu Lake on the PCT. You'll cross an impressive lava flow, contour about Yapoah Crater (the cinder cone that produced the lava), and reach a huge meadow of lupine at the Scott Trail junction (see Hike #45).

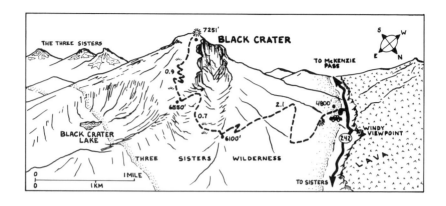

50   Black Crater

Difficult
7.4 miles round-trip
2500 feet elevation gain
Open mid-July to late October
Use: hikers, horses
Map: Three Sisters (Geo-Graphics)

Ice, more than fire, built the craters of this monumental cinder cone. Ice Age glaciers scooped out one bowl for Black Crater Lake and gouged a second, higher chasm that left the peak's summit teetering atop a 500-foot cliff.

The steep trail to Black Crater's former lookout site demands stamina, but offers Central Oregon's best view of the Three Sisters and the McKenzie Pass lava flows.

Start by driving McKenzie Highway 242, the scenic old road between Sisters and McKenzie Bridge. At a hiker-symbol sign 3 miles east of McKenzie Pass, between mileposts 80 and 81, turn south into the Black Crater Trailhead parking area. The path climbs steadily through woods of mountain hemlock, subalpine fir, and pine. After 0.3 mile, a clifftop viewpoint on the left looks out across lava flows to Mt. Washington and distant Mt. Jefferson.

At the 2-mile mark, crest a ridge shoulder and traverse the undulating valley carved by a glacier. Blue and yellow wildflowers brighten meadowed depressions here. Then climb through forest again to another ridge shoulder and enter open alpine country on the butte's east flank. Soon, views open up across Central Oregon to the town of Sisters, Black Butte Ranch, and even Mt. Hood.

The path switchbacks up into the zone of dwarfed, weather-blasted pines known to alpinists as *krummholz*—German for crooked wood. In fact, the whitebark pines here are of a species that only grows above 6000 feet. To withstand winter winds, these trees have limbs so flexible they can literally be tied in knots.

Finally the trail crosses an eerie, barren plateau of black cinders to the summit's 30-foot crag. A lookout building once stood on a flattened spot nearly overhanging the crater cliffs. The trail continues several hundred yards past the summit before dying out, but the view at the top is best. The pinnacles of North Sister and Mt. Washington seem close enough to touch. To the west, black lava flows appear to have oozed like molasses from Little Belknap (Hike #48) and Yapoah Crater, leaving a dozen forested "islands" marooned in rock.

North Sister from Black Crater.   Opposite: Whitebark pine branch.

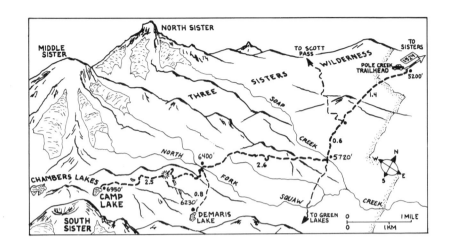

Camp Lake and South Sister.   Opposite: South Sister from the trail in April.

51   Chambers Lakes

Difficult (to Camp Lake)
14.2 miles round-trip
1800 feet elevation gain
Open August to mid-October
Use: hikers, horses
Map: Three Sisters (Geo-Graphics)

The heather ridges around Camp Lake are an alpine wonderland, set smack between towering South Sister and the glaciers of Middle Sister. Wind-sculpted pines cling to crags in scenic poses. Miniature wildflowers turn brilliant blooms to the sun. Icebergs drift in blue waters. The sky seems full of Oregon's most beautiful mountains.

But good things don't come easy. And the price of admission here is more than merely a long, uphill hike—it's a hike that starts with 4.6 miserably dusty, viewless miles. To find the trailhead, drive 1.4 miles west of Sisters on old McKenzie Highway 242 and turn left onto gravel Road 15 for 10.5 miles, following frequent signs for the Pole Creek Trailhead. At the end of the improved road, park at an undeveloped campground distinguished only by an outhouse. The trail begins at a prominent message board on the left.

The path climbs gradually for 1.4 miles to a junction. Turn left for 0.6 mile to Soap Creek, a welcome oasis in this dry lodgepole pine forest. Note the pink monkeyflower on the splashing creek's banks. Cross on a log footbridge to another trail junction. Keep right toward Chambers Lakes and climb more steeply into cooler, lichen-draped mountain hemlock woods.

After 2.6 miles reach Squaw Creek's roaring North Fork and the first clear view of massive Middle Sister. Squaw Creek is milky with rock silt from the peak's Diller Glacier. Cross the stream as best you can on precarious logs and slippery rocks. At a trail junction on the far bank, follow the "Camp Lake" pointer up to the right. This path switchbacks to an alpine ridgecrest with views of all Three Sisters and Broken Top. Camp Lake, the first and most accessible of the Chambers Lakes, is 2 miles along this enchanting ridge.

Despite Camp Lake's name, it's a chilly spot for an overnight stay. There's no shelter from the almost constant winds, and campfires are banned within half a mile of any of the Chambers Lakes.

Other Hiking Options

Demaris Lake is a somewhat closer goal. Though less spectacular, this lake is a good choice on days when wind or threatening weather make the Chambers Lakes uninviting. A sign at the North Fork of Squaw Creek indicates the 0.8-mile side trail. Round-trip distance from the Pole Creek Trailhead is 10.8 miles.

52   Park Meadow

Moderate (to Park Meadow)
7.6 miles round-trip
700 feet elevation gain
Open mid-July to early November
Use: hikers, horses
Map: Three Sisters (Geo-Graphics)

Difficult (to Golden Lake)
11 miles round-trip
1200 feet elevation gain
Open late July through October

Long-time outdoorsmen often have a "secret spot" in the wilderness—an alpine lakelet or a hidden wildflower meadow whose beauty they will gladly describe to you in glowing terms. But ask them just where this paradise is and they only smile.

Many of these secret spots are hidden on the north flank of Broken Top. And the real reason tenderfeet aren't here is not the oath of silence but rather the difficulty of the hike. Park Meadow, the gateway to this wonderland, is nearly 4 miles along a tedious, dusty trail. Golden Lake, with a backdrop of 4 glacier-clad mountains, is another 1.7 miles—partly without any trail at all.

From Highway 22 in downtown Sisters, turn south at a sign for Three Creek Lake and follow Elm Street (which becomes Road 16) for 14 paved miles and another 0.3 mile of gravel until you reach a Park Meadow Trailhead pointer. Eventually the trailhead parking area will be here on Road 16, and hikers will have to walk a dirt road 1.2 miles to the actual trail. In the meantime you can drive 1.1 mile on this track to a sandy parking area where the road turns too rough for most cars. Then walk another 0.1 mile to the old trailhead.

The trail itself is 6 feet wide, churned to dust by horse hooves. But it's not a strenuous route. The round trip has 700 feet of cumulative elevation gain only because of very gradual downs and ups. Beyond the old trailhead 0.8 mile, cross

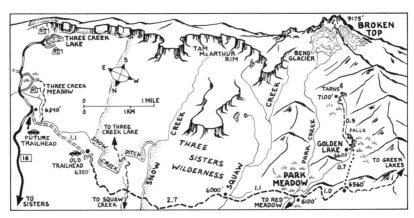

Broken Top from a tarn above Golden Lake.   Opposite: Golden Lake.

an unnamed creeklet and continue straight to the Wilderness boundary at 10-foot-wide Snow Creek. Another 1.5 miles through dry lodgepole pine forest brings you to the footbridge over Squaw Creek, a mossy stream banked with clumps of pink monkeyflower.

From this oasis it's just a mile to the edge of Park Meadow and the first views of Broken Top, South Sister, and North Sister. Brilliant blue, cup-shaped gentians bloom in the grass here each August. If you're backpacking, don't tent in the fragile meadow! Instead look for campsites in the woods, at least 100 feet from trails or water.

Only experienced hikers with map-and-compass skills should attempt to continue to Golden Lake. Cross Park Creek and immediately head left at a trail intersection, following the "Green Lakes" pointer. This path climbs 0.4 mile to a sharp switchback to the right, continues another 0.2 mile to a major, ridge-end curve to the left, and then follows the broad ridgecrest 0.3 mile to a glimpse of Broken Top's peak over a low rise to the left. Watch for a small rock cairn that may still be beside the trail here.

At this point leave the official trail and contour due south (left) toward Broken Top through level, meadowed openings for 0.7 mile to the lake. If you hit a creek, follow it right to the lake. If you come to huge meadows backed by a 500-foot-tall ridge, follow the meadows left to the lake. If you insist on backpacking here, hide your tent well back in the woods. Campfires are banned.

Now here's the real secret: a small, steep trail begins at the waterfall behind Golden Lake and leads 0.9 mile up the meadowed creek to a pair of beautiful timberline tarns.

53   Tam McArthur Rim

Moderate
5 miles round-trip
1200 feet elevation gain
Open August to mid-October
Use: hikers, horses
Map: Three Sisters (Geo-Graphics)

Surrounded by sheer, 500-foot cliffs, the viewpoint on the edge of Tam McArthur Rim is an almost aerial overlook of the Three Sisters. Even in August a few patches of snow remain among the struggling trees and wildflowers of the rim's tablelands. Although hiking to the rim of this enormous fault scarp is not difficult, you arrive at an elevation greater than that of many Oregon mountains. Lewis ("Tam") A. McArthur was secretary of the Oregon Geographic Names Board from 1916 to 1949.

To start the hike, drive to downtown Sisters and turn south on Elm Street at the sign for Three Creek Lake. Follow Elm Street and its successor, Road 16, for 15.7 miles. After 1.7 miles of gravel, notice the trailhead sign on the left, opposite the entrance road to Driftwood Campground. Park at a lot 100 feet down the campground road and walk back to the trail.

The path climbs steeply 0.2 mile, levels off for a bit, and then climbs hard again up to the rim's plateau. Notice how porcupines have gnawed patches of bark off some of the pines. These mostly nocturnal, spiny rodents can also subsist on lupine, though it causes selenium poisoning in other mammals.

The trail climbs gradually for half a mile across the rim's tilted tableland before views begin to unfold. To the north, look for (left to right) Belknap Crater, Mt. Washington, Three Fingered Jack, Mt. Jefferson, Mt. Hood, and the tip of Mt. Adams.

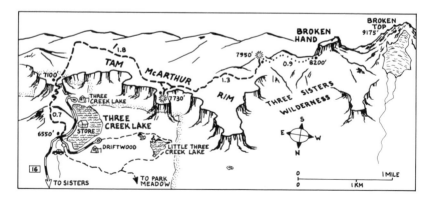

The wildflowers of this sandy plateau grow in scattered clumps to preserve moisture and to fight the winds. The bright purple trumpets are penstemon. The clumps of yellow balls are sulfur plant. And the off-white, fuzzy flowers are dirty socks—source of a suspicious odor wafting across the hot sand.

Finally, at an unmarked fork, take a small right-hand path 200 yards along the rim to the cliff-edge viewpoint. Three Creek Lake and its cousin, Little Three Creek Lake, are over 1000 feet below. To the east, sunlight glints off metal roofs in Bend and Sisters. To the south is snowy Mt. Bachelor, striped with ski slopes.

Other Hiking Options

If you have energy left after reaching the cliff-edge viewpoint, invest it in a relatively level 1.3-mile continuation of this hike along Tam McArthur Rim. Return to the main trail and turn right toward Broken Top. After a mile of sandy, alpine country, climb a snowfield and turn left up what appears to be a small red cinder cone—but which is in fact a ridge end. Stop at the ridgecrest amid a scattering of drop-shaped lava bombs, and admire the view here stretching south to Mt. Thielsen.

It's possible to continue even farther toward Broken Top, but the trail becomes faint and dangerous as it traverses a very steep slope around the left side of Broken Hand's cliffs.

Tam McArthur Rim.   *Opposite: Broken Top from Broken Hand.*

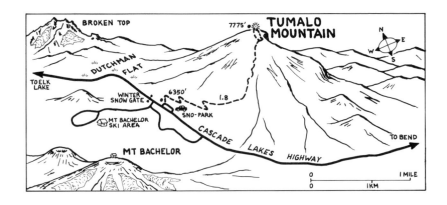

54   Tumalo Mountain

Moderate
3.6 miles round-trip
1200 feet elevation gain
Open mid-July to mid-October
Map: Three Sisters (Geo-Graphics)

Each summer thousands of tourists ride a chairlift to the summit of Mount Bachelor for a view of the Three Sisters. But you can hike up Tumalo Mountain in an hour and get virtually the same view for free. Even better, Tumalo Mountain has no unsightly chairlifts and no throngs of tourists.

Drive 21 miles west of Bend on the Cascades Lakes Highway. Half a mile after the first Mt. Bachelor Ski Area exit, turn right into the Dutchman Flat sno-park, where you'll find a sign for the Tumalo Mountain Trail.

The trail begins at the far end of the parking area and climbs steadily through an open forest of mountain hemlock, true fir, and lupine. Meadowed openings allow glimpses of Mt. Bachelor's snowy cone.

Tumalo Mountain and Mt. Bachelor are cinder cones—gigantic heaps of volcanic shrapnel. Though geologically fresh, they're both old enough to have been bitten by glaciers. Mt. Bachelor is the least damaged; it must have been so smoothly conical before the Ice Age that snow had few places to compact into ice. Tumalo Mountain, on the other hand, probably had a crater that allowed snow to collect. Under the weight of ice, the crater became a glacial cirque, leading to the destruction of the cone's entire northeast quarter.

At the trail's 1-mile mark, views begin opening up across Central Oregon to Sunriver's distant meadow. The trail climbs past gnarled whitebark pines, heads more steeply up a red cinder slope, and finally reaches the summit's long, tilted plain. Because the few struggling plants of this alpine cinder field could easily be damaged by off-trail hiking, approved paths have been clearly outlined with red cinder rocks.

On a cliff edge to the right, notice the concrete foundations of the former lookout tower. The view here extends across the Swampy Lakes' meadow and the seemingly barren valleys of the 1979 Bridge Creek Burn to the rooftops of Bend.

Follow a path along the cliff edge 200 yards to the mountain's highest point. In the forests below are Dutchman Flat and Sparks Lake. And rising above them are the peaks of fame: snowy South Sister and Broken Top.

South Sister from Tumalo Mountain.   Opposite: Broken Top from the summit.

55 Green Lakes via Broken Top

Moderate
9.6 miles round-trip
500 feet elevation loss
Open August to mid-October
Use: hikers, horses
Map: Three Sisters (Geo-Graphics)

The three green lakes in this famed alpine basin reflect South Sister on one side and Broken Top on the other. The picturesque valley also features a glassy lava flow, wildflower meadows, gigantic springs, and a waterfall. But beauty has brought crowds, and crowds have brought restrictions. Several overused lakeshore areas are roped off for restoration. Campfires are banned. Tents are allowed only in posted, designated sites. To avoid the largest crowds, skip August and September weekends.

This trail to the Green Lakes is quieter and less steep than the Fall Creek route (Hike #54), and it has better mountain views. Road access, however, is poor.

Drive the Cascade Lakes Highway west of Bend 22 miles. Two miles beyond the Mt. Bachelor Ski Area, turn right at a sign for Todd Lake Campground. Follow gravel Road 370 half a mile to the campground parking lot and continue on what becomes a steep, miserably rutted dirt road. The route is passable for passenger cars, but demands both caution and courage. After 3.5 arduous miles, turn left at a large "Trailhead" sign and follow this side road 1.3 miles to its end.

The trail follows a barricaded dirt road for 200 yards, then turns left onto a friendlier tread at a sign for Green Lakes. After half a mile, enter a flower-filled meadow overtowered by Broken Top's cliffs. From here Broken Top offers a remarkable cut-away view of a composite volcano. The red, yellow, and black stripes are layers of red cinders, yellow ash, and black lava that built the peak

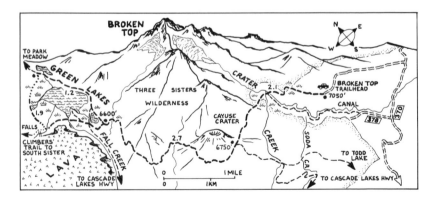

Broken Top from the trail near Green Lakes.   Opposite: Crater Creek meadow.

into a smooth-sided cone. Explosions similar to those at Mt. St. Helens later destroyed the cone's symmetry, hurling 8-foot lava bombs across Central Oregon and burying the entire Bend area under 20 to 50 feet of debris.

At the 1-mile mark cross an irrigation ditch that diverts most of Crater Creek into the Tumalo Creek drainage for use by the Tumalo Irrigation District. The main trail continues straight and 50 yards later crosses the unchanneled remnants of Crater Creek.

The trail then contours around Broken Top, with views across Sparks, Hosmer, and Lava Lakes. On the horizon are snowy Diamond Peak and distant, pointy-topped Mt. Thielsen. Finally the path heads straight for South Sister and drops into the Green Lakes Basin.

Perhaps the best way to explore the valley is with an optional 3.1-mile loop. When you reach the first lake, turn right on an unmarked trail. Skirt the right-hand shore of this lake and the next, larger lake, passing picture-postcard views of South Sister. After crossing a footbridge over the third lake's outlet creek, leave the trail and head cross-country to the left around the largest lake. Stay on the cinder plain; the lakeshore meadows are swampy here. Hike along the far western edge of the valley floor, passing enormous springs, a milky outwash creek from Lewis Glacier, and a blocky lava flow of shiny obsidian. To complete the loop, cross Fall Creek on narrow, tippy logs and go straight.

Other Hiking Options

With a car shuttle you can make this trip all downhill. After hiking to Green Lakes via Crater Ditch, continue 4.2 miles down the Fall Creek Trail (Hike #56) to the Cascade Lakes Highway.

127

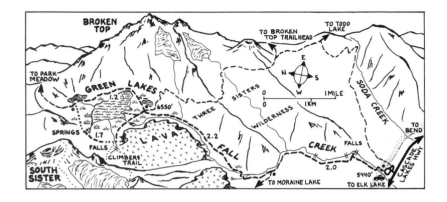

56   Green Lakes via Fall Creek

Moderate
8.8 miles round-trip
1100 feet elevation gain
Open mid-July through October
Use: hikers, horses
Map: Three Sisters (Geo-Graphics)

This classic route to the famous alpine basin of the Green Lakes is a little shorter and more accessible than the less-used Broken Top trail (Hike #55). The path up Fall Creek has other charms as well, for it leads past a string of waterfalls and through a strangely idyllic canyon walled by an enormous lava flow. Although the trail is dusty from extremely heavy use, you can avoid the worst traffic by skipping August and September weekends.

Take the Cascade Lakes Highway 25 miles west of Bend (4.5 miles past the Mt. Bachelor Ski Area) and turn right at a sign for the Green Lakes Trailhead. The path starts at the end of the parking loop on the left.

After 200 yards the trail crosses swift, glassy Fall Creek on a footbridge. Half a mile beyond is the first waterfall, a 25-foot-wide curtain of water. But don't spend all your time here. Just 100 yards upstream is another major cataract. In fact, the creek puts on a trailside performance for the next 1.5 miles, tumbling through chutes, juggling over boulders, and falling headlong into pools.

After a trail splits off toward Moraine Lake on the left, cross Fall Creek again on a footbridge in a meadow with glimpses ahead to South Sister and Broken Top. Blue lupine, yellow composites, and pink monkeyflower bloom here in August.

Then the trail climbs through the woods for a mile before returning to Fall Creek in an eerie meadow flanked by a massive lava flow on the left. This wall of blocky obsidian created the Green Lakes Basin thousands of years ago by damming Fall Creek. Since then, sediment has washed down from the mountains on either side, filling most of the basin and splitting the original single lake into 3 parts.

The obsidian flow itself is a sign of South Sister's old age. Young volcanoes typically spew cinders and pour out fluid basalt lava. As a volcano ages, its magma often becomes richer in silica, the mineral in glass. Silica makes the magma so thick that it can clog up the volcano's vent, causing a Mt. St. Helens-style explosion. If that happens, the silica-rich magma froths out as pumice or shatters into ash. If the volcano is dying quietly, however, the silica may ooze out as obsidian—blocks of shiny glass.

Finally reach a 4-way trail junction just before the lakes. To prowl the lake basin on an optional 2.9-mile loop, continue straight. See Hike #55 for a description of this loop.

The fragile alpine meadows around the Green Lakes have been so severely overused that restrictions are necessary. Many lakeshores are closed to entry as restoration areas. Campfires are banned throughout the entire basin and tents are allowed only at posted, designated sites.

Other Hiking Options

If you'd like to return a different way to your car—and if you don't mind adding 3.1 miles to the day's walk—take the Broken Top trail east from the 4-way trail junction at the Green Lakes. After 2.8 miles turn right at a sign for the Fall Creek Trailhead and follow the Soda Creek Trail 4.5 miles to your car.

South Sister from the largest Green Lake.   Opposite: Lava flow beside Fall Creek.

57 Moraine Lake and South Sister

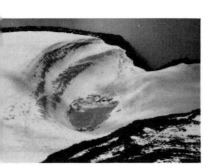

Difficult (to Moraine Lake)
6.8-mile loop
2000 feet elevation gain
Open August to mid-October
Use: hikers, horses
Map: Three Sisters (Geo-Graphics)

Very Difficult (to summit of South Sister)
11 miles round-trip
4900 feet elevation gain

Oregon's third tallest peak has a path to its top. Admittedly, the trail up South Sister is exceedingly steep, long, and rugged, but no technical climbing skills are required and the rewards are great. From the summit—a broad, snowy crater with a small lake—you can see half the state.

If this sounds too demanding, here's a secret: the loop to Moraine Lake, halfway up the mountain, is just as picturesque. This lower hike avoids the final trudge up cinder scree, yet still offers views 100 miles south to Mt. McLoughlin. Moraine Lake itself, a sandy-shored reflecting pool, is set in a dramatic alpine valley strewn with wildflowers and pumice. What's more, the weather's better here. The summit often generates its own wisp of clouds—a scenic feature when viewed from below, but a nuisance at the top.

To begin these popular hikes, drive 27 miles west of Bend on the Cascade Lakes Highway. Beyond the Mt. Bachelor Ski Area 6.5 miles, turn left into Devils

South Sister from Moraine Lake.   *Above: Teardrop Pool atop South Sister.*

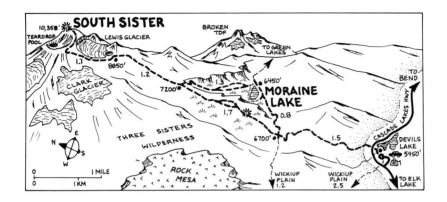

Lake Campground and park at the end of the camp loop.

Start out on the South Sister Climbers Trail—*not* the more obvious path that ducks through a highway culvert. The correct trail crosses a footbridge over glassy Tyee Creek before crossing the highway. This trail promptly launches steeply uphill through a dense mountain hemlock forest. After 1.5 grueling, viewless miles, the path suddenly emerges from the forest at the edge of a vast, sandy plateau. South Sister and Broken Top loom ahead. Signs at a 4-way trail junction indicate Moraine Lake is to the right, but to take the recommended scenic loop to Moraine Lake, follow the "South Sister" pointer straight ahead.

This portion of the hike is a lark—strolling up the open tableland, admiring views of a dozen mountains and lakes. Wind-gnarled trees pose in occasional clusters. Scraggly, red-leaved dogbane plants dot the sand. At one point the trail splits, but the forks soon rejoin.

At the upper end of Moraine Lake's valley a side trail to the right dives down into the canyon. If you're taking the Moraine Lake loop, turn right and descend this steep, slippery trail. Use caution (and your hands) on the first, rugged 100-foot section of this path.

Moraine Lake's U-shaped valley was carved by the Lewis Glacier in the Ice Age. Leftover rock and sand were pushed to the glacier's toe as a *moraine*—the rounded sandpile now cupping the lake. Later volcanic eruptions scattered pumice across the valley. Some of these floatable rocks are as big as basketballs.

To complete the Moraine Lake loop, hike to the far side of the lake and follow the trail up the ridge to the right. The climbers' trail back to Devils Lake is 0.8 mile beyond. If you're backpacking, note that tents near Moraine Lake are allowed only at sites designated by a post. Campfires are banned.

If you're climbing South Sister, however, go straight at the junction at the upper end of Moraine Lake's valley. The next 1.2 miles steepen drastically, finally leading to a resting point in a sandy saddle—the current terminal moraine of Lewis Glacier, overlooking a small green cirque lake. A climbers' trail from Green Lakes joins here on the right. The route to the summit heads up the ridge to the left. After 0.7 mile, crest the lip of South Sister's broad crater. Follow the rim to the right 0.4 mile to the summit, a rocky ridgecrest with a benchmark but no climbers' register. Bend, Sisters, and Redmond are clearly visible in the Central Oregon flatlands. To the north, the green Chambers Lakes dot the barren, glacial landscape below Middle Sister.

58   Sisters Mirror Lake

Moderate (to Sisters Mirror Lake)
8 miles round-trip
700 feet elevation gain
Open mid-July through October
Use: hikers, horses
Map: Three Sisters (Geo-Graphics)

Moderate (to Le Conte Crater)
7 miles round-trip
1000 feet elevation gain

Here's a hike with two very different options. If you enjoy exploring alpine lakes, the heather meadows around Sisters Mirror Lake are ideal. If you're in the mood for a volcanic viewpoint instead, choose the other fork of this trail and climb to Le Conte Crater, a miniature cinder cone wedged between Wickiup Plain and South Sister's rugged Rock Mesa lava flow. If you can't decide, why not do both? The combined loop is still only a moderate, 10.4-mile hike.

Start by driving 27 miles west of Bend on the Cascade Lakes Highway. Beyond the Mt. Bachelor Ski Area 6.5 miles, turn left at Devils Lake Campground. Park on the left of the campground loop at the sign for the Elk-Devils Lake Trail.

The trail promptly passes under the highway through a large culvert. After half a mile the path joins an abandoned, dusty road. This cat track was one of several bulldozed by a California mining company to reach claims staked before the 1964 Wilderness Act. The company's threat to strip-mine Rock Mesa's pumice for cat litter ended with a $2 million buyout by Congress in 1983.

After half a mile on the road, turn right onto a heavily used but poorly marked side trail. Follow this path uphill for 1 mile to a trail junction at the edge of Wickiup Plain, a plateau of pumice and bunchgrass with a dramatic view of South Sister. If you're only going to Le Conte Crater, go straight here and head for the little cinder cone at the far upper end of the prairie. But to see Sisters Mirror Lake, turn left.

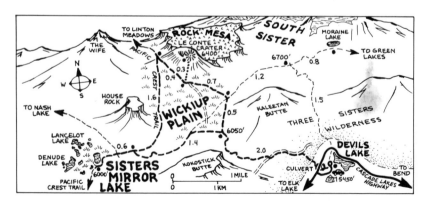

Sisters Mirror Lake.   *Opposite: South Sister from Wickiup Plain.*

If you head left toward the lake, keep left at all junctions for another 1.4 miles to the Pacific Crest Trail. Then turn left on the PCT for 0.6 mile. The lake is too shallow for swimming and doesn't reflect South Sister very well, since only the tip of the peak is visible. But no matter; the alpine ambience here is the main attraction. Sit on the rocks at the far end of the lake to admire the natural rock garden of heather. If you have a compass and some pathfinding skills, try prowling cross-country to find a few of the two dozen ponds clustered within the square mile to the west. If you're backpacking, be sure to tent in the forest—not on the fragile meadow plants. Campfires are banned.

To visit Le Conte Crater on the return trip, hike back on the PCT, following it 2.2 miles as it skirts House Rock and crosses a corner of Wickiup Plain. At a junction, turn right for 0.4 mile to the base of Le Conte Crater, a little, round-topped cinder cone at the upper edge of Wickiup Plain. From here climb cross-country up the meadowed slope to the crater rim. The crater bowl holds snow until mid-August. South Sister rises almost overhead. Rock Mesa is a sea of jumbled lava at your feet. To the southeast are Broken Top, Mt. Bachelor, and the lakes of the Cascade Lakes Highway.

Climb back down the cinder cone, turn left on the trail across Wickiup Plain, and follow signs for Devils Lake to return to the car.

59   Horse Lake

Moderate
8.8-mile loop
600 feet elevation gain
Open late June through November
Use: hikers, horses
Map: Three Sisters (Geo-Graphics)

This popular loop heads deep into the rolling forests of the Three Sisters Wilderness. At Horse Lake, a fisherman's trail leads around the shore to a dramatic rock peninsula—the ideal spot for lunch. On the hike back, take a short, little-known side path to Colt Lake, a miniature version of Horse Lake. Mosquitoes are a problem throughout July.

Drive the Cascade Lakes Highway 31 miles west of Bend to Elk Lake, turn west at the sign for the Elk Lake Trailhead, and park at the turnaround. The trail forks after 50 yards—the start of the loop. Keep right, following the pointer for Horse Lake. This dusty, heavily used path climbs gradually 1.3 miles to a forested pass, crosses the Pacific Crest Trail, and then gradually descends 2 miles to a 4-way trail junction in a meadow. You can't see Horse Lake from here, but if you take the faint, unsigned trail straight ahead 300 yards you'll find the shore.

From this perspective, Horse Lake is likely to be a disappointment. No trace remains of the shelter that once stood here. The beachless shore is densely forested and so heavily trammeled that areas have been closed for restoration. So continue to the right on an unmaintained path around the lake to the much nicer far shore. Tennis shoes may get wet on this route, because some areas are a little boggy. Also expect to step over a few small logs along the way.

The less-visited, far shore of the lake has a view of Mt. Bachelor and a cinder cone named Red Top. Explore the long, blocky rock peninsula that juts far into

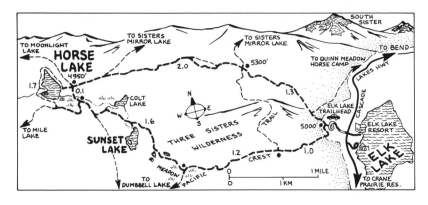

Horse Lake.   Opposite: River otter.

the lake, with cliffs on the left and a forested island on the right. The peninsula itself is off-limits for tents or campfires.

Just beyond the peninsula the path crosses the lake's gurgling outlet creek on stepping stones. After another 0.3 mile the shoreline path joins the well-maintained trail from Mile Lake. Turn left here, skirt some lovely meadows, and reach another trail junction in the woods. Turn right toward Dumbbell Lake. But at the next trail junction, 0.3 mile up this path, *do not* follow the "Dumbbell Lake" pointer. Instead go straight toward Sunset Lake.

The side trail to Colt Lake is not marked, so watch for it carefully. Just 170 steps beyond the trail junction with the "Sunset Lake" arrow, notice a faint path splitting off across a small meadow to the left. Follow this path 0.1 mile to the pretty lake, ringed with small meadow openings.

Continuing the loop on the main trail, notice Sunset Lake through the trees on the right. Nearly a mile later, the path joins the Pacific Crest Trail in an unnamed meadow. Turn left on the PCT for 1.2 miles and then follow signs to the Elk Lake Trailhead.

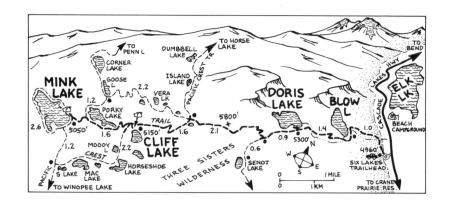

Doris Lake.   Opposite: Cliff Lake Shelter.

60 Doris and Cliff Lakes

Easy (to Doris Lake)
4.8 miles round-trip
400 feet elevation gain
Open late June through October
Use: hikers, horses
Map: Three Sisters (Geo-Graphics)

Difficult (to Cliff Lake Shelter)
14 miles round-trip
1600 feet elevation gain

The Six Lakes Trailhead near Elk Lake is the gateway to far more lakes than merely six. The rolling forests in this portion of the Three Sisters Wilderness are polka-dotted with blue. An easy walk up this trail reaches the first two large lakes, with small beaches suitable for children. For a longer hike, continue to the picturesque shelter at Cliff Lake. Backpackers can explore even farther through these lake-dotted forests to Mink Lake. Expect mosquitoes all of July.

Start by driving 33.5 miles west of Bend on the Cascade Lakes Highway. Beyond the Elk Lake Resort 2 miles, turn right at the "Six Lakes Trailhead" sign and park at the end of the turnaround.

The trail climbs very gradually through a dry forest of lodgepole pine, twice crossing footbridges over the (usually dry) outlet creek of Blow Lake. After the second bridge, short side trails lead to the right to Blow Lake's narrow gravel beach. The main trail continues around the lake to its inlet and then follows this creek more than a mile to Doris Lake. Once again, watch for side paths leading to the shore, where you'll find a view of a small rocky butte. One lakeshore peninsula has been closed for restoration, but other picnic spots abound.

If you're heading onward to Cliff Lake, continue nearly a mile on the main trail to a junction for Senoj Lake. Yes, this is "Jones" spelled backwards. Turn right, following the "PCT" arrow. The trail now switchbacks up a ridge into a cooler mountain hemlock forest with blue huckleberry bushes. Cross a pass and descend gradually to a junction with the Pacific Crest Trail. Turn left on the PCT for 1.6 miles, past small meadows and rock outcroppings.

The unmarked side trail to Cliff Lake is easy to miss. The trick is to watch for the well-marked trail junction to Porky Lake, beside a large rockslide. Stop here and backtrack 20 paces on the PCT. The path to Cliff Lake takes off here, skirting the base of the rockslide 150 yards to the hidden lake, backed by 50-foot cliffs. Flat, shaley rocks from the cliffs provide the foundation—and even some novel furniture—for the 3-sided shelter here.

Other Hiking Options

The 18-mile round-trip hike to Mink Lake will interest backpackers, though the leaky shelter at this large, forest-rimmed lake provides little refuge. A tempting, slightly longer option is to return from Mink Lake on one of the trail loops exploring the countless smaller lakes in this area—either via Mac Lake or Goose Lake.

61   Muskrat Lake

Moderate
10 miles round-trip
200 feet elevation gain
Open mid-June to early November
Use: hikers, horses
Map: Three Sisters (Geo-Graphics)

This remarkably level hike follows the shore of Cultus Lake several miles, and then strikes off through the forest to a rustic log cabin by a pastoral lilypad lake.

To find the trailhead, drive the Cascade Lakes Highway 44 miles west of Bend to the sign for Cultus Lake Resort. Turn right onto paved Road 4635 for 1.8 miles, fork right toward the campground, and then keep to the right on a gravel road marked "Dead End." Half a mile farther, after the road turns to a dirt track, you'll see the trailhead sign on the left.

The trail joins a lakeshore path from the campground after 200 yards and marches around Cultus Lake to the right, offering views across the water to Cultus Mountain, a forested cinder cone. The mixed lodgepole pine and fir forests along the trail host woodland blooms: twinflower, prince's pine, and star-flowered smilacina.

The word *cultus* is a Chinook jargon term used by Northwest Indians to describe wicked spirits and worthless places. Today the value of this clear, 3-mile-long lake is diminished only by the buzz of mosquitoes in July and the buzz of speedboats in August.

After 0.8 mile pass a long, sandy, swimmable beach. The semi-developed campsites here are popular with boaters. A mile beyond, leave the lakeshore at a broad bay. Ignore a side trail that joins from Corral Lakes, but turn right at the second trail junction, following a "Winopee Lake" sign. This nearly level route passes a Wilderness boundary sign and a side trail for the Teddy Lakes before finally reaching a meadow-banked creek and Muskrat Lake.

The shelter here, though not shown on most Forest Service maps, is a spacious 15-by-25-foot log cabin, complete with wooden floor, two stoves, cupboards, folding chairs, and a sleeping loft. It is unlocked and open to the public. A path out the back door leads across a meadow to the lake. Aster, larkspur, and Indian paintbrush bloom in the meadow. Reeds and lilypads line the lake. If you're backpacking, here, don't rely on the shelter being unoccupied.

Other Hiking Options

For a short side trip, continue 0.3 mile around Cultus Lake to the lake's inlet creek. For a slightly longer side trip, follow an 0.6-mile trail past the smaller Teddy Lake to the forested shore of the larger Teddy Lake.

Muskrat Lake.   Opposite: Inside Muskrat Lake Shelter.

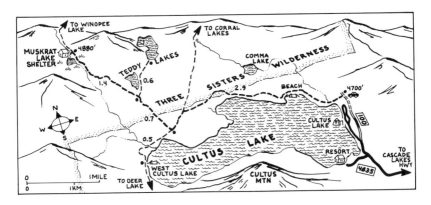

McKenzie
Foothills

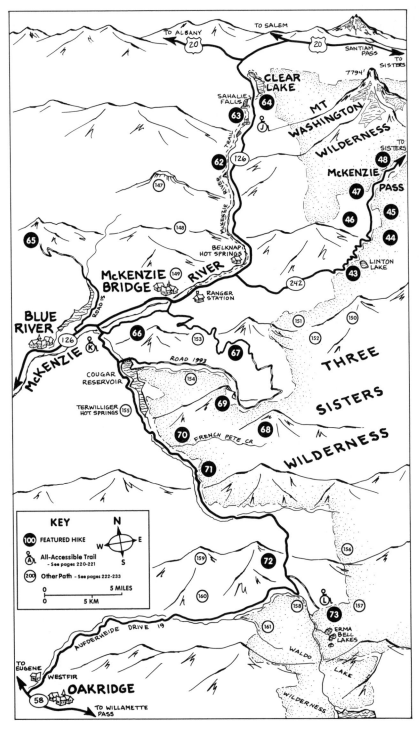

TO SALEM

TO ALBANY

20

20

SANTIAM PASS

TO SISTERS

CLEAR LAKE

7794'

SAHALIE FALLS

64

63

MT WASHINGTON

J

62

126

WILDERNESS

TO SISTERS

48

McKENZIE

47

PASS

65

46

45

44

BELKNAP HOT SPRINGS

148

147

McKENZIE RIVER TRAIL

LINTON LAKE

43

McKENZIE BRIDGE

149

RIVER

RANGER STATION

242

BLUE RIVER

151

150

ROAD 15

126

152

K

66

153

THREE

67

COUGAR RESERVOIR

ROAD 1993

154

McKENZIE

SISTERS

TERWILLIGER HOT SPRINGS

155

69

70

FRENCH PETE CR.

68

WILDERNESS

71

KEY

N

100 FEATURED HIKE

W E

S

A All-Accessible Trail
  - See pages 220-221

200 Other Path - See pages 222-233

0   5 MILES

0   5 KM

159

72

156

160

AUFDERHEIDE DRIVE 19

158

L

157

73

161

ERMA BELL LAKES

TO EUGENE

WESTFIR

WALDO

OAKRIDGE

58

LAKE

TO WILLAMETTE PASS

WILDERNESS

Opposite: McKenzie River (Hike #62).

McKenzie River

Easy (to Tamolitch Pool)
4.2 miles round-trip
200 feet elevation gain
Open April to mid-December
Use: hikers, bicycles
Maps: Tamolitch Falls, Clear Lake (USGS)

Difficult (entire trail)
26.5 one way
1800 feet elevation gain

Perhaps the most astonishing part of the 26.5-mile McKenzie River Trail is the short stretch to Tamolitch Pool, where the river vanishes into a lava flow, tumbles over an eerily dry, phantom "waterfall," and then reemerges from a small turquoise lake. The 4.2-mile walk to this pool is easy enough for hikers with children. For a serious trek—or a mountain bike ride—start at the McKenzie Ranger Station and follow the McKenzie River Trail upstream past two visitable hot springs to Tamolitch Pool.

For the easy walk, start by driving McKenzie Highway 126 east of McKenzie Bridge 14 miles (or south of the Highway 20 junction 10.5 miles). Beside the upper end of Trailbridge Reservoir, turn west at a "EWEB Powerhouse" sign, cross a bridge, and promptly turn right on gravel Road 655. At a curve after 0.4 mile, park by hiker-symbol sign on the right.

The first 1.1 mile of this hike is nearly level, through an old-growth forest of Douglas fir and droopy red cedar alongside the rushing whitewater river. Then the trail climbs through a moss-covered lava flow to an overlook of blue-green Tamolitch Pool. The lake's only apparent inlet is a dry waterfall, yet the McKenzie River rages out of the pool fully grown.

In Chinook jargon, the old trade language of Northwest Indians, *tamolitch* means "bucket." The name fits this cliff-rimmed basin. Lava from Belknap

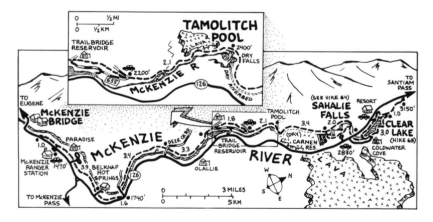

Tamolitch Pool.   Opposite: Footbridge on trail to Tamolitch Pool.

Crater buried 3 miles of the riverbed above here 1600 years ago. Except during rare floods, the McKenzie was left to percolate underground through the porous rock to springs in Tamolitch Pool. A 1963 hydroelectric project has left the dry stretch of riverbed even drier. The Eugene Water and Electric Board catches the river in Carmen Reservoir, diverts it through a 2-mile tunnel to Smith Reservoir, and drops it through a second tunnel to the Trail Bridge power plant.

   If you're interested in a longer trek or a mountain bike ride, tackle a longer section of the McKenzie River Trail. But don't start at the official beginning of the trail, because the path's first mile merely follow the highway shoulder. Instead start at the McKenzie Ranger Station, 2.2 miles east of McKenzie Bridge on Highway 126. If you don't want to drive there, take the Lane Transit District bus from Eugene. It leaves Eugene's downtown transit station at 8:20am weekdays (8:30am weekends), and returns from the McKenzie Ranger Station at 4pm and 7:16pm (6:03pm weekends). One-way fare is $1, and bicycles are free. To check the latest fares and schedules, call 687-5555.

   From the ranger station, walk across the highway from the parking lot's west entrance, take an obvious but unsigned trail 50 yards to the riverbank, and turn right on the McKenzie River Trail amid 6-foot-thick Douglas firs. This lower portion of the trail is usually snow-free all year. By April, dogwood trees fill the understory with their white crosses, and trilliums dot the forest floor. In late May, crowds of fishermen arrive, but so do delicate pink deer-head orchids and great yellow bunches of Oregon grape blooms. And in fall, chanterelle mushrooms sprout in the forest while vine maple turns the river banks scarlet.

   The first few miles of the trail often detour away from the river, approaching within earshot of the highway. At the 3.9-mile mark you'll cross the paved entrance road to Belknap Hot Springs, an old-timey lodge with a 102-degree swimming pool. For a quick swim, detour left 0.2 mile. The riverside pool is open 365 days a year 9am to 9pm. The fee is $3. Simon Belknap, who staked a claim to the springs in 1870, claimed the waters cured "female weakness, inflammations both external and internal, and general debility."

For a free soak in a wilder hot springs, continue 5 miles up the river trail to the Deer Creek Road crossing. A path from the road's bridge heads downstream 200 yards to Deer Creek Hot Springs, a shallow 2-person pool separated from the icy river by rocks. Depending on the river level, the pool can be chilly or hot.

If you're continuing onward, follow the river trail another 7.2 miles upstream to Tamolitch Pool's dry waterfall. Beyond this point, the McKenzie River Trail follows the dry riverbed through a lovely, remote valley for 3.4 miles, passes Sahalie and Koosah Falls (see Hike #63), and continues to the river's source at Clear Lake (Hike #64).

63   Sahalie and Koosah Falls

Easy
2.6-mile loop
400 feet elevation gain
Open May through November
Use: hikers, bicycles
Map: Clear Lake (USGS)

Here's a quick way to impress out-of-state friends with Oregon's roaring rivers, waterfalls, and old-growth forests: Take them on the waterfall loop around the McKenzie River's two grandest cascades. The hike starts at 100-foot-tall Sahalie Falls, a raging cataract that pounds the river into rainbowed mist, descends past 70-foot Koosah Falls, and returns on the river's far shore through forests of 6-foot-thick Douglas fir and droopy-limbed red cedar.

Drive 19 miles east of McKenzie Bridge on Highway 126 (or 5.2 miles south of the Highway 20 junction). Near milepost 5, pull into a large, well-marked Sahalie Falls parking area and walk 100 yards down to the railed viewpoint of the falls. In Chinook jargon, the old trade language of Northwest Indians, *sahalie* meant "top," "upper," "sky," and "heaven." *Sahalie Tyee* (heaven chief) was the pioneer missionaries' translation for God. Natives pronounced the word *saghalie*, accenting the first syllable and using a guttural *gh*.

Start the loop by heading left from the viewpoint, following a "Waterfall Trail" pointer downstream. The river churns through continuous whitewater for half a mile before leaping off another cliff at Koosah Falls. The word *koosah* also meant sky or heaven in Chinook. Notice the massive springs emerging from the lava cliff near the base of the falls. Over the past 6000 years, half a dozen basalt flows from the High Cascades have tortured the McKenzie River, damming it at Clear Lake (Hike #64), squeezing it into a gorge here, and burying it altogether

Sahalie Falls.   Opposite: Dogwood.

on the dry riverbed above Tamolitch Pool (Hike #62).

Keep right at all junctions after Koosah Falls. In another 0.4 mile you'll meet a gravel road beside Carmen Reservoir. Follow the road right 150 yards to a trail sign, take the path into the woods 100 yards, and turn right on the McKenzie River Trail. This route heads upstream past even better viewpoints of Koosah and Sahalie Falls. After 1.3 miles, cross the river on a footbridge and turn right for 0.4 mile to your car.

Other Hiking Options

For a longer hike, continue upstream on the McKenzie River Trail 0.6 mile to the Clear Lake loop (Hike #64), or else head downstream for 3.4 quiet miles along a dry riverbed to a dry waterfall at Tamolitch Pool (Hike #62).

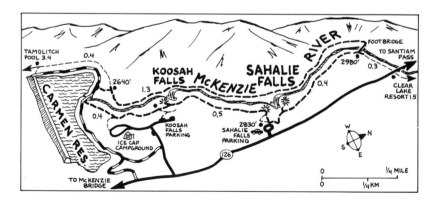

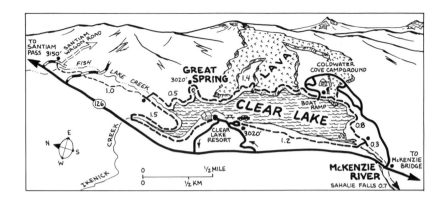

64   Clear Lake

Easy
5.5-mile loop
200 feet elevation gain
Open May to mid-November
Use: hikers, bicycles
Maps: Clear Lake, Santiam Jct. (USGS)

Three thousand years ago lava flows from the High Cascades dammed the McKenzie River, creating a lake so clear, cold, and calm that ghostly tree snags are still visible under its 100-foot-deep waters. The stroll around Clear Lake offers lots of variety: huge springs, lava crossings, old-growth forests—even a resort where a cup of coffee costs less than a dollar.

Start by driving Highway 126 east of McKenzie Bridge 20 miles (or 3.7 miles south of the Y junction with Highway 20). Between mileposts 3 and 4, at a "Clear Lake Resort and Picnic Area" sign, take a paved side road 0.4 mile downhill and turn right to the picnic area's parking loop.

Walk past a log picnic shelter built by the Civilian Conservation Corps in the 1930s and continue on a trail around the lake counter-clockwise. Although the path is set back from the shore in a forest of Douglas fir and mountain hemlock, it offers glimpses across the lake to the spire of Mt. Washington and the snowy tips of the Three Sisters. The forest floor is carpeted with bunchberry, a low, 6-leaved wildflower that's closely related to dogwood trees. Like dogwoods, these dainty plants have cross-shaped white blooms in June (when yellow Oregon grape and white vanilla leaf also flower here) and red berries in fall, when vine maple paints the forest understory with scarlet leaves.

Expect some traffic noise for the hike's first mile. Then the path crosses a footbridge over the lake's glassy outlet, the beginning of the McKenzie River. In another 200 yards, turn left on the McKenzie River Trail for 0.8 mile to the Coldwater Cove boat ramp. Golden-mantled ground squirrels are so bold here that they sit on picnickers' laps. Parts of the trail in this area have been paved to simplify the crossing of rough lava flows.

Continue 1.4 miles to Great Springs, where the trail detours around a rushing, 300-foot-long river that emerges from an astonishing pool in an old lava flow. Though chilly, the springs' constant 38-degree Fahrenheit temperature keeps Clear Lake from freezing in winter.

After another half mile, cross a footbridge over Fish Lake Creek (an inlet stream that only flows during the spring snowmelt), and turn left at a junction. The lakeshore path then climbs over a peninsula, detours around a narrow arm of the lake, crosses Ikenick Creek near the highway, and ends at the Clear Lake Resort, 200 yards from your car. The tiny resort offers a cafe, a few groceries, rustic cabins, and rowboat rentals. In fact, renting a rowboat is the best way to see the eerie snags of the 3000-year-old drowned forest—not petrified, but merely preserved from rot in the lake's cold, pure water.

Other Hiking Options

For a longer hike, combine this loop with the 2.6-mile walk around Sahalie and Koosah Falls (Hike #63). The loops are connected by a 0.6-mile stretch of the McKenzie River Trail that crosses Highway 126.

Rowboats at Clear Lake Resort.   Opposite: Bunchberry.

65 Tidbits Mountain

Moderate
4 miles round-trip
1100 feet elevation gain
Open mid-June through October
Use: hikers, horses, bicycles
Map: Tidbits Mountain (USGS)

This little-known mountain near Blue River is a delightful tidbit for hikers. The pinnacled summit, where a lookout tower once stood, offers sweeping views from the Three Sisters to the Willamette Valley. The trail to the top traverses an old-growth forest of 6-foot-thick giants. Rhododendrons, gentians, and trilliums brighten the way. And although the path gains more than 1000 feet, the grade is gradual enough that the hike is relatively easy.

From Springfield, follow McKenzie Highway 126 east 44 miles. Beyond the village of Blue River 3 miles (near milepost 44), turn left onto Road 15 at a "Blue River Reservoir" pointer. Follow this road 4.8 miles to the end of the pavement, and then go straight on gravel Road 1509 for 8.3 winding miles. Half a mile past a green water tank, turn left on Road 877. Follow this very steep road 0.2 mile up a ridgecrest to a short spur on the left with a rough parking area.

The trail begins at the end of the parking area amid rhododendrons and beargrass, but soon dives into a forest of huge, ancient Douglas firs. Watch for the heart-shaped leaves of wild ginger, the big triple leaves of vanilla leaf, and the tiny white sprays of star-flowered smilacina.

At a saddle after 1.3 miles you'll reach a trail junction beside the remains of a collapsed 1930s Forest Service shelter. Turn left on a path that soon traverses a large rockslide with impressive views over crumpled foothills to the northwest. Above the path are cliffs with interesting pinnacles—the finger-like "tidbits"

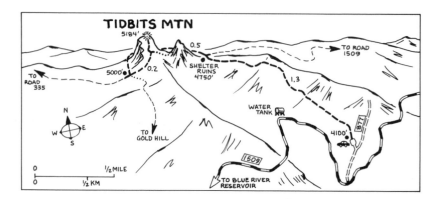

View from Tidbits Mountain.   Opposite: Vanilla leaf.

that give this mountain its name. In the middle of the slope ignore a side path switchbacking up to the left—a rough, alternate return route from the summit. Continue straight, past scattered boards from the fallen lookout tower and huge bouquets of blue, cup-shaped gentian.

When the trail reaches a junction at a ridgecrest, switchback to the left on a path up the ridge. The forest dwindles here to wind-swept bonsai trees in a rock garden of yellow stonecrop and pink penstemon. Remains of a staircase reveal how the lookouts climbed the final 30 feet, but it's not difficult to scramble up the rock without the stairs.

From the top you can survey the entire route of the hike and even spot your car. To the east are Cascade snowpeaks from Mt. Hood to Diamond Peak, with Black Butte and Mt. Bachelor peeking out from Central Oregon. To the west, look down the South Santiam, Calapooia, and McKenzie River valleys to the distant haze of the Willamette Valley.

To try the alternate route back from the summit, hike 50 yards down the main trail and turn left. This fainter path switchbacks through a high saddle before rejoining the main trail in 0.2 mile.

Madrone atop Castle Rock.   Opposite: Oregon grape leaf.

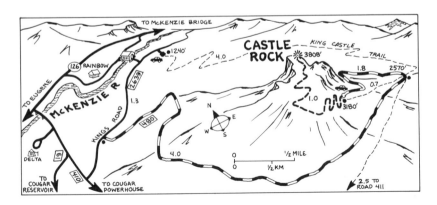

66 Castle Rock

Easy (from Road 480)
2 miles round-trip
630 feet elevation gain
Open April to mid-December
Use: hikers, horses, bicycles
Map: McKenzie Bridge (USGS)

Difficult (from Kings Road)
11.4 miles round-trip
2600 feet elevation gain

Viewpoint climbs don't come much easier than this. After a scant mile of well-graded switchbacks through the forest, this path leads to a cliff-edge lookout site overlooking the McKenzie River Valley from Blue River to the Three Sisters. If the hike sounds *too* easy—or if you're riding a mountain bike—you're welcome to start 4.7 miles farther down the mountain instead.

From Springfield, follow McKenzie Highway 126 east 45 miles. Beyond the village of Blue River 4 miles (between mileposts 45 and 46), turn right at a Cougar Reservoir pointer onto paved Aufderheide Road 19. At a fork after half a mile, keep left on Road 410 toward the Cougar Dam powerhouse. After another 0.4 mile, turn left onto paved Kings Road 2639 for 0.5 mile. Then turn right onto Road 480 and follow this one-lane gravel road uphill 5.8 miles to its end at a very small parking area.

After a few yards the trail forks; head uphill to the right. The Douglas fir forest here is so dense that only the most shade-tolerant vanilla leaf, vine maple, and Oregon grape can grow beneath it. After climbing steadily 0.8 mile, pass beneath some cliffs and enter a steep, dry meadow dotted with manzanita bushes, chinkapin trees, and gnarled black oaks. At a saddle, follow the bare ridge to the summit on the left.

From the old lookout site, the long trough of the McKenzie River Valley is very clearly U-shaped in cross section—evidence the canyon was widened by Ice Age glaciers spilling down from the Three Sisters. Note the green links of Tokatee Golf Course far below and a scrap of Cougar Reservoir to the south. To the east are Mt. Washington and the Three Sisters, while the horizon in all other directions teems with the jumbled ridges of the Old Cascades, patchworked with clearcuts.

Other Hiking Options

If this hike's too short, or if you want to avoid driving the rough gravel on Road 480, consider driving an extra 1.3 miles on paved Kings Road 2639 to park at the King Castle Trailhead instead. The well-graded path that begins here is usually snow-free all year. After 4 miles the path meets a switchback of Road 480 in a saddle. From there you can either cross the road for a final 1.7-mile climb to Castle Rock's summit, or, if you're on a bicycle, you can turn left for a zooming ride down Road 480 to complete a 9.3-mile loop.

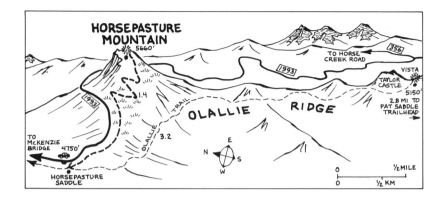

67   Horsepasture Mountain

Moderate
2.8 miles round-trip
910 feet elevation gain
Open late June to early November
Use: hikers, horses, bicycles
Map: Three Sisters (Geo-Graphics)

Mountain views and wildflower meadows highlight the relatively easy climb to this panoramic former lookout site perched on a crag between the Three Sisters and the McKenzie River Valley.

Horsepasture Mountain was named by early forest rangers. While riding the Olallie Trail from McKenzie Bridge to lookout towers on Olallie Ridge, rangers often camped at the (since vanished) Horsepasture Saddle Shelter and let their mounts graze the nearby peak's meadows. Indians, too, once visited this area, drawn by the huckleberries that still ripen on Olallie Ridge each August. In fact, *olallie* is the Chinook jargon word for "berry."

To find the trailhead, drive Highway 126 east of Springfield 50 miles to McKenzie Bridge. Immediately after crossing the village's river bridge, turn right onto paved Horse Creek Road 2638 for 1.7 miles. Just after the Horse Creek Group Campground turn right onto Road 1993, follow this one-lane paved route for 8.6 winding, uphill miles, and park at the second hiker-symbol sign on the right, at the Horsepasture Trailhead.

The trail begins amid a patch of coneflowers—odd brown blooms in the sunflower family, but lacking petals. After just 80 yards, turn sharply left at a 4-way trail junction in Horsepasture Saddle. This path traverses Douglas fir woods with white woodland blooms in early summer: vanilla leaf, bunchberry, fairy bells, and star-flowered smilacina.

After 0.7 mile you'll enter lush meadows with white beargrass plumes, purple aster, goldenrod, coneflower, and the boat-shaped leaves of hellebore. If the trail seems faint at times in the meadow foliage, just keep going onward and upward. The trail's 4 switchbacks are so clear they're hard to miss. When you reach the summit's cliff-edge crags, you'll find 3 large anchor bolts marking the lookout tower's site. The Three Sisters dominate the horizon to the east, with conical Mt. Bachelor to the right and ghostly Mt. Hood far to the left. Below, displayed like a volcanology exhibit, ancient High Cascades lava flows funnel down the great flat-bottomed trough of the McKenzie River Valley toward the blue horizons of the distant Willamette Valley.

Other Hiking Options

For a longer, relatively level hike from the same trailhead, go straight on the Olallie Trail 3.2 miles. This route contours along Olallie Ridge to a viewpoint of the Three Sisters just beyond Taylor Castle's saddle. If you've arranged a car shuttle, you can continue another 2.8 miles along the Olallie Trail to the Pat Saddle Trailhead, described in Hike #68.

North Sister from Horsepasture Mountain.   Opposite: Fairy bells.

68   Olallie Mountain

Moderate
7.2 miles round-trip
1200 feet elevation gain
Open late June through October
Use: hikers, horses
Map: Three Sisters (Geo-Graphics)

Only two lookout buildings survive in the Three Sisters Wilderness—the cliff-edge hut at Rebel Rock (Hike #71) and the well-preserved, unstaffed building here atop Olallie Mountain. This one has the better view, a panorama of the Three Sisters and 8 other snowpeaks. The hike here is easier, too, through beargrass meadows that put on a spectacular summer flower show. And if you're into exploring, short side trips lead to a secret lake and the ruin of a historic guard station.

To find the trailhead, start by driving Highway 126 east of Springfield 45 miles. Beyond the village of Blue River 4 miles (between mileposts 45 and 46), turn right at a Cougar Reservoir pointer onto paved Aufderheide Road 19. After half a mile, keep right at a fork, following Road 19 another 2.5 miles to the reservoir. Then turn left across Cougar Dam and follow Road 1993 for a total of 15.4 miles, partly on gravel, to the well-marked Pat Saddle Trailhead parking loop on the right.

Start out on the Olallie Trail from the far end of the parking loop; don't take the French Pete Trail to the right by mistake. The Olallie Trail traverses at a very gentle grade through a Douglas fir/hemlock forest brightened by pink rhododendrons and white beargrass plumes in July. By late August, expect some ripe blue huckleberries along this trail—no surprise, given that *olallie* is the Northwest Indians' Chinook jargon word for "berry."

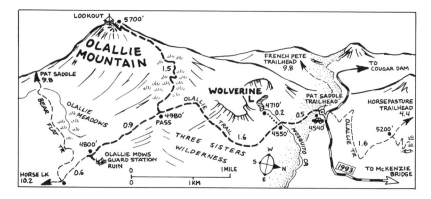

154

Three Sisters from Olallie Mountain.   Opposite: Olallie Mountain lookout.

After half a mile, hop across rocky, four-foot-wide Mosquito Creek in a glen where mosquitoes are rare but salmonberry, bracken fern, salmonberry, and devils club thrive. Make a note of this spot if you're interested in bushwhacking to a hidden lake later on your return trip.

Then continue on the Olallie Trail another 1.6 miles to a trail junction in a sparsely wooded saddle and turn right, following an "Olallie Mountain" pointer. This path is lined with beargrass, and in damp weather the leaves can quickly soak hikers' pants. Beargrass won its name because bears sometimes dig up and eat the plants' fleshy roots. Native Americans wove baskets from the long leaves. But technically, beargrass isn't a grass at all; it's a lily. Some summers the plants hide that secret by not putting out flowers; this helps outwit seed-gathering chipmunks too. But every second or third year they produce a crop of 3-foot plumes, each composed of countless tiny, lily-like white stars.

After 1.5 miles the trail switchbacks up past a display of gigantic white Cascade lilies to the summit's lookout hut. Although the 14-foot-square building is abandoned, its glass windows are mostly intact, protected by openable shutters. The unlocked door allows backpackers to stay here on a first-come-first-served basis. The only furniture is an ancient chair and a rusting fire locator table, but the panoramic view is in perfect condition.

For a little variety on your return trip, consider taking a couple of short detours. To visit the ruin of the Olallie Meadows Guard Station, hike back 1.5 miles to the trail junction in a saddle and turn right, following an "Olallie Meadows" arrow. After an easy 0.9 mile, this path crosses a creeklet and forks in a little meadow. Turn left and climb 100 yards to the large clapboard cabin, built soundly in the 1930s but split down to the floorboards by two falling firs in the winter of 1996.

Only hikers with some routefinding experience should try the trailless side trip to hidden Wolverine Lake. Hike back on the Olallie Trail to the Mosquito Creek crossing (half a mile from your car), and bushwhack upstream to the left through the woods 350 yards to the shallow, reed-edged lake—home to dragonflies and tadpoles, if not wolverines.

69   Lowder Mountain

Moderate
5.6 miles round-trip
900 feet elevation gain
Open late June through October
Use: hikers, horses
Map: Three Sisters (Geo-Graphics)

At first the summit of flat-topped Lowder Mountain seems like any other forest-rimmed meadow. Only when you venture to the wind-bent trees on its eastern side do you discover the mountain's monumental cliffs. Two lakes shimmer nearly 1000 feet below. And beyond, the Three Sisters loom like great white ghosts.

From Springfield, follow McKenzie Highway 126 east 45 miles. Beyond the village of Blue River 4 miles (between mileposts 45 and 46), turn right at a Cougar Reservoir pointer onto paved Aufderheide Road 19. After half a mile, keep right at a fork, following Road 19 another 2.5 miles to the reservoir. Then turn left across Cougar Dam and follow Road 1993 for a total of 11.1 miles, partly on gravel, to a junction at a pass. Park at a hiker-symbol sign here.

Start out on the uphill trail signed for Lowder Mountain. The well-graded path switchbacks a few times in an old-growth Douglas fir forest, then levels off and traverses three sloping meadows. The openings offer views across French Pete Creek's valley (Hike #70) to Olallie Mountain (Hike #68) and snowy Mt. Bachelor. The meadows mix thimbleberry and bracken fern with cone-flower, an oddly unpetaled sunflower relative.

At the 2-mile mark, turn right at a trail junction in another meadow and begin switchbacking steeply uphill. After nearly half a mile of this effort you suddenly reach Lowder Mountain's barren summit plain. The trail's tread is obscure here,

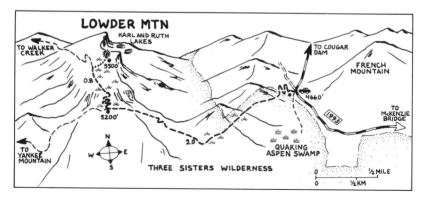

but rock cairns mark the route 0.2 mile across the plain, past clumps of trees. Just before the trail reenters the forest to begin its descent toward Walker Creek, leave the trail and walk up through the field to the right 0.2 mile to the hidden cliffs, and a breathtaking view of the High Cascades from Mt. Hood to the Three Sisters.

Romantic souls sometimes camp atop Lowder Mountain to watch the Three Sisters burn red in the sunset. Tent sites abound, but bring a permit and any water you might need.

Karl and Ruth Lakes from Lowder Mountain.   Opposite: Coneflower.

70   French Pete Creek

Easy (to bridgeless crossing)
6 miles round-trip
600 feet elevation gain
Open late March to mid-December
Use: hikers, horses
Map: Three Sisters (Geo-Graphics)

Moderate (to 5-mile marker)
10 miles round-trip
1000 feet elevation gain

French Pete Creek was Oregon's first low-elevation forest valley to be preserved because of the outcry over Oregon's vanishing old-growth forests. The original Three Sisters Wilderness included only feebly forested, high-elevation land. After 14 years of ardent protest by hikers, students, and environmentalists, French Pete was added to that Wilderness in 1978.

This valley aroused such passion because of the sheer grandeur of the mossy jungle along its cascading mountain creek. Gargantuan Douglas firs and 1000-year-old cedars tower above a green carpet of sword ferns, twinflower, and Oregon grape. But the French Pete Trail's charming footbridges also won a number of converts. Old-growth logs, fitted with handrails, spanned a dozen side creeks and crossed the main stream 4 times.

Now all but one of these scenic bridges have rotted away. The Forest Service, reluctant to cut old-growth trees to replace the spans, surveyed a new trail route entirely on the creek's north bank. With trail funds low, the Forest Service is looking for volunteers to help finish the route. Until then, hikers will find this popular trail a bit rough, with a tricky bridgeless crossing at the 3-mile mark.

To find the trailhead, drive McKenzie Highway 126 east of Springfield 45 miles. Beyond the village of Blue River 4 miles (between mileposts 45 and 46), turn right at a Cougar Reservoir pointer onto paved Aufderheide Road 19. At a fork after half a mile, veer right toward Cougar Reservoir. Then keep on Road

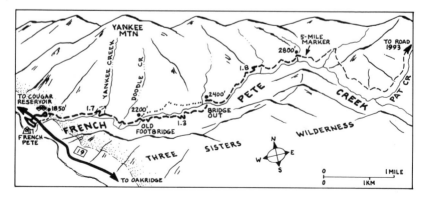

French Pete Trail. Opposite: French Pete Creek.

19 another 10 paved miles. A mile beyond the end of the reservoir turn left into the well-marked French Pete Trailhead parking area.

The path climbs very gradually, at times through wooded benchlands out of sight of the creek. After 0.9 mile the path forks, but you can take either route. Both paths cross 6-foot-wide Yankee Creek in a side canyon and then rejoin.

At the 1.7-mile mark, the trail crosses French Pete Creek on a huge old-growth log with a handrail. Eventually this ancient footbridge will be removed and the trail will continue along the creek's steep north slope. In the meantime, carefully cross the 100-foot span one at a time and follow the trail on the south bank 1.3 miles to a bridgeless crossing of French Pete Creek. This makes a good turn-around point for hikers with children.

If you're continuing, cross the creek as cautiously as possible on the available wiggly logs and slippery rocks—or safer yet, bring old tennis shoes and wade. After the crossing, the French Pete Trail is less well maintained but far less crowded. Continue 1.8 pleasant miles until the trail crosses a large, bouldery side creek. Just beyond is a picnickable flat beside French Pete Creek. A ceramic "5" mile marker is 200 yards up the trail. This makes a good stopping point, because the path now begins a long traverse up the canyon slopes, leaving French Pete Creek for good.

If you're planning an overnight trip, bring a backpacking stove because campfires are banned within 100 feet of water or trails—in other words, virtually everywhere in this narrow canyon.

Other Hiking Options

With a car shuttle, you can hike the 9.8-mile length of the French Pete Valley one-way—and all downhill. Leave a car at the trailhead described above and drive a second vehicle back to Cougar Dam. Cross the dam and follow Road 1993 for 15.4 miles to the Pat Saddle Trailhead, also described in Hike #68.

71   Rebel Creek

Easy (to second bridge)
2.2 miles round-trip
400 feet elevation gain
Open late March to mid-December
Use: hikers, horses
Map: Three Sisters (Geo-Graphics)

Difficult (to Rebel Rock lookout)
12.3-mile loop
3300 feet elevation gain
Open mid-June through October

The old-growth forests along this mountain stream are as grand as those along nearby French Pete Creek, but because this area is less well known, it's much less crowded. What's more, energetic hikers can continue up Rebel Creek on a challenging loop past a hidden lookout building to a viewpoint of the Three Sisters.

Drive McKenzie Highway 126 east of Springfield 45 miles. Beyond the village of Blue River 4 miles (between mileposts 45 and 46), turn right at a Cougar Reservoir pointer onto paved Aufderheide Road 19. At a fork after half a mile, veer right toward Cougar Reservoir. Then keep on Road 19 another 13 paved miles. Four miles beyond the end of the reservoir, pull left into the Rebel Trailhead.

The trail begins at a message board and reaches a fork after 100 yards. Keep left on the Rebel Creek Trail. This path ambles through a second-growth forest for half a mile before switchbacking down to cross the creek on a 100-foot bridge built of a single huge log. Here the trail enters a cathedral-like grove of ancient Douglas fir and drooping cedar, many 7 feet in diameter.

At the 1.1-mile mark cross the creek again on a smaller bridge. Hikers with children should declare victory here and turn back, because the trail beyond this point leaves the creek and climbs for 4.6 miles along a canyon slope. If you're intrigued by the hidden lookout tower, however, and prepared for an athletic loop hike, continue onward.

As the Rebel Creek Trail climbs, the forest changes to mountain hemlock, with an understory of rhododendron and bunchberry. After crossing a small branch of Rebel Creek and switchbacking up the head of the valley, turn right at a trail junction. This route soon traverses a large, steep meadow with waist-high bracken fern and thimbleberry. Look for purple aster and red paintbrush.

When the trail reenters the woods and reaches a windswept ridgecrest, be sure to look behind for a view of Rebel Rock's thumb-shaped rock pillar, because this is as close as the trail comes to that landmark.

Note that the Rebel Rock lookout tower is not on Rebel Rock, but rather on a cliff edge a mile to the west. And since the trail bypasses the tower in the woods, it's easy to miss. As you continue up the ridgecrest watch for 4 large rock cairns beside the trail. Turn left here on a faint trail 100 yards to the hidden lookout. No longer in use but well preserved, the squat, square building has a railed

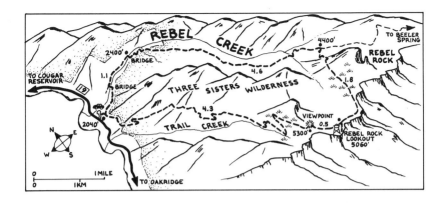

porch with a view across the South Fork McKenzie River Canyon to Chucksney Mountain (Hike #72). To the east is white-topped Mt. Bachelor.

An even better mountain view awaits half a mile farther along the loop trail, where the path crests a meadowed ridge. Here you can finally spot the Three Sisters and Mt. Jefferson.

After the viewpoint the trail dives down a large meadow. Bracken obscures the tread; watch for a switchback to the left 0.6 mile down and a switchback to the right 0.2 mile beyond. The path then reenters the forest for the long descent to the car.

Rebel Rock Lookout.   Opposite: Footbridge over Rebel Creek.

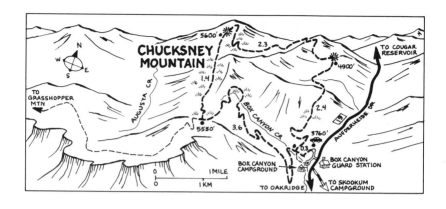

72   Chucksney Mountain

Difficult
10.3-mile loop
2000 feet elevation gain
Open late June through October
Use: hikers, horses, bicycles
Map: Chucksney Mtn. (USGS)

This invigorating loop climbs along forested ridges to the crest of Chucksney Mountain, where it ambles more than a mile through delightful summit meadows with views of the Three Sisters. On the way down, the path visits a hidden glen—the headwaters of Box Canyon Creek.

To drive here from McKenzie Highway 126, take the turnoff for Cougar Reservoir (4 miles east of Blue River, between mileposts 45 and 46) and follow paved Aufderheide Road 19 for 25.5 miles to Box Canyon Campground. To drive here from Highway 58, take the Westfir exit near Oakridge and continue straight past Westfir's covered bridge onto Aufderheide Road 19. Follow this paved route for 31.4 miles to Box Canyon Campground.

A historic guard station opposite the campground entrance has been restored as a rental cabin. The two-room guard station lacks electricity and potable water, but sleeps 4-6 and rents for just $25 a night. Call the Blue River Ranger District at (541) 822-3317 for information.

The trailhead parking area is at the far end of the Box Canyon Campground. The Forest Service promotes the campground as an equestrian center, but horse use of the Chucksney Mountain Trail is light.

Keep right at each of three trail junctions in the first 0.3 mile, so that you end up on Chucksney Mountain Loop Trail #3306. This path climbs in two long switchbacks before traversing north along a steep slope. At first the Douglas fir forest is greened with sword fern, Oregon grape, and star-flowered smilacina. Higher, the forest shifts to mountain hemlock with beargrass and vanilla leaf.

A bare, rocky ridge-end at the 2.7-mile mark provides a nice view across the forests to the Three Sisters and Mt. Washington's distant spire. After climbing another 0.6 mile to a ridgecrest, the trail switchbacks briefly downhill and contours around a large basin—an Ice Age cirque.

Finally the trail switchbacks up to the open crest of Chucksney Mountain's rocky summit ridge. To the east, the Three Sisters, Broken Top, and Mt. Bachelor rise above the chasm of the South Fork McKenzie River. To the west, Grasshopper Mountain and Hiyu Ridge battle an encroaching maze of logging roads.

The loop trail continues on the far side of the crest, heading left through the summit meadows. The route loses a few feet of elevation but then levels off for more than a mile. At the end of the summit ridge descend through a meadow with a glimpse of Diamond Peak and turn left on the Grasshopper Trail. The next mile of this path explores a high basin with scattered meadows. Look here for blue aster, pearly everlasting, purple larkspur, and petal-less brown cone-flower. Finally the path crosses (sometimes dry) Box Canyon Creek and launches downhill through the woods for the steep, 2.9-mile return to the campground.

The Three Sisters from Chucksney Mountain. *Opposite: Chanterelle mushrooms.*

73   Erma Bell Lakes

Easy (to Middle Erma Bell Lake)
4.2 miles round-trip
300 feet elevation gain
Open mid-June to mid-November
Use: hikers, horses
Map: Three Sisters (Geo-Graphics)

Moderate (to Williams Lake)
8.4-mile loop
800 feet elevation gain

Lower and Middle Erma Bell Lakes, separated by a small waterfall, are among the most heavily visited destinations in the high country forests north of Waldo Lake—perhaps because the trail here is so delightfully level that even small children can manage the hike.

To be sure, popularity has brought some restrictions. Portions of the lakes' shores are roped off for restoration. Within 250 feet of any of the 3 Erma Bell Lakes or Otter Lake, camping is only allowed at approved sites marked by a post. But it's not too hard to outdistance the crowds here. Simply continue on a longer loop to Williams Lake, and pick up two other lakes in the bargain.

From McKenzie Highway 126, take the turnoff for Cougar Reservoir (5 miles east of Blue River, between mileposts 45 and 46) and follow paved Aufderheide Road 19 for 25.6 miles. Just after the Box Canyon Guard Station, turn left on gravel Road 1957 for 3.6 miles to Skookum Campground. To drive here from Willamette Highway 58, take the Westfir exit near Oakridge and continue straight past Westfir's covered bridge onto Road 19. Follow this paved route for 31.3 miles to a pass just before the historic Box Canyon Guard Station and turn right on gravel Road 1957 to its end at Skookum Campground.

From the campground parking lot, the trail crosses a creek on a large footbridge. The name Skookum is appropriate for this rushing stream; in Chinook jargon the word means "powerful." The Erma Bell Lakes, on the other hand, are

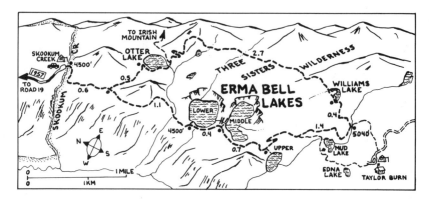

Middle Erma Bell Lake.   Opposite: Reflection in Williams Lake.

named for a Forest Service bookkeeper who died in an automobile accident in Troutdale in 1918. Alongside the broad trail, look for rhododendrons and trilliums blooming in June. Other woodland flowers bloom here in July: bunchberry, star-flowered smilacina, and vanilla leaf.

After 0.6 mile go straight at a trail junction, and in another 1.1 mile reach a "No Camping" sign. A short side trail to the left leads to deep, blue Lower Erma Bell Lake. None of the lakes on this hike has a mountain view or an established trail around its lakeshore.

Continue 0.4 mile up the main trail to Middle Erma Bell Lake. Just above the waterfall, take a side trail left across the outlet creek to find a pleasant stretch of shore where children can dabble sticks in the water and watch dragonflies.

To continue the loop on the main trail, hike past Upper Erma Bell Lake 0.7 mile to a trail junction. Keep left on the Erma Bell Trail for 0.7 mile to the Williams Lake Trail junction, just before a footbridge. Don't cross the bridge. Instead turn left, and in 0.4 mile you'll reach Williams Lake.

Scraped smooth by glaciers during the Ice Age, Williams Lake's bedrock shore shows scratches left by rocks dragged beneath the ice. This entire area is still recovering from glaciation that ended just 6000 years ago. Humps of bare rock protrude from soils so thin that only lodgepole pine and beargrass can grow.

Beyond Williams Lake the trail gradually descends 2.4 miles to the Irish Mountain Trail junction. Turn left and pass Otter Lake to complete the loop.

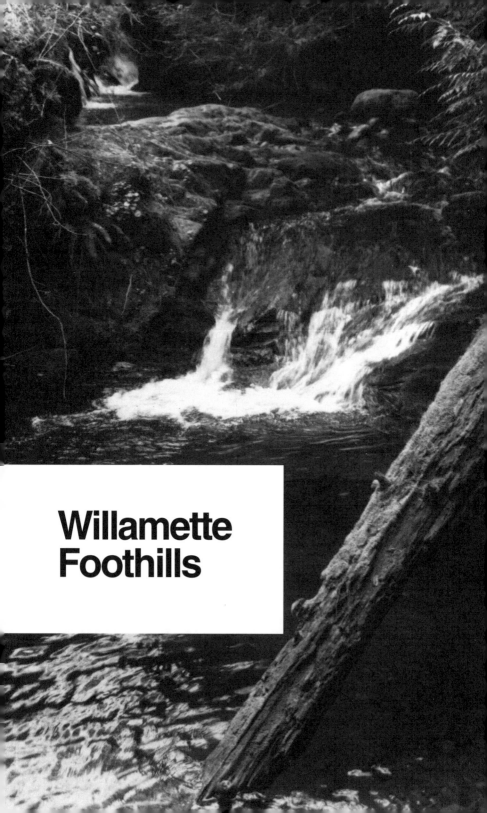

Willamette
Foothills

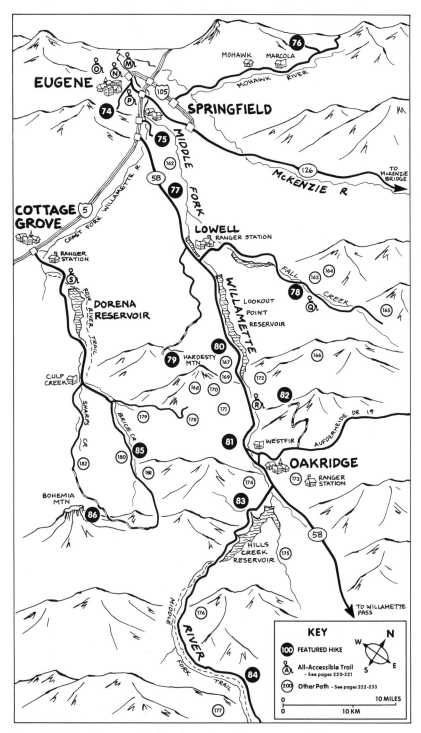

Opposite: Falls on Goodman Creek Trail (Hike #80).

74   Spencers Butte

Easy
1.5-mile loop
800 feet elevation gain
Open all year
Map: Creswell (USGS)

Eugene's skyline is not dominated by buildings, but rather by a long, forested ridge topped with Spencers Butte's haystack-shaped knob. Explore this natural skyline on the South Hills Ridgeline Trail, through forests so thick with Douglas fir and sword fern it's easy to forget city streets lie below.

The Spencers Butte loop is admittedly the steepest and most heavily used part of this trail system, but it's still the best introduction. Children enjoy the challenge of "climbing a mountain" without too much effort, and everyone enjoys the bald summit's 360-degree panorama, extending from Fern Ridge

Sighting toward Cottage Grove from Spencers Butte.   Above: Summit benchmark.

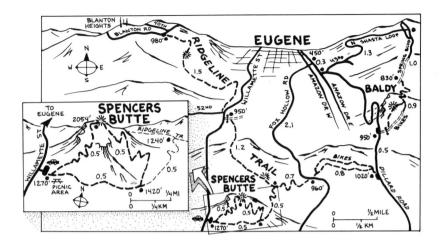

Reservoir to the Three Sisters.

From 8th Street in downtown Eugene, drive 5 miles south on Willamette Street and turn left into the parking lot for Spencers Butte Park. Walk up the broad cement stairs and immediately turn left onto the summit trail.

After 0.3 miles up through forest you'll reach a steep grassy slope with views of the Spencer Creek Valley. As in all grassy, open areas on this hike, poison oak abounds along the trail—be careful to avoid these shrubs' shiny, triple leaflets!

In another 200 yards the trail reaches a forested area where people have attempted shortcuts up to the top, causing erosion. Keep straight on the main trail to a rocky open area. Then scramble up to the right. This final pitch up the summit's bare rock ridge is steep enough you'll have to use your hands.

A bird's-eye view of the Eugene area waits at the top, with Fern Ridge Reservoir to the west, the Willamette Valley to the north, and the Three Sisters on the eastern horizon. The first white man to scale Spencers Butte was Dr. Elijah White, who came here in 1845 hoping to spy an easy wagon train route through the Cascade Range to the east. He named the peak for the then secretary of war.

To continue the loop hike, descend the far side (the east side) of the summit. Traverse down to the right, watching for markers that show where the trail reenters the forest. Then the path zigzags downhill. At a little meadow, ignore a left-hand fork that leads to the rest of the Ridgeline Trail. Curve right on the main path to return to the Willamette Street trailhead.

Other Trail Options

For an easier goal, hike to the second best viewpoint on Eugene's skyline, atop a small knoll called Baldy. The Ridgeline Trail here splits to allow a route for mountain bikes. To find this trailhead from downtown, drive south on Pearl Street to 30th Avenue, turn right on Hilyard to the next light, turn left on Amazon Drive East for 1.2 miles, and turn left on Dillard Road for 1.5 miles to a hiker-symbol sign on the left, under powerlines. Baldy's summit is 0.5 mile up a path through meadows to the left. If you're bicycling, you'll have to take a powerline road below the summit, but then you can continue on a fun 6.9-mile loop, using Spring Boulevard, North Shasta Loop, Fox Hollow Road, and the only other bike-friendly portion of the Ridgeline Trail, as shown on the map.

75   Mount Pisgah

Easy (to summit)
3 miles round-trip
1000 feet elevation gain
Open all year
Map: Springfield (USGS)

Easy (arboretum tour)
1.7-mile loop
100 feet elevation gain

The first Lane County pioneers climbed this grassy hill between the forks of the Willamette River, viewed the green dales at the end of the Willamette Valley, and named the hill Mount Pisgah, for the Biblical summit from which Moses sighted the Promised Land. The view is still dramatic, and the hike is especially fun when coupled with a stroll through the adjacent arboretum's well-tended trail network.

Just south of Eugene, take the 30th Avenue exit (#189) of Interstate 5 and head for the Texaco gas station on the east side of the freeway. (If you're coming from the north you'll have to drive a mile to 30th Avenue, cross the freeway, and double back.) Just past the station, turn right onto Franklin Boulevard for 0.4 mile. Then turn left onto Seavey Loop Road for 1.5 miles, continue straight until you cross the Coast Fork Willamette River bridge, and finally turn right for 0.4 mile to the arboretum parking area.

At a brown metal gate at the upper left edge of the parking area, start hiking uphill on a wide graveled path (Trail #1 on the map). The grassy slopes host a scattering of white oaks and Douglas firs with blackberries and wild roses. Stay on the trail to avoid brushing the shiny triple leaflets of poison oak. Trail #1 passes under powerlines twice before breaking out into the long summit

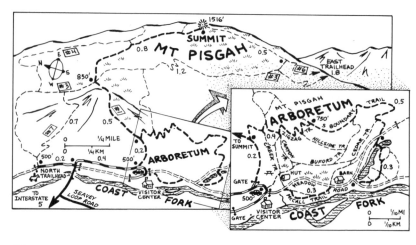

Grassland along Mt. Pisgah trail.   Opposite: Summit sighting pedestal.

meadow. Wildflowers here include purple iris, fuzzy cat's ears, and wild straw-berries. A bronze sighting pedestal, a memorial to Pleasant Hill author Ken Kesey's son Jed, identifies mountains and other landmarks visible from the summit. Bas reliefs on the pedestal's pillars depict more than 300 Oregon fossils.

If you'd like to return from the summit on a longer loop, you have several choices. You could continue straight half a mile to Trail #3, but this trail is rougher and often muddy. You could backtrack 0.8 mile and take Trails #3 and #7 to the North Trailhead, but then you'll have to walk back to your car on a road.

The best bet for a loop hike is probably to return the way you came and then explore the adjacent Mt. Pisgah Arboretum's well-maintained network of short paths. The map shows a suggested 1.7-mile circuit. Admission to the arboretum is free, although donations are accepted. Children are particularly fond of the bridge over a lilypad slough at the far end of the water garden area, where it's fun to watch for bullfrogs and turtles.

Many of the arboretum's trees and flowers are labeled. Detailed plant lists and trail maps are available in the visitor center beside the parking lot. A hangar-like former barn nearby is used for special events—notably a mushroom show on the last Sunday of October and a wildflower exhibition each May on the Sunday after Mothers' Day. For arboretum information, call (541) 747-3817.

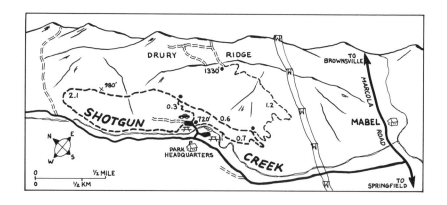

76   Shotgun Creek

Easy
3.4-mile loop
300 feet elevation gain
Open all year
Map: Marcola (USGS)
Left: Shotgun Creek

In the rustic Mohawk Valley just half an hour from Eugene, this woodsy loop is an ideal first hike for small children. In summer, pack a lunch so you can conclude the hike with a picnic beside Shotgun Creek's developed swimming area. In winter, shake off cabin fever by sending the kids around these snowless trails in search of pine cones and orange-bellied newts.

Take the Springfield exit of Interstate 5 and drive east on I-105 to the 42nd Street/Marcola exit. Turn left on Marcola Road for 15 miles—continuing 3 miles beyond the town of Marcola—and then turn left at the Shotgun Creek sign. After another 1.6 miles turn right onto the park entrance road, cross a bridge over Shotgun Creek, and park by the official trailhead on the right.

The main path from this official trailhead leads up into the woods, but if you're hiking with kids, or if you're planning to do the entire 3.4-mile loop, it's actually more fun to start out along the creek itself. So walk across the road from the trailhead parking area and hike past the picnic shelters to find the trail that follows Shotgun Creek upstream. Mossy bigleaf maple, white-barked alder, and droopy red cedar shade this streambank route. After 0.8 mile the path leaves the creek and climbs gradually through a drier, second-growth forest of Douglas fir and salal. The notches visible in old stumps along the trail were originally fitted with springboards to give loggers a place to stand while pulling two-man crosscut saws—tools known to loggers as "misery whips."

At the 2.1-mile mark you can turn right at a trail junction for a shortcut back to your car. But if you're still going strong, continue straight on the Meadow Loop Trail, which contours through meadowless forest, crossing several rustic footbridges over dry side creeks. After 0.6 mile, ignore the Drury Ridge Trail turnoff to the left (this path climbs to a logging road in a viewless clearcut) and instead continue straight on the Lower Trail. This route switchbacks down to Shotgun Creek and follows the creek back to the picnic area.

77   Elijah Bristow Park

Easy (from Channel Lake)
1-mile loop
No elevation gain
Open all year
Map: Park brochure

Easy (from Lost Creek)
2.9-mile loop
No elevation gain
Use: hikers, horses, bicycles
Right: Wild blackberries

These two easy lowland loops along the Middle Fork of the Willamette River near Eugene are pleasant in any season, but they're especially fun in August, when masses of sweet, juicy blackberries ripen along the trail. The state park honors Elijah Bristow, Lane County's first settler. Born in Virginia in 1788, he came to Oregon in 1846 and took up a claim on "a pleasant hill" 5 miles west of here—now the town of Pleasant Hill.

From Interstate 5 just south of Eugene, take Oakridge exit 188A, drive 7.2 miles east on Willamette Highway 58, and turn left at the sign for Bristow Park. After a block turn right on Wheeler Road for 0.7 mile to the park entrance on the left. Don't drive all the way in to the main picnic area. To find the trailhead

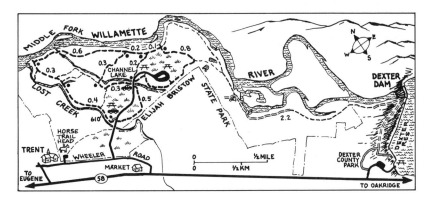

for the short, 1-mile loop (ideal for hikers with small children), drive 0.6 mile on the park entrance road and park on the left, immediately before the road's second bridge. From here, a very easy, hiker-only path ambles left along the shore of Channel Lake, an ancient, abandoned Willamette River channel. Keep right at all trail junctions to complete the loop. Along the way you'll cross a footbridge across Channel Lake and amble briefly along the Willamette river-bank before turning inland to your car.

If you'd prefer a longer, 2.9-mile loop hike, start at a different trailhead. When you enter the park, drive just 0.3 mile on the park entrance road. Immediately after crossing the first bridge, pull into a small picnic area and trailhead on the left beside Lost Creek. From here, a trail follows the lazy creek downstream past blackberry patches and mossy bigleaf maples. Horses and bikes share the route. After crossing a footbridge at the 0.4-mile mark, avoid two side trails to the right, continue across a field of Scotch broom, and then avoid a side trail to the left.

Shortly thereafter reach the beachless bank of the swift Willamette River. Alders and tall, honey-scented cottonwood trees line the shore. Turn right along the river for 0.9 mile. When the path emerges at the main picnic area's lawn, keep along the bank 200 yards to a 4-way trail junction just before a muddy slough. If you turn left 50 feet you'll reach a delightful pebble beach. If you go straight you'll be on the rugged riverside trail to Dexter Dam. (This muddy 2.2-mile route requires rubber boots, and is sometimes closed by floods.) Turn right to continue the loop. The trail now leaves the river and follows an abandoned road through the woods behind the picnic area. Spur trails to the right lead out to picnic lawns. Keep left to skirt a lake and return to your car.

78   Fall Creek

Easy (to Timber Creek)
5.8 miles round-trip
200 feet elevation gain
Open all year
Map: Saddleblanket Mtn. (USGS)

Moderate (to Road 1828 with shuttle)
9 miles one way
700 feet elevation gain

The popular trail along this woodsy, low-elevation creek has attractions for each season: fall mushrooms, winter solitude, spring wildflowers, and best of all, summertime swimming holes. For an easy hike, turn back at Timber Creek. Or shuttle a bicycle to the upper trailhead, hike 9 miles of the trail one-way, and shoosh back on 7 miles of pavement to your car.

To start, drive Interstate 5 south of Eugene to Oakridge exit 188A. Then follow Willamette Highway 58 east for 14 miles, turn left across Dexter Reservoir at a covered bridge, follow the Jasper-Lowell Road through the town of Lowell (where the road jogs left and then right), continue 1.5 miles to another covered

Footbridge beside Fall Creek.   Opposite: Wild iris.

bridge, and turn right on North Shore Road. Follow this paved route 11 miles, around the north side of the reservoir and up Fall Creek. Park at a hiker-symbol sign on the right just before a bridge by Dolly Varden Campground.

The trail begins in an old-growth forest greened with a carpet of sword ferns, oxalis, and delicate maidenhair ferns. White fairy bells and pink bleeding hearts bloom in spring. The trail occasionally dips to creekside gravel beaches, but mostly stays higher on the forested bank.

Look for a nice swimming hole in Fall Creek at the 2-mile mark. In the next 0.9 mile you'll cross three log footbridges over side creeks. The last of these, spanning scenic, 15-foot-wide Timber Creek, is a good place for hikers with children to declare victory and turn back to the car.

Hikers who continue—perhaps having arranged a car or bicycle shuttle back from a more distant trailhead—will soon come to an unmarked fork in the trail. Take the right fork, which detours around a dirt road and meets paved Road 18 at its bridge across Fall Creek. Cross the bridge; the trail now continues on the sunnier, drier north side of the valley. Beyond the bridge a mile the trail crosses Slick Creek on a high bridge, with a small beach on the right and Slick Creek Cave on the left. Native Americans once camped under this overhanging cliff,

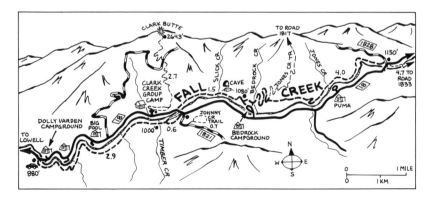

but looters in the 1950s destroyed the site's archeological value. It's still an interesting spot, and a good turnaround point if you don't have a shuttle.

After another 0.4 mile the trail circumvents Bedrock Campground; avoid side trails to the right. Cross Bedrock Creek and climb 5 long switchbacks to a junction with the Jones Trail, high above Fall Creek. Watch for poison oak here. The trail stays high for a mile, then returns to the creek for the final 2.3 miles to the trailhead on gravel Road 1828, a stone's throw from paved Road 18's bridge across Fall Creek.

Other Hiking Options

The Fall Creek Trail continues another 4.7 miles beyond Road 1828. This quiet, scenic upper section starts on the north side of the creek, promptly passes an unusual rock shoreline of water-rounded stone formations, crosses the creek on a long footbridge, and continues on the south bank to trail's end at Road 1833, near that road's junction with paved Road 18.

79   Mount June

Easy (to Mount June)
2.4 miles round-trip
900 feet elevation gain
Open mid-April to mid-December
Map: Mount June (USGS)
Use: hikers, horses

Difficult (to Hardesty Mountain)
9.6 miles round-trip
2100 feet elevation gain

An undesignated wilderness in Eugene's backyard, the Hardesty Mountain area is a popular patch of forested ridges and trails. Each year hundreds of hikers march up the 5-mile Hardesty Trail from Highway 58, arduously gaining over 4000 feet in elevation, only to discover that the former lookout site atop Hardesty Mountain is overgrown with young trees, blocking most of the view.

These hikers obviously don't know about Mount June. Not only is it the area's tallest peak, but the panorama from its former lookout site stretches unimpeded from the Willamette Valley to the Three Sisters. What's more, the Mount June trail is much shorter and less steep, so that even children can taste the success of "climbing a mountain." And if you continue on the ridgecrest beyond Mount June, you'll reach Hardesty Mountain anyway—by an easier route.

To find the Mt. June trailhead, drive Interstate 5 south of Eugene to Oakridge exit 188A. Then follow Willamette Highway 58 east for 11.4 miles to Dexter Dam and turn right at a sign for Lost Creek. After 3.7 miles, turn left across a somewhat hidden bridge onto the signed Eagles Rest Road. Follow this paved, one-lane route up 7.8 miles to a fork. Heeding a hiker-symbol pointer here, keep left on Road 20-1-14 for 2.6 miles of pavement and another 3.5 miles of gravel. At the far end of a fenced tree farm, turn left onto Road 1721, and 0.1 mile later turn left onto steep Road 941 for 0.4 mile to the trailhead sign on the right.

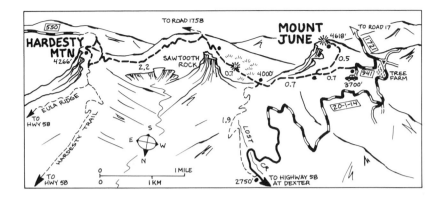

The trail climbs gradually through a Douglas fir forest with a lush understory of sword ferns, shamrock-shaped oxalis, and May-blooming rhododendrons. After 0.7 mile turn right at a trail junction and climb steeply up a ridge toward the summit. The ridgecrests here are known for their eerie fogs, shafted with rays of sun. But the bare rock of Mt. June's summit usually rises above the fog, providing a view from Mt. Hood to Diamond Peak. The route to Hardesty Mountain is spread before you like a map.

To hike on to Hardesty Mountain, backtrack from the summit to the trail junction and turn right on the Sawtooth Trail. This path goes up and down along the ridgecrest through dry woods with chinkapin, beargrass, and yew. After 0.7 mile, turn right at a trail junction. The path now traverses a steep, grassy meadow with a view back to Mt. June. The southern horizon is full of Calapooya Mountains, dominated by square-topped Bohemia Mountain (Hike #86).

At the far end of the meadow the trail makes two short switchbacks. From the top of these switchbacks it's easy to scramble up 100 feet to the base of Sawtooth Rock, a 50-foot monolith with a shallow cave in its south base.

Continuing on the main trail, keep left at a marked trail junction and follow

Mt. June's lookout site.   Opposite: Fog on Sawtooth Trail.

the up-and-down ridgecrest another 1.4 miles to a trail junction on the slope of Hardesty Mountain. To make a small loop to the summit, turn left for 0.2 mile to a trail junction on a ridgecrest and follow the right-hand path up to the old lookout site. To return, continue south along the summit ridge and switchback down to the Hardesty Cutoff Trail. Turn right here for 0.2 mile and then turn left on the Sawtooth Trail to return to the car.

80   Goodman Creek

Easy (to Goodman Creek)
4 miles round-trip
300 feet elevation gain
Open year-round
Map: Mount June (USGS)
Use: hikers, horses, bicycles

Difficult (to Eagles Rest)
13.4 miles round-trip
2100 feet elevation gain
Open mid-March through December

Left: Goodman Creek footbridge.

Just half an hour from Eugene, this hike through the forests below Hardesty Mountain can either be an easy walk to a waterfall—popular with kids—or it can be lengthened to a more strenuous trek past Ash Swale Shelter to the viewpoint at Eagles Rest.

Drive Interstate 5 south of Eugene 2 miles to Oakridge exit 188A. Then follow Willamette Highway 58 east to Lookout Point Reservoir. Just before milepost 21, park at a pullout on the right marked by a hiker-symbol sign.

The trail starts in an old-growth Douglas fir forest brightened in March and April by the white blooms of trilliums. After 0.2 mile, turn right onto the Goodman Trail, which contours through the woods above an arm of the reservoir. In damp weather, expect some muddy spots. Also watch for rough-skinned newts on the trail—the rugged, orange-bellied "waterdogs" that fascinate kids.

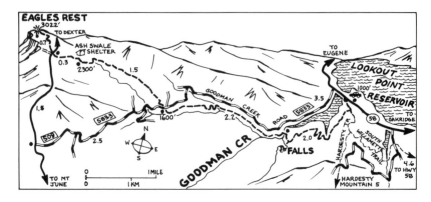

At the 1.9-mile mark you'll pass a grassy campsite and reach an unmarked trail junction within earshot of falling water. The main path goes right, but take the left fork 50 feet through the vine maple to discover a lovely little waterfall sliding into a swimmable, rock-edged pool overhung with droopy red cedars. Return to the main trail and continue 200 yards to a pebble beach and huge log footbridge across Goodman Creek—a good picnic spot, and the turn-around point for hikers with children. Beware of stinging nettles near the creek.

If you're continuing, the next 1.2 miles of trail are nearly level, in a mossy rain forest along the creek. A small gravel road paralleling the trail is mostly out of sight. Next the trail climbs steadily for a mile and crosses Road 5833 to a well-marked trailhead for the Eagles Rest Trail. This trail continues to climb through second-growth Douglas fir—at one point crossing a 1989 clearcut—for 1.7 miles to Ash Swale Shelter. The swale beside this solid, 3-sided structure is a skunk cabbage marsh full of frogs.

Beyond the shelter, the trail skirts two large 1989 clearcuts, crosses the paved Eagles Rest Road, and then climbs another 0.7 mile to the dry, rocky summit of Eagles Rest, with its clifftop view across the Lost Creek Valley.

81   Deception Butte

Difficult (from Highway 58)
8 miles round-trip
2600 feet elevation gain
Open April through December
Use: hikers, horses, bicycles
Maps: Holland Pt., Westfir W. (USGS)

Moderate (from Road 549)
1 mile round-trip
300 feet elevation gain
Right: Summit of Deception Butte.

For a convenient bit of well-paced exercise, start this quiet forest trail at its lower end on Highway 58. After warming up with a virtually level first mile, the path steepens for 3 miles to a mountaintop meadow overlooking Oakridge and Diamond Peak. On the other hand, if the view interests you more than the exercise, you can start at the upper trailhead on gravel Road 549 and take an easier half-mile shortcut to the top.

To find the lower trailhead, take Interstate 5 south of Eugene to Oakridge exit 188 and follow Willamette Highway 58 east for 30 miles. Immediately after the highway bridges Deception Creek (2 miles beyond Shady Dell Campground and 4 miles before Oakridge), park on the shoulder to the right, in front of a trailer park. Then walk 50 yards back across the bridge to the trailhead sign.

This lower end of the path sets out through an old-growth hemlock forest carpeted with shamrock-shaped oxalis, but after half a mile you enter a stand of younger Douglas fir. At the 1.1-mile mark, cross a large tributary of Deception Creek on a 50-foot log footbridge.

The trail now climbs in earnest, promptly switchbacking up to an open rock

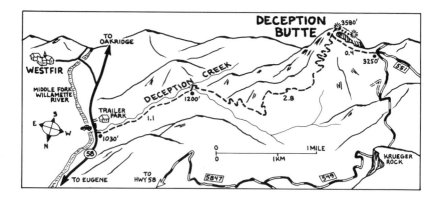

ridge with a view across the valley. Between 1.4 and 1.6 miles switchback through a 1985 clearcut regrown with thimbleberry. From mile 2.7 to 3.0 cross a slightly older clearcut and then climb steeply through woods brightened by pink rhododendrons in early June.

Just 100 feet before the butte's rocky summit, ignore an unmarked trail leading down to the right; this is the path to Road 549. Continue to the summit, a clifftop rock garden of penstemon, paintbrush, and manzanita. The only view here is of Krueger Rock across the valley. For a view of Oakridge and Diamond Peak, bushwhack 100 yards past the summit, descending along the ridge to a steep, mossy field of cat's ears.

If you're driving to the upper trailhead, turn off Highway 58 at Shady Dell Campground 6 miles west of Oakridge and take Road 5847 toward Krueger Rock. Follow this one-lane road 4.5 miles to a saddle, and then turn left on Road 549 for 3.2 miles to the intersection of Road 551 in a pass. A sign on the left marks the half-mile trail to Deception Butte.

82   Tire Mountain

Easy
7.6 miles round-trip
800 feet elevation gain
Open May through November
Use: hikers, horses, bicycles
Maps: Westfir E., Westfir W. (USGS)

If you're eager to get a head start on summer, stroll through the wildflower meadows of Tire Mountain, a little-known retreat near Oakridge where the blooms of summer arrive by early June. The easy path contours 2 miles through sunny meadows with views of Cascade snowpeaks. Then the trail climbs

Tire Mountain's meadows.   Opposite: Bleeding hearts.

through forest to Tire Mountain's former lookout site.

From Interstate 5 just south of Eugene, take exit 188A and follow Willamette Highway 58 east for 30 miles, almost to Oakridge. Then veer left at the Westfir exit for a mile to a stop sign beside a covered bridge, continue straight 4.5 miles on paved Road 19, turn left on gravel Road 1912 for 6.6 steep, winding miles to Windy Pass, go straight onto Road 1910 for 0.4 mile, and finally fork right onto Road 1911 for another 0.4 mile to the "Alpine Trail" sign on the left.

After a few hundred yards through a 1975 clearcut, the trail enters a lovely old-growth forest packed with woodland blooms: twin fairy bells, pink bleeding hearts, yellow wood violets, and 5-petaled candyflowers. In another half mile the path traverses the first of a series of steep meadows. Diamond Peak dominates the skyline to the right while Mt. Bachelor and two of the Three Sisters cluster to the left. Below are Hills Creek Reservoir and the oak-dotted ridges of Oakridge, surrounded by clearcuts.

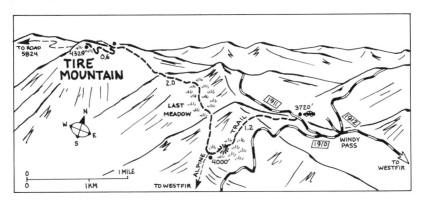

At the 1.2-mile mark, turn right at a trail junction in a summer patch of tall purple larkspur. The path ducks into the forest for half a mile and crosses two small meadows before emerging at the last and largest field, covered each June by a carpet of tiny pink flowers. Also look here for yellow monkeyflower, sunflower-like balsamroot, and blue camas.

If you're tired, turn back at this final meadow. Otherwise, follow the virtually level path 1.1 mile through the woods to a trail junction on the slope of Tire Mountain. Take the uphill fork, switchbacking to the broad, brushy summit. Trees block much of the view. A few boards remain from the unusual lookout tower that once stood atop the truncated tree in the middle of the summit field.

Tire Mountain is named for Tire Creek, where story has it that an early traveler on the old military wagon road to Oakridge left a broken wagon wheel.

83   Larison Creek

Easy (to small pool)
6 miles round-trip
200 feet elevation gain
Open all year
Use: hikers, horses, bicycles
Map: Oakridge (USGS)

Moderate (to fork in creek)
10.4 miles round-trip
700 feet elevation gain

This easy trail, open even in winter, starts along a sunny shore of Hills Creek Reservoir and then follows a small creek through a deep, forested canyon.

Start by driving Willamette Highway 58 east of Oakridge 1.3 miles. Between mileposts 37 and 38, turn south at a sign for Hills Creek Dam. After half a mile, turn right onto paved Road 21 for 3.3 miles. A hiker-symbol sign on the right marks the trail's parking area beside an arm of the Hills Creek Reservoir.

The first 1.5 miles of the trail contour around deep, green Larison Cove, cut

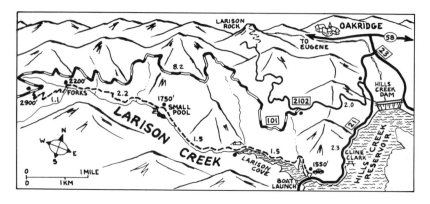

Trail beside Larison Cove.   *Opposite: Poison oak.*

off from the main reservoir by the road's causeway. Only non-motorized boats are allowed on the cove. The rocky hillsides here host sparse Douglas fir and some poison oak; don't let children touch triple-leaved bushes. At the end of the cove the path crosses a side creek and reaches an established picnic/camping area sometimes used by boaters. Cattails fringe the shore.

Beyond the reservoir the trail follows the creek through a cooler, mossier forest of old-growth Douglas fir, red cedar, and twisted yew trees. Lily-white trillium and shamrock-like oxalis bloom here in April, followed by pink rhododendron and yellow Oregon grape in May.

The path climbs very gradually, staying within a stone's throw of the creek. Beyond the reservoir 1.5 miles watch carefully for a small water chute and pool through the trees to your left. Bushwhack 50 feet to this small but pleasant picnic spot, where the creek swirls down a 10-foot-long bedrock slide into a pool so clear you can count the fingerling fish. This makes a good turnaround point for hikers with children.

Beyond the small pool 0.7 mile, the trail climbs away from the creek. Briefly cross a 1976 clearcut at the 4.4-mile mark. Finally return to the creek at another nice picnic site—a pleasant, mossy bower just before the creek forks and the trail begins its switchbacking climb out of the canyon.

Other Trail Options

If you're mountain biking, consider doing this trail as part of an 18.8-mile loop. Ride the entire trail 6.3 miles up to its steep, switchbacking top, turn right on gravel Road 101 for 8.2 miles, turn right on paved Road 2102 for 2 quick downhill miles, and turn right on paved Road 21 back to your starting point.

84   Chuckle Springs

Easy (to Chuckle Springs)
3.3-mile loop
200 feet elevation gain
Open April through December
Use: hikers, horses, bicycles
Map: Rigdon Point (USGS)

Difficult (entire Middle Fork Trail)
33.1 miles one way
4000 feet elevation gain
Open June through November

Where does the mighty Willamette River start? The Middle Fork Trail answers that question by following the river's main stem 33.1 miles up a remote Cascade Range canyon. Trek the entire trail if you like, but for an easy day hike take a shortcut to the most spectacular of the river's secret sources—a cluster of massive springs in an old-growth forest.

Start by driving Willamette Highway 58 east of Oakridge 1.3 miles. Between mileposts 37 and 38, turn south at a sign for Hills Creek Dam. After half a mile, turn right onto Road 21 and follow this completely paved route past Hills Creek Reservoir. Road 21 passes nearly a dozen different trailheads for the Middle Fork Trail, so it's possible to trek the path in segments.

To warm up with a 0.2-mile hike around the most visitable of the river's springs, drive Road 21 for a total of 28.7 miles. Between mileposts 28 and 29, turn left into the primitive (and free) Indigo Springs Campground. Go straight to a hiker parking spot and walk a little loop path around a mossy glen where Indigo Springs spill out of the ground in half a dozen major fountains.

To move on to the more substantial 3.3-mile Chuckle Springs loop, drive (or

Middle Fork Willamette River.   *Above: Lady's slipper orchids.*

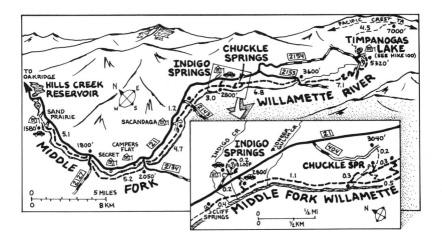

walk) 100 yards back to Road 21, turn left for 150 yards to a sign for the Middle Fork Trail, and turn right on a grassy spur road for 100 feet to a trailhead on the right. Hike a connector path down 200 yards toward the river and turn left on the Middle Fork Trail.

The rushing, 40-foot-wide Middle Fork Willamette River tumbles through a forest of giant Douglas fir, western hemlock, red cedar, and alder. Along the riverside path, Oregon grape, thimbleberry, yew, and vine maple sprout from a thick carpet of moss. After hiking a mile upstream, turn left at a "Horse Trail" pointer and keep left at all junctions for 0.3 mile to Chuckle Springs. Surrounded by droopy-limbed red cedars, the glassy, 10-foot-wide springs slide out from a hillside, zip across a mossy pool, and charge down a gulch toward the river.

To return on a loop, hike back 150 yards and turn left at another "Horse Trail" sign. After 0.2 mile turn right at a fork and switchback down to the river on a steep path that crosses several gushing springs before rejoining the main Middle Fork Trail in half a mile.

If you'd like to add a short side trip to Cliff Springs, head back on the Middle Fork Trail a mile, but then continue straight past the trailhead cutoff, following the river downstream 0.4 mile. You'll cross a footbridge over Indigo Creek before reaching a spring that erupts from the trail at the base of a 15-foot rock cliff. Then return to your car.

For a longer trek on the 33.1-mile Middle Fork Trail (and especially if you're riding a horse or bicycle), start instead at the trail's actual beginning, near milepost 12 of Road 21, south of Sand Prairie Campground 0.6 mile. The path's first 5.1 miles to the Road 2127 bridge are nearly flat and are usually open even in winter. Tall cottonwoods line the river's pebbled bank at this lower elevation, filling the air with honeyed fragrance. Great blue herons wade the riffles, mallards start up from oxbow sloughs, and alders show beaver toothmarks.

Farther upstream, near Sacandaga Campground, the Middle Fork Trail follows the route of the Oregon Central Military Wagon Road, built 1865-66 to connect Western and Eastern Oregon. Beyond Chuckle Springs, the Middle Fork Trail steepens as it climbs to Timpanogas Lake, the official source of the Willamette. From there, trails described in Hike #100 lead onward to the Pacific Crest Trail and Indigo Lake.

185

85 Brice Creek

Easy (entire trail, with shuttle)
5.5 miles one way
600 feet elevation gain
Open all year
Use: hikers, bicycles

Easy (to Trestle Creek Falls)
3.4-mile loop
1000 feet elevation gain

The trail along this lovely creek leads past small waterfalls and swimmable pools under the canopy of an old-growth forest. The route is fun for children and open even in winter. A paved road unobtrusively parallels the trail on the creek's opposite shore, making access easy at several points. To hike the entire trail one way, plan on leaving a shuttle car or bicycle at the upper trailhead. If waterfalls are your goal, however, consider starting at the upper trailhead instead. From there a 3.4-mile loop (scheduled for completion in 1999) climbs to Trestle Creek's spectacular falls.

Drive Interstate 5 to Cottage Grove exit 174 and follow signs to Dorena Lake. Continue on the main, paved road through Culp Creek and Disston (bear right at this village) for a total of 21.7 miles from the freeway. A mile past the Umpqua National Forest entrance sign, where the road first bridges Brice Creek, look for a trail sign on the left marking the lower trailhead. (If you're driving on to the upper trailhead, continue up Road 22 to the next bridge, near Champion Creek.)

From the lower trailhead, the Brice Creek Trail starts out across a dry slope but soon plunges into a more typical, mossy old-growth forest of Douglas fir and red cedar. Sword ferns, oxalis, and twinflower thrive here.

After 1.5 miles, take a short side trip to the right to inspect the 150-foot-long footbridge to Cedar Creek Campground. Then continue on the main trail. A quarter mile beyond is a charming, 8-foot waterfall surrounded by smooth rock

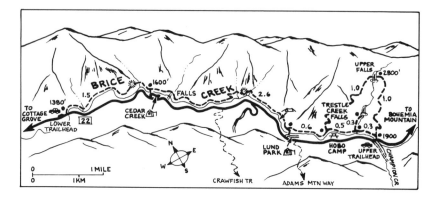

Waterfall on Brice Creek.   Opposite: Footbridge at Lund Park.

terraces ideal for sunbathing or picnicking. Children can play on a small beach nearby, while swimmers will find the clear, 15-foot-deep pool beside the terrace tempting. The next mile of trail passes half a dozen other creekside sites almost as attractive.

At the 3.3-mile mark the trail climbs a bluff 300 feet above the creek. When the path finally returns to the creek there's a large campsite on the right—a fine spot to take children on a first backpack. Another 200 yards farther is the trail junction for Lund Park Campground. A long footbridge crosses the creek to this virtually undeveloped roadside meadow.

Note that Lund Park is not a park. It was the site of a wayside inn popular with travelers to the Bohemia gold mining district in the late 19th century, and was named for its owners, Alex *Lund*gren and Tom *Park*er. With similar profundity, Brice Creek is a drawling commemoration of Frank *Brass*, an early prospector who once fell into the stream.

Beyond Lund Park 0.6 mile, a steepish side trail to the left climbs on an optional 2-mile loop to Trestle Creek's upper waterfall. This demanding little detour is set for completion in 1999. Until then, continue straight on the main trail another half mile to Trestle Creek, where an easier, completed side trail leads 0.3 mile to a misty rock grotto at the base of a 100-foot lower falls. Beyond Trestle Creek, the Brice Creek Trail ambles a final 0.3 mile to the upper trailhead, following an old water ditch that once supplied a power plant at Lund Park.

If you love waterfalls, and if the Trestle Creek loop trail is finished, you might prefer to start at Brice Creek's upper trailhead instead. From the parking pullout, take the right-hand trail. This path switchbacks up a mile, ducks behind Trestle Creek's upper falls, and continues a mile down to the Brice Creek Trail. Turn left for half a mile to the Trestle Creek bridge, detour left 0.3 mile to the lower falls, and then return to Brice Creek for 0.3 mile to complete a 3.4-mile loop.

86   Bohemia Mountain

Easy
1.6 miles round-trip
700 feet elevation gain
Open mid-June through November
Map: Fairview Pk. (USGS)

Cliff-edged Bohemia Mountain towers above the gold-mining ghost town of Bohemia City. A short steep trail to the top features a view from the Three Sisters to Mt. McLoughlin. Although the hike up usually takes less than an hour, you can easily fill a day here by prowling the ghost town, picking huckleberries, or driving up to the 60-foot lookout tower on neighboring Fairview Peak.

Drive Interstate 5 to Cottage Grove exit 174 and follow signs to Dorena Lake. Continue on the main, paved road through the villages of Culp Creek and Disston, and continue straight on the paved road along Brice Creek a total of 30.5 miles from the freeway. Along the way the road number changes from Lane County 2470 to Forest Service 22. Finally, at a pointer for Fairview Peak, turn right onto gravel Road 2212. Follow this route 8.4 miles to Champion Saddle and turn left onto Road 2460, heeding another sign for Fairview Peak. The road now becomes narrow, steep, and rough. Continue carefully 1.1 mile to a 4-way junction at Bohemia Saddle. Park here and walk 100 yards to the left to the signed start of the Bohemia Mountain Trail.

The path climbs a sparsely forested ridge where blue huckleberries ripen in late August. Switchbacks lead to the summit plateau, capped by a layer of tough andesite lava. Thick-leaved stonecrop plants hug the rock. Diamond Peak looms large to the east. The patchwork forests of the Calapooya Mountains stretch in all directions like a rumpled quilt. Far to the northwest are the flats of the Willamette Valley.

The buildings visible at the base of the mountain are the remains of Bohemia City—a boomtown named for James "Bohemia" Johnson, a wandering Czech immigrant who discovered gold here in 1863. During the town's heyday from 1880 to 1930, 1750 pounds of gold were mined.

Though the ghost town is on Lane County parkland, the traditional access road from Road 2460 crosses private land and may be gated on a slope where it's difficult for cars to turn around. Mining has not ceased altogether in this area. Hikers need to avoid private land, mining equipment, and dangerous mine shafts. But you can still bushwhack to the ghost town on public land. Return to the start of the Bohemia Mountain Trail and head due east, scrambling 0.3 mile down a steep, brushy hillside to the town's two remaining buildings.

For an easier side trip from Bohemia Saddle, drive the steep, 1-mile road to Fairview Peak's climbable fire lookout tower, staffed in summer. On a clear day,

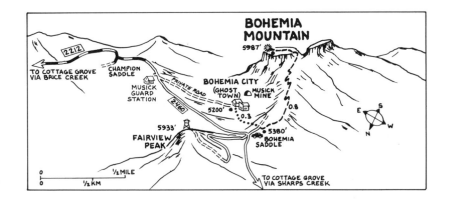

the view stretches from Mt. Hood to Mt. Shasta. If you'd like to stay overnight in the area, consider spending $40 to rent the historic Musick Guard Station, 0.7 mile east of Bohemia Saddle on Road 2460. Built by the CCC in 1934, the cabin sleeps 10 and has a woodstove, but no potable water or electricity. Call the Cottage Grove Ranger District at (541) 942-5591 for reservations.

To drive home via a loop, drive west from Bohemia Saddle on Road 2460. This shorter but rougher route to Cottage Grove follows Sharps Creek to the main road at Culp Creek.

Summit of Bohemia Mountain.   Opposite: Abandoned post office at Bohemia City.

Willamette
Pass

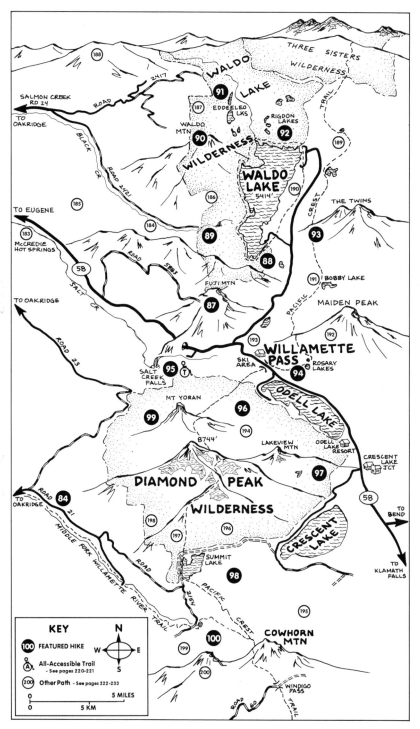

Opposite: Mount Yoran and Divide Lake (Hike #99).

87 Fuji Mountain

Easy (from Road 5833)
3 miles round-trip
950 feet elevation gain
Open mid-July through October
Use: hikers, horses, bicycles
Map: Waldo L. Wilderness (USFS)

Difficult (from Road 5897)
11.2 miles round-trip
2200 feet elevation gain

When a delegation from Eugene's sister city in Japan visited Oregon, officials took them on a hike up Fuji Mountain.

It wasn't a bad choice. The former lookout site atop this cliff-edged peak has a 360-degree view of some of Oregon's greatest treasures: virgin forests, vast Waldo Lake—one of the purest in the world—and pristine snowpeaks from the Three Sisters to Mt. McLoughlin. A popular new shortcut up Fuji Mountain begins on gravel Road 5833. The longer, traditional route from paved Road 5897 provides a more thorough athletic workout.

To take the shorter route, drive 15 miles east of Oakridge on Willamette Highway 58. By the railroad trestle between mileposts 50 and 51, turn north onto Eagle Creek Road 5833. After driving 11.5 miles up this gravel road, park opposite a hiker-symbol sign on the left.

The trail traverses a clearcut for 100 yards, then enters a mountain hemlock forest where blue huckleberries ripen in late August. After 0.3 mile, turn left at a junction. As you climb, the path gradually steepens and the switchbacks shorten. The trees begin to dwindle, making room for fields of blue lupine and views south to snowy Diamond Peak. Finally follow a ridge to the rocky summit, with its vista of 7-mile-long Waldo Lake to the north and Bunchgrass Ridge to the west.

To start from the lower trailhead instead, turn off Highway 58 at the sign for

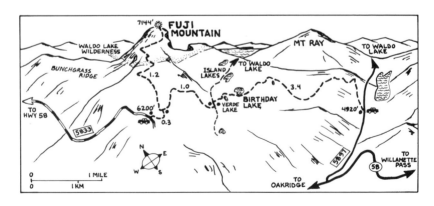

Waldo Lake from Fuji Mountain.   Opposite: Pond on the lower Fuji Mountain Trail.

Waldo Lake, 3 miles west of Willamette Pass. Follow paved Road 5897 exactly 2 miles to the trailhead sign on the left. Park on the shoulder on the right.

This lower portion of the Fuji Mountain Trail climbs steeply for a mile, then strikes off across a broad, forested benchland. Green, tree-rimmed Birthday Lake, 3 miles from the trailhead, is often warm enough for a dip. Just beyond is a smaller green pool, appropriately named Verde Lake. Continue 0.2 mile to a trail junction and head left for 100 feet to a second junction. This time turn right and climb 1 mile to the summit shortcut trail described above.

South Waldo Lake

Easy (to South Waldo Shelter)
3.4 miles round-trip
No elevation gain
Open mid-June to early November
Use: hikers, horses, bicycles
Map: Waldo L. Wilderness (USFS)

Moderate (to Black Meadows)
9.8-mile loop
1000 feet elevation gain
Use: hikers, horses

Perhaps the prettiest portion of the shoreline trail around mile-high Waldo Lake, this hike starts at a popular sailboat landing and leads past a sandy beach to a shelter in a meadow. More ambitious hikers can add a loop through a remote corner of the Waldo Lake Wilderness, passing Black Meadows and the prodigious huckleberry fields near Bingo Lake. Visit in August for berries; avoid July because of mosquitoes.

Oregon's second largest natural lake, Waldo covers 10 square miles to a depth of 417 feet. Despite its size the lake has no inlet, leaving its waters so pure and clear they are virtually devoid of plant life. Boaters can watch fish swimming 100 feet deep. The lake is named for Judge John B. Waldo, an early devotee of the Oregon Cascades who trekked from Willamette Pass to Mt. Shasta in 1888.

To drive here, turn off Willamette Highway 58 at the sign for Waldo Lake, 3 miles west of Willamette Pass. Follow paved Road 5897 for 6.8 miles, turn left at the Shadow Bay Campground sign, and continue 2 miles to the boat ramp parking area.

The trail begins by a water faucet at the left edge of the vast parking lot. The path's first half mile is graveled, following the shore of Shadow Bay. Sailboats strike romantic poses in the bay. The growl of powerboats damages the idyll. Despite the ardent pleas of environmentalists, the Forest Service continues to endanger this fragile alpine lake—surrounded on 3 sides by Wilderness—by allowing motors. A decline in the lake's fabled clarity has, however, led the government to redesign the campgrounds' sewage system and stop dumping game fish into the lake from helicopters.

At the 1.3-mile mark, reach a sandy beach sheltered by a small wooded island—a nice wading spot on a hot day. After this the trail leaves the lake and skirts a meadow to the shelter, a rustic, 3-sided structure not near the shore.

The loop trail beyond the shelter is faint in places, and is off-limits to bicycles, which are only allowed on the trail around Waldo Lake. If you're an adventurous hiker, continue on the main trail (following the "High Divide Trail" arrow), cross a large footbridge, and 100 feet later watch for an obscure side trail to the left marked "South Waldo Trail." This path climbs through the woods 1.1 mile to a pass and then descends past a small lake to a 4-way trail junction. Turn right, climb to another wooded pass, dip to a smaller saddle, and then descend steeply for a mile to Black Meadows.

The upper end of this meadow is damp, with marsh marigolds and a pond

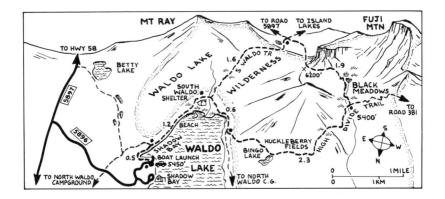

reflecting Fuji Mountain (Hike #87). But as you continue downhill the vale grows drier. Tall grass and the boat-shaped leaves of green hellebore obscure the tread. Continue to a large brown trail junction sign. Turn right, following trail blazes shaped like exclamation points. Cross a (usually dry) creekbed and look for a cut log, where the tread again becomes clear.

Half a mile beyond Black Meadows the trail crosses a smaller meadow. The tread is faint here, too, but simply go across the meadow to its far right end.

Next the path enters a first-rate huckleberry patch. Wildfire killed most trees on this hillside; the resulting sunshine makes the berries particularly fat and juicy. Continue purple-fingered past Bingo Lake and over a rise to the Waldo shoreline trail. Turn right and pass a lovely swimming beach en route back to the shelter.

Waldo Lake's Shadow Bay.   Opposite: South Waldo Shelter.

89 Lillian Falls

Easy (to Lillian Falls)
2.4 miles round-trip
600 feet elevation gain
Open mid-April through November
Use: hikers, horses
Map: Waldo L. Wilderness (USFS)

Difficult (to Klovdahl Bay)
7.6 miles round-trip
2200 feet elevation gain
Open mid-June through October

A vast glacier capped the Cascade crest during the Ice Age, gouging Waldo Lake's basin and spilling long, snake-like streams of ice down half a dozen valleys to the north and west. When the glacier melted from its mile-high plateau, Waldo Lake was left to choose a single outlet. It opted for a rugged and remote valley to the north. But the huge lake also nearly overflows to the west, into Black Creek's 2000-foot-deep canyon.

In 1912, engineer Simon Klovdahl set out to exploit this coincidence for hydroelectric power and irrigation. He spent two years blasting a diversion tunnel from Waldo Lake to the headwaters of Black Creek. When his tunnel didn't work, the project was abandoned to the wilderness.

Today the Black Creek Trail climbs up this dramatic, unspoiled canyon amid old-growth trees 6 feet in diameter. For an easy hike, stop at Lillian Falls' 150-foot series of mossy cascades. For a more challenging trip, continue up to Waldo Lake and the headgates of Klovdahl's failed tunnel.

To start, drive Willamette Highway 58 to the traffic light in the middle of Oakridge. Turn north across the railroad tracks to a stop sign in the old downtown area and turn right on what becomes Salmon Creek Road 24. Follow this paved route for 11 miles to a Y-shaped junction. Keep right on Road 24 to the end of pavement in another 3.2 miles, and then continue straight on gravel Road 2421 for 8.2 miles to the trailhead at road's end.

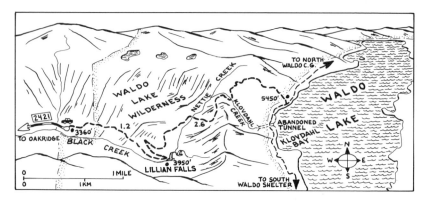

View across Waldo Lake's Klovdahl Bay to Mt. Ray.   *Opposite: Blue huckleberries.*

The trail begins in a 1970 clearcut, but soon passes the Waldo Lake Wilderness sign and enters a magnificent old-growth forest of mountain hemlock and red cedar. Look for white woodland blooms: big trilliums in May, tiny twinflower in June, and delicate sprays of star-flowered smilacina in July.

After 1.2 miles the path switchbacks at the base of Lillian Falls, a nice picnic spot and the turning-back point for hikers with children. This turbulent cascade is also known as Lithan Falls.

After the falls the trail climbs steeply 0.7 mile before leveling off in a densely forested upper valley. Rhododendrons bloom here in June. Then the path climbs again, traversing a sunny rockslide with views across the canyon. The trail ducks into the scenic, hidden glen of Klovdahl Creek, switchbacks up through a forest full of huckleberry bushes, and finally descends to the shore of Klovdahl Bay.

Waldo Lake is so large and wild it feels like a fjord in Alaska's Inside Passage. Waves crash on boulders. Gray lichen beards the snow-bent trees. The far shore, miles away, is a silhouette of forest-furred ridges.

Follow the shoreline trail half a mile to the right to view the rotting headgates of Klovdahl's tunnel, which nearly succeeded in reducing this mighty lake to a reservoir. Then return as you came.

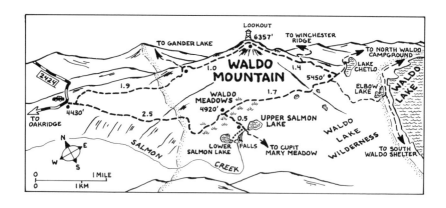

90   Waldo Mountain Lookout

Difficult
8.5-mile loop
2000 feet elevation gain
Open July through October
Use: hikers, horses
Map: Waldo L. Wilderness (USFS)

Waldo Mountain's lookout building, staffed in peak fire season, features a view from Mt. Hood to Diamond Peak, with Waldo Lake a pool of melted silver at your feet. Visit the lookout on a loop hike that returns through Waldo Meadows, hip-deep in wildflowers. A short, optional side trip leads to Upper Salmon Lake and a small waterfall.

To find the trailhead, turn north off Willamette Highway 58 at the traffic light in the middle of Oakridge. Cross the railroad tracks to a stop sign and turn right on what becomes Salmon Creek Road 24. Follow this paved route for 11 miles to a Y-shaped junction and veer left onto Road 2417 for 6 miles. Half a mile after Road 2417 turns to gravel, fork to the right onto Road 2424 and drive 3.7 miles to a hiker-symbol sign on the right marking the trailhead.

After 200 yards the trail forks; this is the start of the loop. Turn left and climb through a mixed forest of mountain hemlock and true firs. As you ascend, the slope grows drier. The lush understory of vanilla leaf and coolwort yields to rhododendron, which in turn gives way to drought-resistant beargrass. Turn right at a junction 1.9 miles along the trail and continue steeply uphill another mile to the towerless lookout building.

The Three Sisters line up to the south. Directly across Waldo Lake are The Twins (Hike #93) and Maiden Peak. To the right, Diamond Peak rises above Fuji

Mountain (Hike #87). If you set down your backpack while enjoying the view, be forewarned that the lookout's half-tame ground squirrels probably will ransack its pockets for goodies.

To continue, head toward Waldo Lake down an open, rocky ridge. Ignore a faint side trail to the left halfway down. At the base of the mountain turn right at a well-marked, T-shaped junction. After another 300 yards ignore a left fork for Elbow Lake. Go straight for 1.4 miles and enter Waldo Meadows. The tread can be obscure here amidst the profusion of giant hellebore leaves, brown coneflower, red paintbrush, and purple aster. Simply hike through the middle of this long, narrow field 0.3 mile to a signed trail junction at the meadow's edge.

If you'd like to take a short side trip, turn left here, cross the meadow, and hike half a mile through the woods to shallow Upper Salmon Lake. To find Salmon Creek's 20-foot waterfall, follow the lake's outlet 150 yards downstream.

When you return to the Waldo Meadows junction, turn left to complete the loop back to your car. This final 2.5-mile segment of the trail descends gradually along a hillside to the trailhead.

Other Hiking Options

Ambitious hikers will be tempted to extend this loop down to Waldo Lake. From the trail junction at the eastern base of Waldo Mountain, it's only 0.8 mile to Elbow Lake, near Waldo Lake's shore. To return on a loop, follow the shoreline trail 2.4 miles north to Waldo Lake's outlet (a nice backpacking goal) and turn left on a 1.2-mile trail back to the base of Waldo Mountain via Chetlo Lake.

Waldo Mountain Lookout.   Opposite: Waldo Mountain from Upper Salmon Lake.

91 Eddeeleo Lakes

Moderate
9.2 miles round-trip
700 feet elevation gain
Open mid-June through October
Use: hikers, horses
Map: Waldo L. Wilderness (USFS)

Ed, Dee, and Leo were three early Forest Service employees who hiked into this string of lakes to plant fish. Hikers have been carrying fish the other way ever since. Note that the path leads *downhill* to the lakes, leaving the elevation gain for the return trip. Along the way, the route emerges once from the hemlock forests for a view of the Three Sisters. Expect rhododendron blooms in June, buzzing mosquitoes in July, and delicious blue huckleberries in August.

Drive Willamette Highway 58 to Oakridge and turn north at the traffic light in the middle of town. Cross the railroad tracks to a stop sign and turn right on what becomes Salmon Creek Road 24. Follow this paved route for 11 miles to a Y-shaped junction, veer left onto Road 2417 for 10.9 miles, and then turn left onto Road 254 at a "Winchester Trail" arrow. After just 0.3 mile on this gravel spur, park at a wide spot on the right. If the trailhead sign is missing, watch carefully for the large parking area.

Huckleberry bushes line the first, level portion of the trail. Turn left after 0.8 mile, and then, at the Blair Lake Trail junction 0.3 mile beyond, turn right. After hiking downhill another half mile, watch for a short side trail to the left. This leads 30 feet to the hike's best viewpoint—a cliff overlooking Fisher Creek's forested canyon. On the horizon are Irish Mountain and the tops of the Three Sisters.

The trail continues downhill, crosses Lower Quinn Lake's outlet creek (the

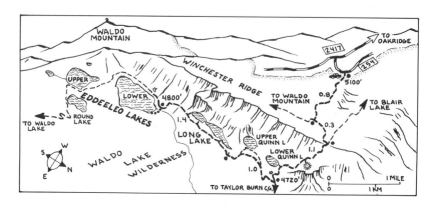

lake itself is visible through the trees to the right) and then climbs to a trail junction. Take the right-hand fork, even though it may have no sign. In half a mile this path forks again. The right fork loops past the shore of Upper Quinn Lake, while the left fork is a slightly shorter bypass. The routes soon rejoin and continue together to a meadow at the start of Long Lake.

Although the trail parallels Long Lake and then Lower Eddeeleo Lake for most of the next 2.5 miles, the path stays in dense woods away from the shoreline. To get views of the lakes you have to watch for short side trails leading through the rhododendrons to the brushy shore. The shore access at the end of Long Lake is less appealing since a runaway campfire burned the site, but if you continue to the start of Lower Eddeeleo Lake, a faint side trail on the left descends to the outlet creek and continues 200 yards to a lovely lakeshore picnic site with a view of Waldo Mountain (Hike #90).

Other Hiking Options

For a 16-mile backpacking loop, continue 2.4 miles to the outlet of Waldo Lake, follow the Waldo Shore Trail 2.4 miles south to Elbow Lake, turn right for 0.8 mile, turn right for 300 yards, head left toward Waldo Mountain for half a mile, and then turn right on the Winchester Ridge Trail for 5.7 miles to the car.

Backpackers should plan on only using camp stoves because campfires are banned within 100 feet of water, yet rhododendron thickets make tenting difficult outside the few established sites near lakes. Use low-impact camping techniques and dispose of waste water well away from lakes.

Long Lake.   Opposite: Thimbleberry.

Rigdon Lakes

Moderate
8-mile loop
200 feet elevation gain
Open mid-June through October
Use: hikers, horses
Map: Waldo L. Wilderness (USFS)

A forest fire that swept down to Waldo Lake's north shore in 1996 left the once-popular Rigdon Lakes surrounded by miles of blackened snags, but the area is recovering with huckleberry bushes and some wildflowers. The crowds have thinned, too. For a quick look at the fire's handiwork, take a level, 2.4-mile walk to Upper Rigdon Lake. For a more thorough tour, continue on an 8-mile loop that includes a list of other attractions: Waldo Lake's outlet river, a secluded swimming beach, and an optional bushwhack up to Rigdon Butte's viewpoint.

To start, turn off Willamette Highway 58 at the "Waldo Lake" sign 3 miles west of Willamette Pass and drive 13 miles on paved Road 5897, following signs to the Boat and Swim Area parking lot at North Waldo Campground. Park on the right-hand side of the lot near the sign for the Waldo Lake Trail.

Near the start of the Waldo Lake Trail, a horse path joins from the right and a shoreline trail joins from the left. Consider veering left on the shoreline trail. Though it is not the shortest route, the shoreline path offers almost constant views of 10-square-mile Waldo Lake, while the official Waldo Lake Trail has almost none. Both trails enter the burned area and rejoin within a mile.

Once the trails rejoin, continue another mile on the Waldo Lake Trail, turn right at an obvious (but possibly unmarked) trail junction and hike 0.7 mile to Upper Rigdon Lake. The main trail skirts the lake on the right, but a fisherman's trail also follows the shoreline to the left, passing the lake's two islands. For an

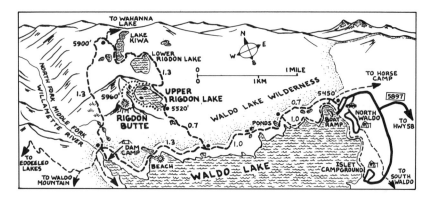

Upper Rigdon Lake.   Opposite: Waldo Lake's Dam Camp.

easy hike, circle the lake and head back to the car.

If you're wishing for a panoramic viewpoint above this area's burned woods—and if you're up to a steep little cross-country scramble—detour 0.6 mile from Upper Rigdon Lake to the rocky summit of Rigdon Butte. Start from the far lakeshore (near the larger island), scramble up a bluff, and then head left to a cliff-edged promontory overlooking the Rigdon Lakes and the whole of Waldo Lake. To the north are the Three Sisters and—on a clear day—the tip of Mt. Hood. The rumbling railroad sound you hear is the North Fork Middle Fork Willamette River, deep in the canyon to the west.

To hike the 8-mile loop, return to the main trail at Upper Rigdon Lake and turn left. You'll pass Lower Rigdon Lake and long, narrow Lake Kiwa before reaching the Wahanna Trail junction. Turn left and hike 1.3 miles through more burned woods to a trail junction at the rushing, 10-foot-wide outlet of Waldo Lake—the North Fork Middle Fork Willamette. The loop continues to the left, but first take a 0.2-mile detour, following the river up to primitive Dam Camp on Waldo Lake.

When you continue on the loop, you'll pass a lovely lakeshore beach after 0.7 mile. This secluded stretch of sand is just the place to wash off the trail's dust with a swim. A rocky peninsula nearby serves for sunbathing, although camping is banned along this north side of the lake. Then it's back to the loop and 2.3 miles to the car.

93   The Twins

Moderate
6.6 miles round-trip
1600 feet elevation gain
Open mid-July through October
Use: hikers, horses, bicycles
Map: Waldo L. Wilderness (USFS)

Admittedly, Maiden Peak is the most popular viewpoint hike east of Waldo Lake. But why join the crowds trudging up 2900 feet in 11.6 miles when you can gain a similar view for about half the effort on the less well-known trail to The Twins? From the airy top of this volcano, vast Waldo Lake sprawls through the forests at your feet while the peaks of the Central Oregon Cascades march along the horizon. Like its bigger sister, Maiden Peak, The Twins is a geologically recent cinder cone with broad, forested flanks and a cute summit crater. The Twins earns its name because a gap in the crater rim has left two summits.

Drive Willamette Highway 58 to the Waldo Lake turnoff 3 miles west of Willamette Pass, head north on paved Road 5897 for 6.2 miles, and park at the "Twin Peaks Trail" sign on the right.

At first the trail climbs very gradually through a dry forest of lodgepole pine, mountain hemlock, and red huckleberry bushes. Cinders and volcanic ash from the volcano's eruptions have left the soil porous.

After 1.6 miles cross the Pacific Crest Trail and begin climbing more steeply. Pass a 100-foot snowmelt pond and then a number of smaller tarns—many dried to mere grassy basins by summer. Here the forest changes to mountain hemlock. Watch for trunks that zigzag, forever locked in deep knee-bends from the snow burdens of winters past. Snow reaches 12 feet deep here, judging from the gray-green usnea lichen that beards trees only above that height.

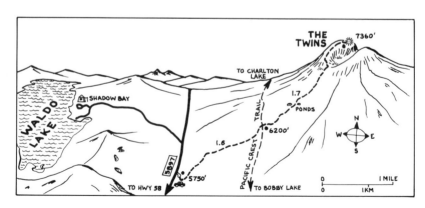

View of South Twin from North Twin.   Opposite: Mountain hemlock burl.

At the 2.9-mile mark, where the trail climbs onto the red cinder sand of the crater rim, you'll gain your first views south to Diamond Peak. (If you're on a bicycle, park it here to protect the fragile summit area.) Follow the rim clockwise amid wind-gnarled whitebark pines to the highest point of the north Twin—one of the few Cascade peaks with a full-length vista of 7-mile-long Waldo Lake. To the north are Charlton Lake and the peaks of the Three Sisters Wilderness.

For a look east, bushwhack 100 feet farther along the crater rim to red lava cliffs marking the headwall of a vanished Ice Age glacier. Below are the vast lakes and reservoirs of Central Oregon.

If you're up to a short cross-country jaunt, cross an open saddle and climb The Twins' south summit. From here you can sight across Bobby Lake to Maiden Peak, and across Gold Lake to Diamond Peak. On the way down, stop in the crater basin's peaceful meadow. Tiny white partridgefoot and pink elephant's head bloom here in late July.

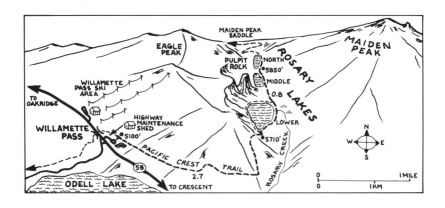

Pulpit Rock from Lower Rosary Lake.   Opposite: Subalpine fir branches.

94   Rosary Lakes

Easy
7 miles round-trip
800 feet elevation gain
Open late June to early November
Use: hikers, horses
Map: Diamond Pk. Wilderness (Imus)

Blue beads on a mountain's necklace, the Rosary Lakes sparkle along this popular portion of the Pacific Crest Trail beside Maiden Peak. If you're hiking with children, you can shorten the trip to 5.4 miles by stopping at the first, largest lake. Just don't expect solitude, especially on crowded summer weekends. Nor is this a lonely place to backpack. Since it's the only campable area for miles along the PCT, tents have worn the lakeshores brown.

Turn off Willamette Highway 58 at a hiker-symbol sign 0.3 mile east of the Willamette Pass Ski Area, immediately turn right at a highway maintenance gravel shed, and pull into the Pacific Crest Trail parking area.

Take the path uphill from the parking area and turn right on the PCT. The first 2 miles of the trail climb very gradually along a forested slope without a single switchback or satisfactory viewpoint. Squint through the forest to glimpse snowy Diamond Peak and huge Odell Lake. At times distant railroad trains can be heard across the lake.

It's hard to imagine the 1000-foot-thick Ice Age glacier that gouged Odell Lake's basin. The ice would have buried the PCT and connected with a smaller side glacier from the Rosary Lakes' basin. With the ice gone, that side valley has been left hanging 700 feet above Odell Lake.

This part of the trail is a good place to watch for prince's pine, a small pinkish wildflower that blooms in July. Its dark green leaf-whorls are the dominant ground cover here. Also notice the subalpine firs. Usually spire-shaped to shed snow, they have grown huge on this protected slope. Recognize them by their tidy, bluish branches, arranged with a geometric precision that makes neighboring Douglas fir branches look sloppy.

After 2 miles, the trail curves sharply left into the Rosary Lakes' valley. Then the trail levels through mountain hemlock woods, skirts a rockslide inhabited by peeping pikas ("rock rabbits"), and switchbacks up to Lower Rosary Lake. The crag beyond the lake is Pulpit Rock, while the low mountain to the right is Maiden Peak. This is the only lake of the cluster ringed by a fisherman's trail.

Follow the PCT around the lake to the right, cross the outlet creek, and climb through the woods to Middle Rosary Lake. North Rosary Lake is just beyond, separated from the middle lake only by a severely overused campsite. If you need more exercise, continue 1.1 mile up the PCT to Maiden Peak Saddle. Though the pass itself is wooded, the trail along the way has views south to Odell and Crescent Lakes.

95

Salt Creek Falls

Easy (to Diamond Creek Falls)
3.4-mile loop
400 feet elevation gain
Open May through November
Map: Diamond Pk. Wilderness (Imus)

Moderate (to Vivian Lake)
8 miles round-trip
1600 feet elevation gain
Open mid-June through October

Waterfalls! This stroll starts at magnificent Salt Creek Falls, the state's second tallest, and loops along a canyon rim to lacy Diamond Creek Falls, hidden in a mossy grotto. For a longer hike, continue up a steep trail past churning Fall Creek Falls to Vivian Lake and its tranquil reflection of Mt. Yoran.

Turn off Willamette Highway 58 at the sign for Salt Creek Falls (5 miles west of Willamette Pass or 1 mile east of the highway tunnel) and follow the paved entrance road to a turnaround with an information kiosk, restrooms, and picnic tables. Park here and walk 100 feet past the kiosk to an overlook of 286-foot Salt Creek Falls. The falls have cut a dramatic canyon in the edge of a High Cascades basalt lava flow.

To start the loop hike, follow a concrete pathway upstream, cross Salt Creek on a footbridge, and look for a small sign directing hikers 200 feet through the woods to a well-marked trail junction. Turn right and climb 0.2 mile to a viewpoint of Salt Creek's canyon. Here the trail crosses rock worn smooth by Ice Age glaciers. Notice the honeycomb-shaped fracture pattern characteristic of basalt.

In another 200 yards a short side trail to the left leads to Too Much Bear Lake, a brushy-shored pond. Continue on the main trail 1.2 miles, passing numerous viewpoints, profuse rhododendrons (blooming in June), and two small clearcuts before reaching the signed turnoff for Diamond Creek Falls on the right. Take

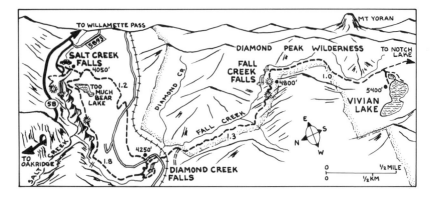

Salt Creek Falls.   Opposite: Vivian Lake.

this steep, 0.2-mile side trail down to a footbridge and through a narrow canyon to a misty grotto below the fan-shaped, 100-foot cascade. A surprising mix of lowland wildflowers, watered and cooled by the falls, bloom throughout summer in this hidden glen. Look for scarlet salmonberry blossoms, yellow monkeyflowers, and pink bleeding hearts among the ferns.

Then return to the main trail and switchback up past another viewpoint to a trail junction. If you're hiking with children, turn left here to complete the loop to the car. The 1.2-mile return route crosses a gravel road twice. If you're headed on to Vivian Lake, however, turn right. This path crosses Diamond Creek on a road's cement bridge, ducks through the woods for 300 yards, crosses the Southern Pacific tracks, and climbs into the Diamond Peak Wilderness.

The trail steepens as it climbs, always within earshot of Fall Creek. Beyond the railroad tracks 1.1 mile you'll reach the first viewpoint of Fall Creek Falls. Continue 0.2 mile to the second, superior overlook of this churning, twisting, 40-foot cascade.

The path stays close to the scenic mossy, tumbling creek for most of the next mile up to the Vivian Lake turnoff. Turn right, cross a meadow, and keep to the right-hand shore of this shallow lake for the view of Mt. Yoran's chunky monolith. In August, fields of ripe blue huckleberries surround the lake.

96　　　　　Yoran Lake　　　

Difficult
12.1-mile loop
1300 feet elevation gain
Open late June through October
Use: hikers, horses
Map: Diamond Pk. Wilderness (Imus)

This woodsy lake, with two small islands and a view of Diamond Peak, is a worthy destination even if you merely hike 5 miles up and return the same way. But if you have some pathfinding skills you can bushwhack 800 yards beyond Yoran Lake through open, level country to the Pacific Crest Trail. And from the PCT you can return on a loop past half a dozen wilderness lakes and ponds.

Just east of the Willamette Pass summit, turn off Willamette Highway 58 at the "West Odell Lake Campgrounds" sign and follow Road 5810 for 2.3 miles. Just before Shelter Cove Resort, pull into the Trapper Trailhead on the right.

Cross the Southern Pacific railroad tracks and follow the trail up into a dense forest of mountain hemlock and subalpine fir. At a fork after 0.2 mile, veer right across a footbridge over Trapper Creek. After another level half mile, turn left on the Yoran Lake Trail. This path climbs steadily for 3 miles to a nameless but pleasant green lake on the left. After another half mile, the trail crosses Yoran Lake's outlet creek. This rocky torrent dries up by July, when blue lupine and wild strawberry bloom along its meadowed banks.

A half mile beyond, you'll reach an obscure trail junction at the bank of another (dry) creek. The Yoran Lake Trail ducks across the creek on a log and then bypasses Karen Lake. For a look at Karen Lake, take the more obvious left-hand path, following the (dry) creek up to the lakeshore. Then take a rough fisherman's trail 100 yards around to the right to return to the main path.

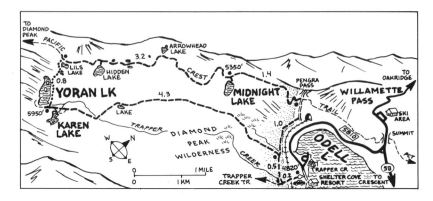

Diamond Peak from Yoran Lake.   Opposite: Pond reflection along trail.

Just beyond Karen Lake, when Yoran Lake peeks through the trees to the right, the trail forks. The left branch leads to a small beach and an overused campsite. The smaller, right-hand fork ends at the lake's outlet, with a view across the lake to Diamond Peak's red-and-black-banded crags.

If you're heading for the PCT, take this right-hand fork, cross the outlet, and bushwhack above the shore almost to the far end of Yoran Lake. Opposite the second small island, cross a small inlet creek to find a campsite on a low bench.

Leave the lakeshore here, following your compass true north (20 degrees left of magnetic north). In the first 300 steps you'll cross a meadow, crest a small rise, and reach a pond. In another 150 steps you'll reach Lils Lake. The PCT is in the woods on the far shore. Bushwhack left around the lake to a low cliff on the far side. Then walk north away from the lake 100 steps to find the PCT's obvious, 3-foot-wide tread.

Once on the PCT, it's an easy, 4.6-mile downhill roll to Pengra Pass, where the trail meets a dirt road. Follow the road 0.4 mile to the right, and then fork to the right on a trail marked by blue diamonds for skiers. Keep left on this path for 1.3 miles to return to your car.

97   Fawn Lake

Moderate
7.3-mile loop
1000 feet elevation gain
Open late June through October
Use: hikers, horses
Map: Diamond Pk. Wilderness (Imus)

An oasis in the dry lodgepole pine forests blanketing the High Cascades' eastern slope, Fawn Lake is one of the most popular destinations in the Diamond Peak Wilderness. Alas, popularity has left many of the trails here beaten to dust. There is one exception: an unmaintained path via Pretty Lake. To make a loop, the suggested route climbs to Fawn Lake on the easy, well-graded trail from Crescent Lake and then returns on this quieter, more difficult path.

Turn off Willamette Highway 58 at the "Crescent Lake Campgrounds" sign in Crescent Junction (7 miles east of Willamette Pass). Follow paved Road 60 for 2.2 miles, turn right at a pointer labeled "Camping," and in another half mile turn left onto the Crescent Lake Campground entrance road. At the first exit to the right, drive to the far end of a huge parking lot (built for boat trailers) and park by the Fawn Lake Trail sign.

The trail crosses the paved road and a horse trail before heading up past lodgepole pines and aromatic manzanita bushes into the Wilderness. The path climbs at such a gradual, steady grade that it doesn't need a single switchback. After a mile, cross an abandoned road and enter cooler woods with Douglas fir and the small pinkish blooms of prince's pine. Eventually the hot pine woods return, making it all the more pleasant to reach Fawn Lake's shimmering waters. The craggy peak across the lake is Lakeview Mountain, while the rounded summit to the left is Redtop Mountain.

At the lakeshore the main trail turns right toward a severely overused campsite. But if you turn left you'll find yourself on a much quieter, fainter shoreline path. This is the unmaintained route to Pretty Lake. Return via this loop only if you have some skill at pathfinding—and if you don't mind stepping over a few small logs.

The path circles halfway around Fawn Lake and then curves away from the shore through a sparse stand of lodgepole pine. Watch for i-shaped blazes on tree trunks. Beyond the lake 0.3 mile the trail climbs a more densely forested ridge, faintly switchbacking three times to a low pass. Here the path veers left and descends 0.3 mile to an old-fashioned enamel sign announcing Pretty Lake. The shallow, moss-banked pool, 100 feet to the left of the trail, offers a distant reflection of Lakeview Mountain.

Beyond Pretty Lake the path descends a manzanita-covered slope with a view of cone-shaped Odell Butte. After a steady, 2.3-mile downhill grade, rejoin the main trail to Crescent Lake and turn right. Notice that this unmarked junction

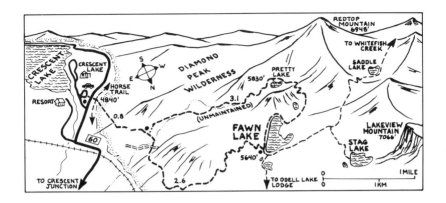

is only clear when hiking in this direction. Do not try to hike this loop in reverse, as fallen trees make this end of the Pretty Lake Trail virtually invisible from the maintained trail below.

Other Hiking Options

Stag Lake, overtowered by Lakeview Mountain's cliffy face, makes an excellent side trip. Turn right at the shore of Fawn Lake and in 0.2 mile keep left at the Odell Lake turnoff. After another mile of gradual climbing, turn right on the 0.4-mile side trail to Stag Lake.

Pretty Lake.   Opposite: Driftwood at Fawn Lake.

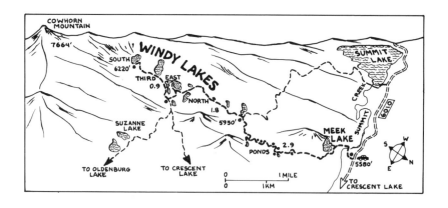

98   Windy Lakes   ⛰

Moderate
11.2 miles round-trip
900 feet elevation gain
Open mid-July to mid-October
Use: hikers, horses, bicycles
Map: Diamond Pk. Wilderness (USFS)

If you love mountain lakes, try this route through the High Cascade forests south of Diamond Peak. The path passes 6 major lakes and 22 ponds. Some have lilypads or meadowed banks; others feature rock outcroppings or forested peninsulas. The Third Windy Lake even has a long sandy beach suitable for swimming.

The suggested route begins from the rough, primitive dirt road to Summit Lake. This is not the most heavily used route to the Windy Lakes. Most hikers innocently start at the large developed trailhead beside Crescent Lake. To be sure, that steep, dusty alternative is half a mile shorter, but it's crowded with horses and it passes no ponds at all.

Start by driving Willamette Highway 58 to Crescent Junction, 7 miles east of Willamette Pass. At a "Crescent Lake Campgrounds" sign in the middle of the village, turn onto paved Road 60. After 2.2 miles, the road turns right at an intersection; follow the pointer labeled "Camping." Exactly 5 miles beyond this intersection, turn right onto an easily overlooked dirt road marked "6010 Summit Lake." (If you pass a large sign for the Windy/Oldenburg Trail, you've missed the dirt road by half a mile.) Road 6010 is steep and rutted, but passable for passenger cars except in wet weather when it fills with giant puddles. Follow this road 3.9 miles to a sign for the Meek Lake Trail on the left.

The trail starts by descending 0.2 mile to a crossing of Summit Creek. Then the path begins a long, very gradual ascent through lichen-draped mountain hemlock forests. After 0.5 mile a large fork to the right leads to a campsite on a peninsula of deep Meek Lake. Continue on the fainter left fork. The ponds commence at the 1.2-mile mark and pop up along the trail every few hundred yards from then on.

After 2.9 miles turn left at a trail junction at the head of a long, green lake. Continue 1.6 miles, passing North Windy Lake, to an unmarked trail junction beside East Windy Lake. The right-hand fork deadends at a peninsula campsite, so turn left. In 300 yards you'll reach a marked junction with the heavily used trail from Crescent Lake. Turn right, following the "S. Windy Lake" pointer.

This route leads around the end of East Windy Lake (with the barest glimpse of Diamond Peak, the hike's only mountain view) and heads through the woods to the Third Lake's delightful, heather-banked beach. Although the water is usually warm enough for bathing, the beach really is windy much of the time because the lake is set right at the Cascade crest.

The trail deadends in another half mile at South Windy Lake, the greenest of all, in a deep, forested basin. Return by the same trail.

Third Windy Lake.   Opposite: Deer tracks on lake beach.

99   Divide Lake

Moderate
8 miles round-trip
1200 feet elevation gain
Open July through October
Use: hikers, horses
Map: Diamond Pk. Wilderness (Imus)

Diamond Peak does indeed have the kind of idyllic alpine scenery that draws crowds to more famous Oregon peaks. But here most of the alpine idylls are packed into one miniature cove: the little-known Divide Lake basin between Diamond Peak and Mt. Yoran. If you have extra energy after hiking up to Divide Lake, an 0.8-mile climb leads to a pass with a view across Central Oregon.

Turn off Willamette Highway 58 at the sign for Hills Creek Dam (1.3 miles east of Oakridge, between mileposts 37 and 38). After half a mile on Road 21, continue straight at an intersection onto Road 23. Follow this route for 15.6 miles of pavement and another 3.9 miles of gravel to a pass beside Hemlock Butte. Turn left at a hiker-symbol sign immediately beyond the pass, drive 200 yards on a spur road, and park at the Vivian Lake Trailhead.

The trail starts in a clearcut with a view ahead to Diamond Peak's snowy ridges and Mt. Yoran's massive plug. Then the path enters uncut mountain hemlock woods with loads of blue huckleberries in August. After 0.6 mile ignore the Diamond Peak Tie Trail branching off to the right; this connector was built so backpackers can trek all the way around Diamond Peak on trail. A few hundred yards beyond, you'll reach the start of Notch Lake. Continue to the lake's far end for the best overview of this scenic, rock-rimmed pool.

At a trail junction 0.2 mile beyond the lake, turn right onto the Mt. Yoran Trail. This path climbs in earnest for 1.6 miles before leveling off along a ridgecrest.

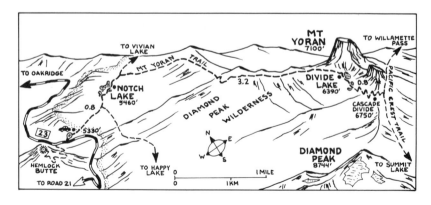

Mt. Yoran from Divide Lake.   Opposite: Clark's nutcracker.

The ridge has occasional views south to Diamond Peak and north across Salt Creek's forested valley. After a mile along the ridge, Mt. Yoran's massive monolith suddenly appears above the woods ahead. Then the trail contours to the right across a rockslide to Divide Lake.

Though very small, this blue-green lake is fortuitously situated to reflect three different peaks from different shores. Walk around the shore to the right, following a pointer labeled "Pacific Crest Trail." Notice how the rock at the far end of the lake has been rounded and polished by the Ice Age glacier that carved this scenic basin. A bit farther along the trail you'll find a second heather-rimmed lake. If you're backpacking, be a sport and pitch camp out of sight of these delicate lakelets so other visitors won't find tents in their scenery.

Few hikers to Divide Lake will be able to resist continuing 0.8 mile up the trail to the actual divide—a pass with a view down the forested eastern slope of the Diamond Peak Wilderness. The Pacific Crest Trail is a few hundred yards down the far side, but that hiker byway offers no better views.

Other Hiking Options

Vivian Lake (Hike #95) is 2.9 miles downhill from the trail junction near Notch Lake. For a more satisfying side trip, however, climb to Hemlock Butte's panoramic view. Return to your car and drive 200 yards back on Road 23 to a hiker-symbol sign at the pass. A half-mile trail here climbs 500 feet to a former lookout tower site atop a rocky knob.

217

Sawtooth Mountain from Indigo Lake.   Below: Indigo Lake from Sawtooth Mountain.

100   Timpanogas Lake

Easy (around Indigo Lake)
4.8 miles round-trip
600 feet elevation gain
Open late June through October
Use: hikers, horses, bicycles
Map: Cowhorn Mtn. (USGS)

Difficult (to Cowhorn Mountain)
11.9-mile loop
3100 feet elevation gain
Open late July through October

Sawtooth Mountain rises like a 1000-foot wall above Indigo Lake, arguably the prettiest pool in this portion of the Cascades. But it's almost too easy a walk up to Indigo Lake from the campground at Timpanogas Lake. For a more challenging trek, continue on a grand loop around a High Cascade basin, where a 2-mile detour scrambles to a breathtaking view atop Cowhorn Mountain.

Timpanogas was actually an early name for Utah's Great Salt Lake, which an imaginative 1830 map mistakenly identified as the Willamette River's source. When the Forest Service later determined that the river's main stem actually originates at a lake below Cowhorn Mountain, they applied the name here. Cowhorn Mountain itself suffers from a different kind of identity crisis. Ever since its original, horn-shaped summit spire fell off in a 1911 storm, this has been the least widely recognized of the High Cascades' major peaks.

To find the trailhead, turn south off Willamette Highway 58 at "Hills Creek Dam" sign 1.3 miles east of Oakridge, between mileposts 37 and 38. After half a mile bear right onto Road 21 and follow this paved route 31.2 miles. Three miles beyond Indigo Springs Campground turn left onto Timpanogas Road 2154.

Then follow signs for Timpanogas Lake 9.3 miles to Timpanogas Campground, where a hiker-symbol sign points to the trailhead parking area on the right.

Start out from the left side of parking area on the Indigo Lake Trail. This path switchbacks up through a forest of mountain hemlock and fir for 0.7 mile to a 4-way trail junction. Keep left, following the "Indigo Lake" pointer. In another 1.2 miles, just 200 feet before Indigo Lake, the loop trail toward Cowhorn Mountain takes off to the left. Ignore it for a moment and continue straight 50 yards to a primitive campground on Indigo Lake's shore. An outhouse is discreetly set back in the woods. A sandy beach invites wading or swimming. To see the lake's indigo coloring, at the far end, take the 1-mile shoreline loop.

If you'd like to tackle the longer loop to Cowhorn Mountain, walk back to the trail junction and turn right. This path switchbacks steadily up 1.7 miles to a sparsely wooded pass. At a junction just beyond the pass, turn left on the Windy Pass Trail, a fainter route that recrosses the ridgecrest, switchbacks once downhill, and then traverses a wooded slope for more than a mile before switchbacking again—this time uphill. *Watch closely for this very faint, final uphill switchback.*

Beyond the switchback 0.4 mile you'll reach a junction where a large sign points right toward the Pacific Crest Trail. For the difficult side trip up Cowhorn Mountain, turn right for 0.3 mile and then turn right on the PCT for another 0.3 mile. At a small rock cairn where the PCT veers downhill to the right, follow a faint side path up a ridge to the left. At timberline the route steepens in cinder scree. Crest a false summit, cross a cinder hogback, and scale the actual summit crag on the left—a non-technical scramble requiring the use of hands.

The view of Crescent Lake steals the show up here. To the left are the Three Sisters, the sinuous shore of Summit Lake, snowy Diamond Peak, and the U-shaped canyon of the Middle Fork Willamette River (Hike #84). To the south look for broad Mt. Bailey, Crater Lake's jagged rim, and Mt. Thielsen's spire.

After admiring the view, return to the Windy Pass Trail and turn right to complete the loop. In another 2.7 miles, just beyond a small lake, turn left at a Timpanogas Lake pointer for 1.1 mile. Then turn right on the Timpanogas Lake shoreline trail to complete the loop back to the campground and your car.

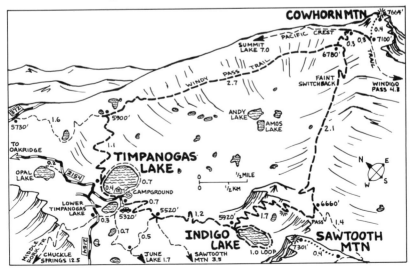

All-Accessible Trails in the Central Oregon Cascades

People with limited physical abilities need not miss the fun of exploring new trails. Here are 20 nearby paths accessible to everyone. Nearly all are surfaced with asphalt or packed gravel. Entries with a bicycle symbol are great for bikers, too. Unless otherwise noted, the paths are open year round. For more information, contact the trail's managing agency, listed at the end of each entry.

SANTIAM FOOTHILLS (map on page 13)

A. Minto-Brown Island. Salem's largest and wildest park, on a pair of former islands in the Willamette River, features a paved 3.2-mi bike path loop past riverfront cottonwood trees, farm fields of geese, and wildlife-rich sloughs. From downtown Salem, take Commercial Street 4 blocks south past the Civic Center, turn right on Owens Street to River Rd for 1 mi to park entrance on right. (Salem Parks, 503-588-6261)   ⊛

B. Silver Creek Falls. Paved bike path follows creek 0.5 mi from campground to South Falls Picnic Area, extends 1.2 mi along hwy to a 1.9-mi loop in nearly level woods. Also, pedestrian-only gravel paths from North Falls parking area lead right for 0.1 mi to a falls overlook and left under the highway bridge for 0.2 mi to Upper North Falls. See Hike #1. (Silver Falls Park, 503-873-8681)   ⊛

C. Hoover Campground. Detroit Reservoir campground offers a 200-foot fishing pier, short nature trail, and 13 barrier-free campsites. (Detroit Ranger Dist, 503-854-3366)

D. Walton Ranch Viewpoint. 0.3-mi path to decked overlook of a farm with a wintering elk herd. See Hike #14. (Sweet Home Ranger Dist, 541-367-5168)

E. Yukwah Campground. South Santiam riverside campground has 15 barrier-free campsites and a 0.3-mi nature trail to a fishing pier where rainbow trout are stocked. See map for Hike #14. (Sweet Home Ranger Dist, 541-367-5168)

F. Hackleman Creek Old Growth Trail. 400-year-old Douglas firs, a creek, and a historic wagon road are featured on this interpretive 1.2-mi loop off Hwy 20, 1.5 mi W of Lost Prairie CG (see map for Hike #13). Expect gravel trail surface to be rough. Open May-Nov. (Sweet Home Ranger Dist, 541-367-5168)

BEND AREA (map on page 79)

G. Lava Lands Visitor Center. Two paved, interpretive loops start from the back patio of Forest Service visitor center. The Trail of the Molten Lands loops 0.8 mi across lava, steeply in places. The easier, 0.3-mi Trail of the Whispering Pines skirts a lava flow edge. Monument Pass fee required. (Lava Lands Visitor Center, 541-593-2421)

H. Lava Cast Forest. Paved 1-mi trail, open May-Nov, is steep in spots. See Hike #37. (Lava Lands Visitor Center, 541-593-2421)

THE THREE SISTERS (map on page 101)

I. Dee Wright Memorial. Atop McKenzie Pass on Hwy 242, paved nature path loops 0.5 mi through lava flow. (McKenzie Ranger Dist, 541-822-3381)

MCKENZIE FOOTHILLS (map on page 141)

J. Sahalie Falls. A 200-ft all-accessible trail leads from a parking area on Hwy 126 to a viewpoint of this roaring McKenzie River falls. See Hike #63. Open May-Nov. (McKenzie Ranger Dist, 541-822-3381)

K.Delta Old Growth Trail. Giant trees and wildlife-rich McKenzie R sloughs highlight this 0.5-mi loop, rebuilt in summer 1998. Starts at Delta Campground (3 accessible campsites). Drive 4 mi E of Blue River on Hwy 126 and turn right toward Cougar Reservoir for 0.2 mi. (Blue River Ranger Dist, 541-822-3317)

L. Lower Erma Bell Lake. Wide dirt trail into Three Sisters Wilderness is all-accessible for 1.7 mi to first large lake. See Hike #73. Open July-Oct. (Oakridge Ranger Dist, 541-782-2291)

Walton Ranch Trail's viewpoint deck.

WILLAMETTE FOOTHILLS (map on page 167)

M. Eugene North Bank. Paved bike path traces Willamette River shore 4.4 mi from Springfield's D Street to the Valley River Center mall through Eugene's Alton Baker Park. Cottonwoods, herons, whitewater views abound. Three bike bridges connect to South Bank Trail (see below). (Eugene Parks, 541-682-4800 ⊛

N. Eugene South Bank. 4.3-mi paved bike path follows the Willamette River's scenic south bank entirely through Eugene. Connects with North Bank Trail (see above) via 4 bike bridges. (Eugene Parks, 541-682-4800)　　⊛

O. West Eugene Amazon Creek. Paved bike path along an urban creek extends 4.6 mi from the county fairgrounds (15th and Madison Street) to Terry Street at Eugene's western city limits. (Eugene Parks, 541-682-4800)　　⊛

P. South Eugene Amazon Creek. Promenade through grassy Amazon Park begins at South Eugene High School (19th and High) and follows a channeled creek 1.2 mi to 30th and Hilyard Streets. (Eugene Parks, 541-682-4800)　　⊛

Q. Johnny Creek Nature Trail. Interpretive 0.7-mi loop path through an old-growth forest. Drive 3 mi past the Fall Creek trailhead (see map for Hike #78), turn right on Rd 1821 for 0.2 mi. (Lowell Ranger Dist, 541-937-2129)

R. Black Canyon Campground. West of Oakridge 8 mi on Hwy 58, this campground has 7 all-accessible campsites and a 1-mi nature trail (not yet fully accessible) along the Middle Fk Willamette River. (Lowell Ranger Dist, 541-937-2129)

S. Row River Railroad. Historic railroad grade, converted to a scenic 12.7-mi paved bike path, skirts Dorena Lake's reservoir and passes near 3 covered bridges. From I-5 take Cottage Grove exit 174, follow "Dorena Lake" signs 3.2 mi, turn R on Layng Road 1.2 mi. (Eugene BLM, 541-683-6600)　　⊛

WILLAMETTE PASS (map on page 193)

T. Salt Creek Falls. Short concrete trail from picnic area (with 5 all-accessible tables) leads to viewing platform of Oregon's 2nd tallest waterfall. See Hike #95. Open May-Nov. (Oakridge Ranger Dist, 541-782-2291)

100 More Hikes in the Central Oregon Cascades

Adventurous hikers can discover plenty of additional trails in the mountains between Bend and the Willamette Valley. The list below covers the most interesting—from easy, paved nature trails to rugged, faint wilderness paths. Directions are brief, so be extra careful to bring appropriate maps. Estimated mileages are one-way. Most paths are open only in summer and fall, but symbols note which hikes are open all year, and which are suitable for kids, horses, bicycles, or backpacking. For more information, check with the trail's administrative agency.

The appropriate ranger district or other offices are abbreviated: (B)-Bend & Fort Rock, (BR)-Blue River, (C)-Crescent, (CG)-Cottage Grove, (D)-Detroit, (L)-Lowell, (M)-McKenzie, (O)-Oakridge, (R)-Rigdon, (S)-Sisters, (SH)-Sweet Home. Agency phone numbers are on page 11.

Easy Moderate Difficult

SANTIAM FOOTHILLS (map on page 13)

101. Shellburg and Stassel Falls. Walk a closed forest road 1.5 mi to short paths that lead L to Shellburg Falls and R to Stassel Falls. One of the closest hiking areas to Salem, this scrap of Santiam State Forest is scheduled for the development of an even better trail network. Drive Hwy 22 E of Salem 22 mi to a yellow light in Mehama by the Gingerbread House and turn L on Fern Ridge Rd 1.1 mi to a yellow gate on the R. (Oregon Dept of Forestry, 503-859-2151)

102. Whetstone Mountain. Strenuous 5.5-mi climb up 3000 ft to lookout site in the Bull of the Woods Wilderness has huckleberries and views from Mt Rainier to Marys Pk. Park as for Opal Creek (see Hike #4), walk 0.6 mi past gate, and turn left at Gold Cr. (D)

103. Mt. Beachie. Pleasant 2.5-mi climb in Bull of the Woods Wilderness provides views of Mt Jefferson and the Opal Cr Valley. Gains 800 ft. Park as for Battle Ax (Hike #6), walk road to Beachie Saddle, and turn left. (D)

104. Battle Creek. Downhill 4-mi hike through rhodies and old-growth Doug firs descends 900 ft to campable creek confluence deep in the Bull of the Woods Wilderness. Drive as to Battle Ax (Hike #6), but only take the horribly rocky final Elk Lk Rd for 1.4 mi. At the first glimpse of Elk Lk, by a creek crossing, park at an unmarked pullout on the R. Then walk 150 yds farther on the rd to an X trailhead sign on the R. (D)

105. Gold Butte Lookout. Unstaffed 1934 cabin overlooks Mt Jefferson and Elk Lk. From Hwy 22 in Detroit, take Breitenbush Rd 46 for 4.4 mi, turn left at a "Elk Lake" sign on Rd 4696 for 0.8 mi, turn right on Rd 4697 for 4.7 mi to a saddle, turn right on Rd 451 for 0.1 mi, and park at a junction. Walk to the right on rough, possibly gated Rd 453 for 1.2 mi and continue on a 0.3-mi trail to the summit, gaining 800 ft in all. (D)

106. Stahlman Point. Convenient 2.5-mi climb to lookout site above Detroit Reservoir gains 1300 ft. Open mid-Mar to Dec. Drive 2.5 mi E of Detroit on Hwy 22 and turn right on Rd 10 for 3.5 mi. (D)

107. Daly Lake. Lovely 1.1-mi path loops around a fishing lake with old-growth Doug fir, beavers, and June rhody blooms. Drive 7.5 mi N of Santiam Y jct on Hwy 22. Near milepost 74, turn W on Parrish Lk Rd 2266 for 4.6 mi. Then turn right on Rd 450 for 0.5 mi. (SH)

108. Parrish Lake and Riggs Lake. Short paths near Daly Lk (see above) lead 0.4 mi down to brushy Parrish Lk or 0.5 mi up to little Riggs Lk. Drive as to Hike #107, but take Parrish Rd 2266 a total of 5 mi to the Parrish Lk trailhead on the left. After the hike, drive another 1.5 mi on Rd 2266 to find the Riggs Lk trailhead on the right. (SH)

109. Trapper Butte and Scar Ridge. New portion of the Old Cascade Crest Tr (see map for Hike #9) gains 1500 ft in 3.9 mi to a viewpoint cliff atop Trappers Butte, then continues up and down 2.8 mi to another viewpoint cliff atop Scar Mtn. Drive 7.5 mi N of Santiam Y jct on Hwy 22. Near milepost 74, turn W on Parrish Lk Rd 2266 for 4.4 mi to a large trail sign on the right. (SH)

110. Echo Basin. Huge, rare, shaggy-barked Alaska cedars line this 2-mile loop, which gains 940 ft on its way to a cliff-rimmed wildflower meadow. Drive Hwy 20 E of Sweet Home 39 mi. Between mileposts 66 and 67, turn L on Rd 055 for 2.1 mi. (SH)

111. Tombstone Nature Trail. Interpretive 0.7-mi nature loop from the Tombstone Pass sno-park on Hwy 20 visits wildflower prairie, woods, and the gravesite of a pioneer boy who died in a 1891accident. See map for Iron Mtn Hike #12. (SH)

112. Chimney Peak. The well-graded, woodsy McQuade Cr Tr gains 1500 ft in 5 mi to a rustic shelter. Then continue 1.1 mi to the base of Chimney Pk's volcanic plug, where 100 yds of artful scrambling reaches a summit lookout site overlooking the Middle Santiam Wilderness. Drive Hwy 20 E of Sweet Home 4 mi and turn left on Quartzville Cr Rd for 24.7 mi to a 3-way fork. Keep right on Rd 11 for 2.6 mi and turn right on Rd 1142 for 4 mi to a trail sign on the left. (SH)

113. Gordon Lakes. A downhill, 0.4-mi path leads to 2 lakes popular with children. The path continues 3.2 mi to marshy Gordon Mdws. Turn S off Hwy 22 at House Rock CG (see Hike #13), follow Rd 2044 for 5.5 mi, and turn right onto Rd 230 for 2.6 mi to road's end. (SH)

114. Falls Creek. This woodsy 4.3-mi path, partly along a creek, climbs 1000 ft to marshy Gordon Meadows. The trail continues to Gordon Lks (see above). Drive Hwy 22 E of Sweet Home 18 mi to milepost 46 and turn right past Longbow Camp on Rd 2031 for 5 mi. (SH)

MOUNT JEFFERSON (map on page 47)

115. Spotted Owl Trail. This very popular trail network, named for a rare owl nest found during construction, begins near the Breitenbush Hot Springs Retreat Center. From Hwy 22 at Detroit, take Breitenbush Rd 46 for 9.2 mi, turn right across a bridge, and keep left for 1.4 mi to a junction. Don't park in the retreat center's private lot to the left! Instead park on the shoulder and walk past a gate on the right (toward summer homes) for 100 ft to the trail. See map for Hike #18 for sketch of routes to Devils Pk's ridge. Only retreat center guests may take a 3.5-mi loop that crosses the river twice and returns across private land. (D)

116. Crown Lake. A 1.2-mi path climbs gradually through a Mt. Jefferson Wilderness forest to the largest of the Firecamp Lakes group. Expect plenty of mosquitoes in July. Drive Breitenbush Rd 46 from Detroit 11.3 mi and turn right on Rd 4685 for 8.3 mi to its end. (D)

117. Bear Point. This envigorating 3.8-mi climb to Wilderness lookout site gains 3000 ft to a grand view of Mt Jefferson. Drive Breitenbush Rd 46 from Detroit 11.3 mi and turn right on Rd 4685 for 5 mi. (D)

118. Jeff Park via South Breitenbush. The quietest route to this Wilderness mecca, this path gains 2800 ft in 6.2 mi and starts at the same trailhead as Bear Pt Hike #117. (D)

119. Woodpecker Ridge. This 2-mi Wilderness path to the PCT on the shoulder of Mt Jefferson has only one good viewpoint. Drive 11.7 mi E of Detroit on Hwy 22, turn left on Rd 040 for 5 mi to its end. (D)

120. Hunts Cove. Gorgeous 15.9-mi alpine Wilderness loop with 3000 ft of elevation gain does not require Pamelia Lk's usual advance permit reservations *if you camp beyond Pamelia Lk.* Walk to Pamelia Lk (Hike #21), continue past Hunts Cove to Cathedral Rocks, turn left on the PCT 4.8 mi around base of Mt Jefferson, and turn left to return to Pamelia Lk. (D)

121. Independence Rock. Convenient viewpoint path gains 300 ft in 1 mi to a clifftop overlooking the N Santiam area. Continue 0.7 mi on the trail and turn right for 0.5 on a road to complete a 2.2-mi loop. Turn off Hwy 22 at Marion Forks and park along Rd 2255 after 100 yds. (D)

122. Eight Lakes Basin. Backpackable 15.2-mi loop visits wildflower meadows and crowded Wilderness lakes. Walk to Marion Lk (Hike #22), turn right on the Blue Lk Trail for 4 mi to Jorn Lk and turn left to return to Marion Lk. Gains 1800 ft of elevation in all. (D) OH

123. Pika and Fir Lakes. An easy path through the woods leads 0.5 mi to 3-acre Pika Lk and another 0.4 mi to trail's end at larger Fir Lk. Drive Hwy 22 E of Detroit 26 mi to milepost 76, turn left on Big Mdws Rd 2267 for 1 mi and turn left on Rd 2257 for 2.5 mi. (D)

124. Maxwell Butte. A panoramic viewpoint atop a Wilderness volcano is the goal of this 4.8-mi trail. The route passes swimmable Twin Lks and gains 2500 ft. Drive 2.5 mi N of the Santiam Y jct on Hwy 22 and park at the Maxwell Butte sno-park near milepost 79. (D)

125. Washington Meadows. This 5.5-mi section of the PCT climbs 1300 ft through Wilderness woods to a viewpoint below Mt Washington's spire. Take the Hoodoo Ski Area turnoff of Hwy 22 at Santiam Pass, follow Big Lake Rd 3.1 mi to a fork, and turn L on Rd 811 for 0.6 mi to the Pacific Crest Trailhead. (M)

126. Blue Lake. This trail loops 4.5 mi through Corbett State Park beside

Paulina Lake from Paulina Peak (Hike #134).

Easy
Moderate
Difficult

a deep, blue lake. Park beside Hwy 20 at a sno-park 4.3 mi E of Santiam Pass. The trail begins behind the restroom and drops 600 ft in 1.3 mi to the lake loop. (S)

127. Suttle Lake. A level 3.7-mi path circles this popular lake, passing a lodge and 3 campgrounds. Drive Hwy 20 E of Santiam Pass 7 mi to milepost 87. (S)

128. Round and Square Lakes. A fairly flat 2.2-mi Wilderness path from Round Lk passes Long Lk and joins Hike #25 at Square Lk. Drive Hwy 20 E of Santiam Pass 8 mi, turn N on Rd 12 for 2.8 mi, and turn L on Rd 1210 for 5 mi. (S)

129. Head of Jack Creek. Less well known than the Head of Metolius springs, these massive springs are the goal of a 0.3-mi loop. Drive Hwy 20 E of Santiam Pass 8 mi, turn N on paved Rd 12 for 3.7 mi, continue straight on Rd 1230 for 0.3, and follow signs left for 2 mi. (S)

130. Table Lake. Challenging, remote 22-mi Wilderness backpack loop up Jefferson Cr Trail and down Sugarpine Ridge passes wildflowers, lava, and views of Mt Jefferson. Drive 8 mi E of Santiam Pass, turn N on Rd 12 for 13 mi, and turn left on Rd 1292 to its end in 3 mi. (S)

131. Metolius Breaks. Remote 1.5-mi path traces the lower Metolius River. Drive W from Hwy 97 through Cove Palisades Park and Grand-view to the end of Rd 64. (S)

● **132. Green Ridge.** A popular 9.5-mi horse and bicycle trail follows a wooded ridgecrest (with views of Mt Jefferson) to the rentable Green Ridge Lookout tower. For overnight reservations, call the Sisters Ranger Station at 541-549-2111. Drive 5.5 mi W of Sisters on Hwy 20 to Indian Ford CG, turn right 4.4 mi on Green Ridge Rd 11, and go straight 1.2 mi on Rd 1120 to the trail on the right. (S)

BEND AREA (map on page 79)

● **133. Swampy Lakes.** Stroll 2.1 mi amid lodgepole pines to a rustic 3-sided shelter with a woodstove. Turn right for 200 yds to a large meadow with a view of S Sister and wander right to ponds with ducks and lilypads. 550 ft elev gain. Drive Cascade Lks Hwy W from Bend to the Swampy Lks sno-park between mileposts 16 and 17. (B)

● **134. Paulina Peak.** Dusty 2-mi path climbs 1500 ft to a breathtaking view of the Newberry Caldera and Central Oregon. Drive to Paulina Lake (Hike #40), but turn R just after the fee booth onto Rd 500 for 1 mi to the trailhead. Since Rd 500 continues to the summit, the trail can also be hiked one-way, downhill. (B)

● **135. Newberry Caldera Rim.** 21-mi loop path follows the wooded crest of a gigantic, collapsed volcano's rim in Newberry Nat'l Volcanic Monument, passing super viewpoints at N Paulina Pk, Cinder Hill, and Paulina Pk (Hike #135). The route has no water. (B)

● **136. Squaw Creek Canyon.** This trailless route traces a high desert gorge. Drive 4.5 mi E of Sisters on Hwy 126, turn left on Goodrich Rd 8 mi, turn left on Rd 6360 for 3.4 mi, turn right on Rd 6370 for 0.8 mi, and park at a gate. Walk 1 mi down the road (keeping left at forks), cross the creek, scramble up the far shore, and hike right 1.2 mi to a riverbend oasis. Closed Dec 1 to Mar 31. (Crooked R Nat'l Grasslands, 541-447-9640)

● **137. The Island at Cove Palisades.** The Island, an other-worldly mesa peninsula in Billy Chinook Reservoir, retains ungrazed high desert bunchgrass, lava formations, and countless clifftop views. Drive Hwy 97 N of Redmond 15 mi, follow signs for The Cove State Park about 8 mi to a pass. Park at a petroglyph pullout and walk N on a dump road 100 yds to its end, where a rough 0.2-mi tr scrambles to the trailless, 2.4-mi-long plateau. (Crooked R Nat'l Grasslands, 541-447-9640)

THE THREE SISTERS (map on page 101)

● **138. Robinson Lake.** Level 0.5-mi path leads to a quiet, swimmable lake. Drive 16 mi E of McKenzie Br on Hwy 126 and turn right onto Rd 2664 for 4.7 mi to road's end. (M)

● **139. Linton Meadows.** Scenic 9.1-mi Wilderness backpacking trail climbs to alpine wildflower fields beside Middle Sister, with Husband and Eileen Lks nearby. Take the Obsidian Trail (Hike #44) to the PCT, follow PCT 2 mi S, and turn right for 1.3 mi. (M)

● **140. Squaw Creek Falls.** 1.5-mi trail leads to a 30-ft falls in the Three Sisters Wilderness. From Sisters, take Elm St (which becomes Rd 16) south for 8 mi, turn right on Rd 1514 for 5 mi, turn left on Rd 600 to a T-jct, and turn onto Rd 680 a mile to a sign at road's end. (S)

141. Little Three Creek Lake. Charming, level 3-mi loop visits a lake below Tam McArthur Rim's cliffs. Park as for Hike #53. (S)

142. Mount Bachelor. Arduous 2.5-mi trail from Sunrise Lodge gains 2700 ft to a picture-postcard view at Mt Bachelor's summit, also accessible by a chairlift. (B)

143. Todd Lake. An easy 1.7-mi shoreline loop begins at Todd Lk's walk-in campground. A tougher 3-mi cross-country circuit of the ridge behind the lake yields better views and still more wildflowers. Drive 2 mi E of Mt Bachelor on Cascade Lks Hwy and turn right on Rd 370 half a mile. (B)

144. Soap Creek. A little-known 4.2-mi Wilderness route accesses a meadow below N Sister's craggy face. Hike 2 mi on the trail toward Chambers Lks (Hike #51), turn right 100 ft before Soap Cr bridge, and follow a faint, unmarked path up the splashing, flower-banked creek, gaining 1500 ft. (S)

145. Sparks Lake to Lava Lake. Hikable 11-mi horse/bike path traverses lodgepole pine woods from Soda Creek CG (4 mi E of Mt Bachelor on Cascade Lks Hwy) to Lava Lake Lodge, crossing some lava. A car shuttle is recommended for hikers. (B)

146. Lucky Lake. Woodsy 1.3-mi Three Sisters Wilderness path leads to Lucky Lk, then continues 4.7 mi to Senoj Lk (see Hike #60). Park at signed trailhead 5 mi S of Elk Lk on Cascade Lks Hwy. (B)

MCKENZIE FOOTHILLS (map on page 141)

147. Carpenter Mountain Lookout. A 1-mi path climbs to this lookout building atop a cliff-edged peak with huckleberries and panoramic views. Drive 3 mi E of Blue River on Hwy 126, turn N on Rd 15 for 3.5 mi, turn right on Rd 1506 for 7 mi, and turn left on Rd 350 for 6 mi to saddle. (BR)

148. Lookout Creek Old Growth. Built to study ancient trees in the Andrews Experimental Forest, this rough, 3.5-mi path is now open to all tree lovers. Drive 3 mi E of Blue River on Hwy 126, turn N on Rd 15 for 3.5 mi, and turn R on Rd 1506 for 7 mi to the lower trailhead (or 10 mi to the upper trailhead). (BR)

149. Frissell Trail. Gaining 2500 feet in 4.7 mi to a forest road, this tough but convenient climb provides a good workout and a view across the McKenzie Valley to the 3 Sisters. Drive Hwy 126 W of McKenzie Br 1.2 mi to a Refuse Disposal Site sign, turn right on Rd 705, keep right at all jcts for 2.2 mi, and fork left on Rd 700 for 0.7 mi to its end. (M)

150. Substitute Point. Climb gradually 4.3 mi on the Foley Ridge Trail for 4.3 mi through viewless mtn hemlock woods, then turn R on a 0.7-mi path to this rocky knob's spectacular, close-up view of the 3 Sisters. Gains 2000 ft of elevation. Drive Hwy 126 E of the McKenzie Br Ranger Station 0.5 mi and turn right on Foley Ridge Rd 2643 for 11.3 mi to its end. (M)

151. Rainbow Falls Viewpoint. A nearly level 1-mi Wilderness path ends at a viewpoint of a distant but massive falls and the 3 Sisters. Drive 3 mi E of McKenzie Br on Hwy 126 and turn right on Rd 2643 for 6.5 mi to a sign. (M)

152. Separation Creek. This remote Wilderness path descends 800 ft in 3.4 mi to a roaring creek in deep woods. Drive 3 mi E of McKenzie Bridge on Hwy 126, turn right on Rd 2643 for 8 mi, and turn right on Rd 480 to its end in 1.5 mi. (M)

153. Lower Olallie Trail. Climb 1900 ft in 4.5 mi up wooded Olallie Ridge to Horsepasture Saddle, where trails split to Horsepasture Mtn (Hike #67), Taylor Castle, and an upper trailhead. Drive as to Hike #67, but only go 2.8 mi up Rd 1993. (M)

154. East Fork McKenzie. This creekside path, climbing 6.5 mi through Wilderness old-growth woods, parallels Rd 1993, so a car shuttle would be handy. Drive to Cougar Reservoir and cross the dam on Rd 1993 to Echo CG. (BR)

155. Terwilliger Hot Springs (Cougar Hot Springs). A heavily used half-mile path leads to a crowded series of natural hot spring pools in a shady forest canyon. Closed after dark. Drive McKenzie Hwy 126 E of Blue River 4 mi to a Cougar Reservoir pointer, turn right on Rd 19, and keep right for 7.5 mi to a well-signed parking area on the left. Cross the road and walk back along it 300 yds to the trail. (BR)

156. Mink Lake via Crossing Way Trailhead. Wilderness backdoor route to Mink Lk gains just 600 ft in 7.7 mi, passing Blondie Lk and Corral Flat. Drive as to Chucksney Mtn (Hike #72), but turn E off Rd 19 0.5 mi N of Box Canyon CG and take Rd 1958 for 3.2 mi. (BR, M)

157. Irish Mountain via Otter Lake. Park as for Erma Bell Lks (Hike #73), but keep left past Otter Lk, climbing 2000 ft in 5.8 mi to an alpine huckleberry field (and a view of Waldo Lk) on Irish Mtn's rocky shoulder. (O)

158. North Fork Middle Fork Willamette River. Some of the Cascades' largest old-growth trees line this amazingly level 3-mi Wilderness path to a bridgeless crossing of the Willamette's wildest fork. If you cross on downed logs, the trail beyond gains 1300 ft in 4.9 mi to Moolack Lk. From Hwy 58 just W of Oakridge, take the Westfir exit and follow Aufderheide Rd 19 for 29.4 mi to a hiker-symbol sign on the right where the road curves sharply left. (O)

159. Hiyu Ridge to Grasshopper Mountain. This quiet 4-mi ridgetop path traverses alpine mdws and woods to a grassy viewpoint, gaining 1200 ft. Drive 6.5 mi past the upper end of Cougar Reservoir on Rd 19 and turn right on Rd 1927 for 6.3 mi to Lowell Pass. (BR)

160. Grasshopper Mountain Shortcut. This refreshing 1.4-mi climb gains 1000 ft to alpine meadows with mountain views. From Hwy 58 just W of Oakridge, take the Westfir exit and follow Rd 19 for 13 mi. Then turn left on Rd 1926 for 3 mi, turn right on Rd 1927 for 2.1 mi, and turn right on Rd 1929 for 5.5 mi. (O)

161. Fisher Creek. The first 2.3 mi of this Wilderness creekside trail are nearly level, through ancient forest. Then the path crosses the creek and climbs steeply. Drive Rd 19 from Oakridge 23.2 mi to a hiker-symbol sign and turn right for 2 mi. (O)   🐴🏠

WILLAMETTE FOOTHILLS (map on page 167)

162. Jasper Bridge Park. All-year, level path follows the Middle Fk Willamette riverbank 1.5 mi. From I-5, drive E on Hwy 58 for 5.3 mi, turn left on Jasper Rd 2.7 mi to a bridge, and walk downstream. (Oregon State Parks, 503-378-6305)   🎣🚶🏇🏠

163. Clark Creek Nature Trail. Easy 1-mile loop in deep woods starts at Clark Creek Group Camp. Drive 2.5 mi past the first Fall Creek trailhead (see Hike #78) to the camp and trailhead. (L)   🎣🚶

164. Clark Butte. Convenient 2.7-mi trail climbs 1300 ft to an overgrown summit viewpoint, crossing 2 roads along the way. Start from the Clark Creek Group Camp (2.5 miles past the first Fall Creek trailhead in Hike #78) and hike to the right, halfway around the Clark Creek Nature Trail 1-mi loop to find the Clark Butte Trail junction. Open Mar to Dec. (L)

165. Gold Point. Scenic 4.3-mi ridgecrest path to lookout site gains 2300 ft. Open only Aug 1 to Dec due to endangered species nearby. Drive 5.8 mi past Fall Creek trailhead (see Hike #78), turn right on Rd 1825 for 2.7 mi, and keep left at junctions for another 0.8 mi. (L)   🐎

166. Saddleblanket Mountain. Viewless, subalpine 1.4-mi stroll from Little Blanket Shelter to unclimbable 80-ft lookout tower. Drive 5.3 mi past Fall Cr trailhead (Hike #78), turn right on Rd 1824 for 6.2 mi, turn left on Rd 142 for 1.1 mi, and turn right on Rd 144. (L)   🏠

167. Hardesty Mountain, Lower Trailhead. Arduous 5-mi climb gains 3300 ft through forest to overgrown lookout site. Park beside Hwy 58 as for Goodman Creek Trail (Hike #80). (L)   🐎🏠

168. Hardesty Mountain, Upper Trailhead. This 0.9-mile back route to Hardesty Mountain's summit lookout site gains only 600 ft. Turn S off Hwy 58 between mileposts 24 and 25, follow Patterson Mtn Rd 5840 for 5.1 mi to a pass and turn right on narrow Rd 550 to its end. (L)

169. South Willamette Trail. Relatively level, all-year 5-mi path through the forest above Hwy 58 can be traveled one-way with a shuttle. Park 1 car as for Goodman Creek Trail (Hike #80) and leave the other at the Eula Ridge trailhead 3 mi farther east on Hwy 58. (L)   🐎🏠

170. Eula Ridge. Steep, less-used 4-mi route to Hardesty Mtn summit gains 3300 ft. Park on Hwy 58 near milepost 24. (L)   🐎

171. Lone Wolf Shelter. The relatively level 1-mi path that leads to this rustic shelter and meadow from Rd 555 is a better bet than the steep 5.6-mi Lawler Tr that climbs here from Rd 535. To find the easy trailhead, drive 6 mi W of Oakridge on Hwy 58 to Shady Dell CG, turn S on Rd 5847 for 7.8 mi, and turn right on Rd 555 for 0.3 mi. (L)   🐴🐎🏠

172. Cloverpatch Trail. This 2.5-mi path above the tip of Lookout Point Reservoir climbs 1200 ft to Rd 124, passing grassy terraces, a waterfall, and some clearcuts. From Eugene, drive 2 mi south on I-5 to Oakridge exit 188A and take Hwy 58 east 31 mi. Just before Oakridge, take the Westfir exit for 1 mi, turn left across a bridge onto N Shore Rd 5821 for 5 mi, and turn right on Rd 5826 for 3 mi. (L)

173. Flat Creek. Almost within Oakridge, this 4.3-mi route climbs 2000 ft to a viewpoint atop Dead Mtn. Drive 2 mi E of downtown on Salmon Cr Rd 24 and turn left on Rd 2404 for 0.7 mi. Take the Flat Cr Tr 2.5 mi up to closed Rd 210 and keep right on the road to the summit. Open Mar-Dec. (O)

174. Larison Rock. For a quick hike, take the switchbacking 0.3-mi trail up to Larison Rock's view of Oakridge and the High Cascades. For a challenging bike ride, take an 11-mi loop that gains 2400 ft on a paved road and descends on a 4-mi trail. Drive 1 mi E of Oakridge on Hwy 58, turn right at a Hills Cr Dam sign for 0.5 mi, fork right on Rd 21 for 1 mi (park here if you're biking), and turn right on Rd 2102 for 4 paved miles up to the trailhead on the right. The trail soon forks. Either go left to the summit or turn right for the long loop. Open Apr to Dec. (R)

175. Tufti Trail. Year-round 0.5-mi path between mossy Hills Cr gorge and Rd 24 features waterfalls and pools. Drive 1.3 mi E of Oakridge on Hwy 58 to Hills Cr Dam sign and turn right on Rd 23 for 5.8 mi to a bridge on the right. (R)

176. Moon Point. Stroll 1.1 mi to a bluff with a sweeping view. A fork of the trail descends steeply through old-growth 4 mi to Rd 21. Drive 18.4 mi S of Hwy 58 on Rd 21 past Hills Cr Reservoir and turn left on Rd 2129 for 9 mi. (R)

177. Dome Rock. A picturesque 2.2-mi ridgecrest path from Little Dome Rock leads to a lookout site on a crag. From Hwy 58, drive S past Hills Cr Reservoir 21.5 mi on Rd 21, turn right on Rd 2134 for 12 mi, turn right on Rd 250 for 2.5 mi, and turn right on Rd 251 for 2.7 mi. (R)

178. Moon Falls and Spirit Falls. An 0.4-mi path descends to lacy, 40-ft Spirit Falls, and an 0.6-mi trail nearby ambles to 80-ft Moon Falls. From I-5 at Eugene, drive Hwy 58 E past milepost 24, turn right on gravel Patterson Mt Rd 5840 for 5.1 to a saddle, veer right toward Rujada CG for 4.4 mi to the start of pavement on Rd 17, and veer left onto Rd 1790 for 0.1 mi to a pullout for the Spirit Falls Tr on the right. To continue to Moon Falls, drive another 0.1 on Rd 1790, fork left onto Rd 1702 for 2.7 mi, and turn right on Rd 728 for 0.3 mi. (CG)

179. Swordfern Trail. Ferns line this all-year 1-mi creekside loop at Rujada Campground. Take I-5 to Cottage Grove exit 174, follow signs for Dorena Lk 17 mi, and veer left on Layng Cr Rd for 2 mi. (CG)

180. Adams Mountain Way. Challenging 11.2-mi loop gains 2400 ft. See map for Brice Cr (Hike #85) for trailhead near Lund Park. Take Adams Mtn Way 3.6 mi uphill, veer R on Knott Tr for 1 mi, turn R on Crawfish Tr for 5.4 mi downhill, and turn R on paved Rd 22 for 1.2 mi. (CG)

181. Parker Creek Falls. All-year 0.7-mi path skirts Brice Cr gorge to 2 falls on a side creek. Drive 7.2 mi past the trailhead for Hike #85 on Rd 22. (CG)

Parrish Lake (Hike #108).

Easy
Moderate
Difficult

182. Fairview Creek. This tumbling stream in a wooded canyon is accessed by an all-year, 1-mi trail from Mineral CG. Drive 15.5 mi E of Cottage Grove past Dorena Lk to Culp Creek and turn right along Sharps Cr for 12 mi. (CG)

WILLAMETTE PASS (map on page 193)

183. McCredie Hot Springs. Surprisingly convenient, this 25-ft-wide natural hot springs pool beside Salt Creek is just a 200-yd walk from Highway 58. Swimsuits are optional. Near milepost 45 (E of Oakridge 9.5 mi), look for an unmarked gravel parking lot on the south side of the hwy, opposite a sign for McCredie Sta. Road. (O)

184. Joe Goddard Old Growth. Doug firs and red cedars 9 ft in diameter highlight this level 0.4-mi loop trail. From Oakridge, take Salmon Cr Rd 24 east for 11 mi, fork right to keep on Rd 24 another 3.2 paved mi, and continue straight on gravel Rd 2421 for 7 mi to the trailhead at the Rd 393 bridge. (O)

185. Bunchgrass Ridge. Hike as far as you like on this alpine path with beargrass meadows and views. The trail leads 6 mi to Big Bunchgrass and 14 mi to Black Mdw (see Hike #88). Drive 6.5 mi E of Oakridge on Salmon Cr Rd 24, turn right on Rd 5871 for 2.7 mi, turn left on Rd 2408 for 7.0 mi, and turn right on an unmarked spur for 0.3 mi to the trailhead at the Little Bunchgrass lookout site. (O)

186. Koch Mountain. This nearly level 2-mi trail is a Wilderness shortcut to the remote W shore of Waldo Lk. Drive 13.5 mi E of Oakridge on Salmon Cr Rd 24, turn left on Rd 2422 for 13.7 mi. (O)

187. Swan and Gander Lakes. Descend 1.2 mi to this pair of Wilderness lakes, or continue on an 8.8-mi loop to Waldo Mtn lookout (Hike #90). Drive 11 mi E of Oakridge on Salmon Cr Rd 24 and fork left on Rd 2417 for 7.2 mi. (O)

188. Blair Lake to Mule Mountain. Climb gradually 4.5 mi through alpine meadows past a broad summit. Drive 9 mi E of Oakridge on Salmon Cr Rd 24, turn left on Rd 1934 for 8 mi, and turn right on Rd 733 for 1.3 mi to Blair Lake CG. (O)

189. Lily Lake. Take a woodsy 2.3-mi stroll via the PCT from Charlton Lk down to Lily Lk. An optional return loop circles Charlton Butte. Drive Hwy 58 to the Waldo Lk exit (W of Willamette Pass 3 mi), turn N on Rd 5897 for 11.8 mi, and turn right on Rd 4290 for 1 mi. (B)

190. Waldo Lake Loop. The 20.2-mi circuit of this huge alpine lake's shore is a classic backpack trek or mountain bike ride. Shortcuts are possible only with a boat. Park as for Hikes #88 or #92. (O)

191. Bobby Lake. The level 2-mi stroll to this large alpine lake is a great trip for kids. Drive Hwy 58 to the Waldo Lk exit (W of Willamette Pass 3 mi) and turn N on Rd 5897 for 5.5 mi. (O)

192. Maiden Peak. This rigorous 5.8-mi climb gains 2900 ft to a sweeping summit view. Just 1 mi W of Willamette Pass on Hwy 58, turn N on Gold Lk Rd 500 for 1.5 mi. (O)

193. Marilyn Lakes. A kid-friendly 1.7-mi loop visits 2 cute lakes. Drive Hwy 58 W of Willamette Pass 1 mi, turn N on Rd 500 for 2 mi to the Gold Lake CG. Park here, hike 1 mi on the Marilyn Lks Tr, and walk back 0.7 mi on Rd 500 to complete the loop. (O)

194. Diamond View Lake. A pleasant 5.4-mi path up Trapper Creek gains 1000 ft to the Wilderness source of Whitefish Creek. Start as for Yoran Lake (Hike #96), but turn left at the first trail junction. (C)

195. Oldenburg Lake. This forested 5.2-mi path passes Pinewan and Bingham Lks before reaching Oldenburg Lk. Drive as to Fawn Lk (Hike #97), but continue on Rd 60 to the W end of Crescent Lk. (C)

196. Effie Lake. Dozens of Wilderness lakelets line this 2.8-mi path, which gains just 400 ft. Park as for Windy Lks (Hike #98) but hike N instead. (C)

197. Diamond Peak Shoulder. Hike the Pacific Crest Tr above timberline to Wilderness wildflowers, views, and springs at the head of Mountain Creek, gaining 1400 ft in 6 mi. Park at Emigrant Pass by Summit Lk on dirt Rd 6010. Access is either via Crescent Lk (see Hike #98) or Oakridge (take Rd 21 past Hills Cr Reservoir). (R)

198. Marie Lake. This charming meadow-fringed lake in the Wilderness has a close-up view of Diamond Pk. The trail here gains 600 ft in 3.3 mi. Park as for Diamond Pk Shoulder (above), hike PCT 2.7 mi N, and turn left. (R)

199. June Lake. The pleasant 5.3-mi loop to this lake crosses a ridge with a view of Mt Thielsen, and gains only 300 ft. Park as for Timpanogas Lk (Hike #100) and refer to the map for that hike. (R)

200. Sawtooth Mountain. A 9.7-mi loop gains 2200 ft to the fabulous views atop this Cascade peak, but routefinding skills are needed on faint trails and on a final 0.4-mi scramble to the summit. Hike 0.7 mi toward Indigo Lk (see Hike #100), but then veer right on a fainter path for 3.5 miles to Sawtooth Mtn's shoulder ridge. From here, detour 0.4 mi left to the summit. Then continue on the loop trail 1.4 mi to a junction, turn left across a pass 1.7 mi to Indigo Lk, and keep right for 1.9 mi to your car. (R)

North Sister from Soap Creek (Hike #144).

Index

About the Author

William L. Sullivan is the author of 6 books and numerous articles about Oregon, including a regular outdoor column for *Eugene Weekly.* A fifth-generation Oregonian, Sullivan began hiking at the age of 5 and has been exploring new trails ever since. After receiving an English degree from Cornell University and studying at Germany's Heidelberg University, he earned an M.A. from the University of Oregon.

In 1985 Sullivan set out to investigate Oregon's wilderness on a 1,361-mile solo backpacking trek from the state's westernmost shore at Cape Blanco to Oregon's easternmost point in Hells Canyon. His journal of that two-month adventure, published as *Listening for Coyote,* was a finalist for the Oregon Book Award in creative nonfiction . Since then he has authored *Exploring Oregon's Wild Areas* and a series of *100 Hikes* guidebooks to the regions of Oregon.

He and his wife Janell live in Eugene, but spend summers in a log cabin they built by hand on a roadless stretch of Oregon's Siletz River. They have two children, Karen and Ian.